Caribbean Light

Donna Shields

Doubleday

New York   London   Toronto   Sydney   Auckland

Caribbean Light

All the Flavors of the Islands,
Without All the Fat

PUBLISHED BY DOUBLEDAY

a division of Bantam Doubleday Dell Publishing Group, Inc.

1540 Broadway, New York, New York 10036

DOUBLEDAY and the portrayal of an anchor with a dolphin are
trademarks of Doubleday, a division of Bantam Doubleday Dell
Publishing Group, Inc.

Book design by Maria Carella
Map on page 8 and illustration on
page 52 by Kris Tobiassen

List of hot sauces on pp. 54–56 from *The Great Hot Sauces Book* by Jennifer
Trainer Thompson, Berkeley, CA.: Ten Speed Press, Copyright © 1995.
Reprinted by permission of the author.

Library of Congress Cataloging-in-Publication Data
Shields, Donna.
Caribbean light: all the flavors of the islands, without all
the fat / Donna Shields.—1st ed.
p.   cm.
Includes index.
1. Cookery, Caribbean.   2. Low-fat diet—Recipes.   I. Title.
TX716.A1S52   1998
641.5′638—dc21   98-10573
CIP

ISBN 0-385-48714-2

Printed in the United States of America

October 1998

First Edition

1 3 5 7 9 10 8 6 4 2

This book is lovingly dedicated to
the sweetest guy in the world, and
our soon-to-arrive baby, who is
being born the same month as this book.

Acknowledgments

I could never have imagined that the process of writing a cookbook would be so all-consuming. It stays with you day in and day out until it's finished. Whether it's just thinking about new recipe ideas, grocery shopping, cooking, writing up recipes, or doing nutrition analysis, it means staying motivated for a long time. So I'd like to thank my number-one cheerleader, Ted, who constantly reminded me that writing this book was a good idea. His taste buds and honest opinions provided the necessary feedback for making the food as good as it could be.

But before I could get started in the kitchen, I had to sell the idea of a healthy Caribbean cuisine cookbook. And for that, I am very grateful to my agent, Susan Ginsburg at Writers House. I can now appreciate her being such a tough taskmaster as I revised—and revised again—the proposal for this book. She knew when it was finally right and then made the book become a reality for me. Once work was in progress, Judy Kern at Doubleday was a patient and thorough editor, answering all my little questions and helping me learn the ropes as I went along.

Contents

Caribbean Light

Introduction

Caribbean Light: the Best of the Caribbean Rim

When people are asked what Caribbean food is all about, I hear answers like, "Lots of fish, some of those unusual tropical fruits, and a rum-something drink." That, in reality, is the extent of most people's food knowledge, when it comes to the Caribbean rim.

Everyone gets a sharp, mental picture when asked to describe the Caribbean. It's the dramatic, kaleidoscopic colors of the ocean, from azure blue to ethereal pale green; baby-powder-fine, white beaches with towering coconut palms that offer a hint of shade against the blinding, bright sun; lush, tropical bougainvillea and hibiscus in a colorful medley of purples, pinks, reds, oranges, and yellows; and charming, scrubbed little cottages, adorned with brilliant-colored shutters and gingerbread framework, looking like something right out of a picture book.

But you know what? Some of the adjectives used to describe this beautiful region are the same words I'd use to explain the cuisine. The food is a medley of brilliant, bright colors, with dramatic, bold flavors, and a lush, tropical presentation. There is nothing subtle about Caribbean cuisine. It steps right up to the plate, and lets you know what it's all about. The cooking techniques are down-home, a melting pot from several hundred years of European, African, Indian, and Chinese influence, and the result is some great eating. This is food with a big personality.

Now here's the good part. This cookbook has married the best of Caribbean cuisine with the principles of good nutrition. By using selected authentic ingredients and recipes, contemporary, lighter cooking techniques, and moderate portion sizes, everyone can create healthier Caribbean-style food at home. Some peo-

ple think island food is inherently a lighter way to eat (you know, it's fish and fruit), so why the need for a special cookbook? That logic holds true to a certain extent, because the cuisine relies heavily on seafood, tropical fruits, root vegetables, and lots of spices and herbs. But there's another side to the menu that you won't find on these pages. Traditional dishes like Jamaican stamp and go (deep-fried codfish fritters), Trinidad's kachouris (chickpea) fritters, Puerto Rico's mofongo (mashed plantains and pork crackling) and tostones (sliced, fried plantains), just couldn't make it into the contents. They're terrific dishes, but not fit for a lighter, healthier eating style.

So let me tell you about the primary criteria for the recipes that did make it into the book. One of my goals was to use dishes that represent typical, home-style Caribbean cooking. This means you won't see lots of gussied-up recipes with non-native ingredients like sun-dried tomatoes or pine nuts. With few exceptions, I have stuck to using meats, produce, and seasonings that are typical of the Caribbean basin. You won't see fancy, multistep recipes: those with two or three recipes within a master recipe. This is not how the locals cook, and besides, when experimenting with a new cuisine, easy and quick recipes are the best way to get your feet wet.

While many cookbooks featuring a regional cuisine may weave in other ethnic influences, such as Mediterranean or Asian, fusion cuisine has not been my intention. However, there are a few recipes where I borrowed ideas from something I enjoyed in another part of the world, and blended them into this book. While I've tried to develop recipes typical of the Caribbean rim, American taste buds and the availability of certain ingredients must still prevail. Let's be real: morcillas (spicy blood sausages) may be fine and dandy, and delicious, but they're not going to be a must-try dish for most American consumers.

Besides paying homage to authenticity, my second goal was to create recipes using native ingredients in new and nontraditional ways. So, while a particular dish may not have any history behind it, the ingredients are certainly part of the Caribbean pantry. You won't find Mango, Tomato, and Coconut Mix (page 50) in the archives of Caribbean cooking, but mango, tomato, and coconut are all ubiquitous ingredients used throughout the region. Newly created recipes such as this one were very often inspired by tried-and-true dishes, such as mango chutney.

Unfortunately, in the past, much of the food experienced by tourists in large hotels was very Americanized, and not true to local island cooking. Today, chefs and hotel management have realized that their local cuisine is a marketing gold mine. Many restaurateurs have adapted local flavors to appeal to a diverse customer base, providing a high-quality dining experience to vacationers. Because of this new mind-set in the hospitality industry, vacationing Americans now have a much better chance of understanding and experiencing local Caribbean food.

I would be remiss, however, not to also credit the significant influence immigrating Caribbeans and South Americans have had on broadening our culinary horizons by bringing their regional food right to our doorstep. There isn't a city in America today that doesn't have a Hispanic/Caribbean food market or restaurant, or at least a supermarket shelf or two stocked with Hispanic products.

So, while recipes had either to be authentic or to include indigenous ingredients, they also had to meet certain nutritional criteria. Not only should the dish be moderate in calories, fat, cholesterol, and sodium but it should also have some positive nutritional value, such as providing fiber, vitamins, or minerals. This often meant tweaking original recipes so that they didn't lose their authenticity yet were lightened up just a bit. Such is the case with Blaff (page 152), a naturally low-fat, one-pot seafood meal that needed only minor adjustments. In some cases, I've taken a traditional recipe such as Cuban boliche (pot roast), and used a traditional ingredient, Cuban coffee (buche), in a totally unorthodox way, to create a coffee-based gravy for Buche Boliche (page 237).

Nutritional Details

The most important criteria in developing these recipes was that they taste really good. I didn't go into the kitchen with set nutritional criteria and then cook to make the numbers fit. The idea was to create recipes that were moderate in calories, fat, cholesterol, and sodium, based on their portion size and type of recipe.

It's only logical that entrees will be higher in calories and fat than a vegetable side dish, or that cooking condiments or rum cocktails will not deliver your daily nutritional requirements. The recipes should be evaluated based on their context within a whole day's diet.

You will notice that the nutrition analysis for each recipe does not provide percentage of calories from fat, but rather lists grams of fat per serving. Listing fat content as a percentage of the calories would be okay if people understood what that really meant. Unfortunately, many folks have this magical "30 percent of calories from fat" drilled into their head, and think that every recipe should meet that criteria. While that's a nice round number to shoot for when developing recipes, it should not be the litmus test. For example, salad dressings, because most of their calories come from fat (due to the oil), will most likely not meet a 30 percent guideline (unless they are reduced-fat or fat-free products). The daily recommendation that says 30 percent of our calories should come from fat is exactly that: a daily guideline, not a criteria for individual recipes. So, rather than zero in on the small picture, i.e., each recipe's fat percentage, I prefer to list a recipe's nutritional value in absolute terms.

You will find that calorie, fat, cholesterol, and sodium values have been rounded to the nearest "5." If the fat content, per serving, is less than 1 gram, it is listed as 0. If cholesterol and sodium values per serving are less than 5 milligrams, they are listed as 0. These are benchmark values, and anything less represents an insignificant amount of those nutrients.

In addition to the "worry" nutrients (those that people worry about getting too much of), there's also the nutritionally positive story, an equally important part of any recipe. I'd be shirking my responsibilities as a nutritionist, and would have the dietitian gods after me, if I didn't also include vitamin, mineral, and fiber values. This information is listed as "% Daily Value," which are the same values used on product labels. This means that one serving of the recipe contributes that given percentage of a nutrient, to be counted toward your daily tally.

Nutrients get listed in this category if they are of major interest and concern, such as Vitamin C, iron, and calcium. Nutrients are also included only if their value is 10 percent or greater, and are listed in de-

scending order. For many recipes, there are other nutrients present in smaller quantities, but given space limitations, and not wanting this to look like a textbook, 10 percent is my cutoff point. When recipes don't contribute any nutrients in a particular category, it is so noted.

All recipe analyses have been done using computer software. While databases now contain some 12,000 foods, inevitably there are some foods you just can't find. This is especially true when working with exotic fruits and vegetables not grown in the United States or other foreign ingredients. When specific foods couldn't be located, a reasonable alternative was used. The analyses include all ingredients listed, excluding suggested accompaniments or optional garnishes.

Recipe Philosophy

When trimming calories, fat, or sodium, you need to pick up the slack with something else. You can't just keep taking ingredients away without seeing the dish eventually falling flat on its face in terms of flavor, color, texture, and aroma. That's why, no matter what kind of ethnic or regional cuisine you're preparing, if you're cooking light, you'd better understand the concept of contrast cooking.

Contrast cooking is something that all well-trained chefs inherently understand and incorporate into their work. In light-style cooking, you are obviously reducing and eliminating certain higher-fat ingredients. This means that the ingredients you *are* using must worker harder, and contribute more to the net result of the dish. One of the ways to do this is by using ingredients that contrast, or play off each other. Contrasts in flavor, color, texture, shape, and temperature are what make food exciting to the palette and to the eye. If you can't rely on butter, cream, or lots of oil to provide flavor and mouth feel, and you're not frying food to provide textural crispness, then you must find other ways to create sensory excitement. This is contrast cooking.

There are quite a few recipes throughout the book that utilize contrast-cooking concept, and you'll find mention of this in specific recipe introductions. Have you ever noticed that spicy, salty, and other savory flavors seem to taste better when paired with something sweet? When you take a bite, there's so much going on in your mouth that you never even notice how little oil may have been used. Texture contrasts are also important, especially when preparing fish fillets, which have a soft, rather unexciting texture. I like to put crusted coatings on fish fillets, and use shrimp in combination with other ingredients to provide a variety of textures. Color contrast, an easily understood concept, is, I hope, something you keep in mind with every plate of food that goes on your table. Lastly, no one can deny the importance of temperature contrast. Isn't that why hot fudge sundaes taste so good? You will find the same hot-cold principle holds true for warm Electric Carambola Compote (page 277) when it's poured over frozen vanilla yogurt.

The other key tenet of healthy cooking is to use the best and most flavorful ingredients available. That's why in most of my recipes I use olive oil, historically used for Spanish-style dishes. Other fats favored by island cooks have been coconut oil, a high saturated fat, or butter, traditionally used in French cooking. Olive oil delivers so much flavor that I can use less of it than I would if cooking with a blander vegetable oil. You will also find high-flavor, high-fat ingredients, such as chorizo sausage, used in small quantities.

For foods like chorizo, avocado, or cream, a little bit goes a long way. Sometimes reduced or non-fat products, especially dairy items, are helpful for creating a recipe base, such as Mamey Cheesecake (page 250), which you can then flavor accordingly.

Finally, I've tried to use portion sizes that I consider to be ample. Anyone can reduce calories and fat by limiting the serving size. My goal has been to provide realistic portions without compromising the nutritional bottom line. You will note that several seafood dishes call for 6-ounce portions of fish, a generous amount, while some beef and pork recipes kick in with 4–6 ounce portions. And I purposely did not skimp on the dessert section, proving that there is lots of variety for the sweet tooth.

Because I've had the good fortune to make my home in Key West for the past 10 years, island food is a way of life in my kitchen. And so, this is a book about the food I love to eat. I hope these recipes will become favorites in your kitchen, too. For those who have traveled to the Caribbean, some of these recipes may ring familiar. For those seeking a new, big-flavored, healthful style of cooking, this book will be a culinary adventure.

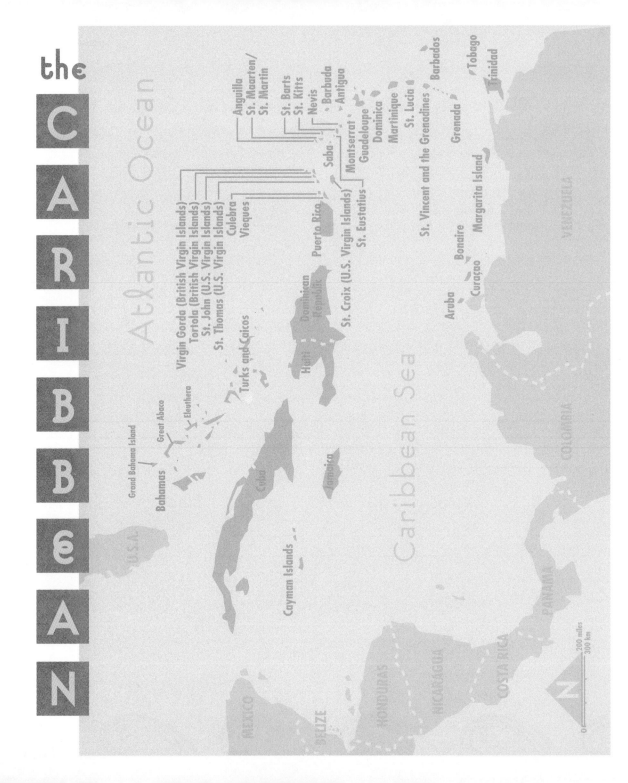

Food Map
of the Caribbean

Unless you've traveled extensively to the Caribbean, you probably don't have a clear vision of where specific islands are located. While the accompanying map can help your geography, its real purpose is to correlate certain dishes with their island of origin.

To make this simple, the following symbols serve as a key, or code, for a specific island. Find the symbol on the map, then look below to see the dishes native to that island, and where to find them in the book. Realize, however, that these lighter recipes may be adaptations of the authentic dish, not exact replicas of what you will find in local restaurants. The dish may also have been inspired by a chef from that island, or based on a locally grown ingredient, or a variation on a restaurant's signature dish.

Because many dishes, like Callaloo, are commonly eaten throughout the Caribbean rim, I've listed the dish next to the island with which it seems to be most closely associated. And then there are some, such as Empanadas, that are actually South American in origin but have migrated throughout the Spanish islands. Flan, a dessert with its roots in Spain, is also found on many island menus throughout the region. So, the idea here is to give you a general sense of food geography, which might come in handy on a future vacation.

ANTIGUA	Pepper Pot Soup	*page 116*
ARUBA	Veal with Sweet Potatoes, Mangoes, and Plantain Chips	*page 241*

Cooking
Condiments

These are the basic flavor foundations that go into cooking at its earliest stages. Like other cuisines, Caribbean cooking has base recipes that are essential to creating a variety of finished dishes. They are rubbed on, stirred in, mixed in, and slathered on. And while some flavoring foundations are subtle, like the French mirepoix of celery, onion, and carrot, there is nothing timid about the recipes in this chapter. Their bold, big flavors will jump-start your cooking, helping to create healthy dishes that need very little assistance from butter or oils.

There are numerous recipes throughout other chapters that call on these cooking condiments as a starting point. So most of what's in this chapter is designed for multiple use. Make a batch, then store it on the shelf, in the fridge, or in the freezer, for future cooking. But don't hesitate to incorporate these condiments into your own favorite dishes, too. Use Sour Orange Mix, for example, to marinate all your grilled meats, and make a Sofrito whenever you're cooking beans, soups, or stews. In essence, you'll be creating your very own Caribbean flavor pantry.

Spiced Lime Juice

You find this ubiquitous green liquid in recycled hot pepper sauce bottles on just about every tabletop and lunch counter from Trinidad to Miami. It's like salt and pepper, a staple of the table setting. Like Pepper Sherry (page 17), it's a catch-all flavoring, used in similar ways. It's the finishing touch on a Cuban sandwich, roast pork, or whatever else comes out of the restaurant kitchen. Please don't use bottled lime juice; it just won't work. Try and store this in a bottle with a small shaker hole on top, to use it sparingly. And by all means, leave the bird peppers in there so someone doesn't mistakenly think it's plain lime juice. Besides, they look nice and keep the flavor bumped up. This makes only ¼ cup, but you'll find a little bit goes a long way.

¼ cup fresh lime juice
2 garlic cloves, smashed

1–2 bird peppers, cut in half
⅛ teaspoon salt

Combine all ingredients in a clean, glass bottle with a shaker top and a lid. Let the mixture sit, at room temperature, for at least 1 week before using. This allows the heat of the peppers to permeate the juice. It keeps indefinitely at room temperature or refrigerated.

Makes ¼ cup

Per Teaspoon: Calories: 2; Fat, Cholesterol, and Sodium: 0; No other significant nutritional value

Turning Up the Heat

Hot peppers were a crop indigenous to the Caribbean before the Spaniards arrived. I guess you could call the Carib Indians the original "chili heads," as they were quite adept at making hot pepper sauce. Apparently, they hadn't figured out how to extract salt from the sea, and turned to hot peppers as their primary method of seasoning food. To this day, West Indian food is among the hottest of island cuisines.

Botanically speaking, hot peppers are in the Capsicum family, covering a very broad spectrum of flavor and heat intensity. Whether the peppers are fresh or dried, most of their heat is contained in the seeds and the membranes. Thus, one way to reduce the heat level in a recipe is to eliminate those portions of the pepper. The hottest pepper around also happens to be the one most commonly used in Caribbean cooking: the Scotch bonnet pepper. It looks like a squatty hat that someone might have sat on, an immediate clue to the origin of its name. Although it comes in shades of green, yellow, orange, and red, the different colors do not necessarily indicate lesser or greater heat intensity. Store Scotch bonnets in the refrigerator, since they are fresh, and will turn moldy if left at room temperature for too long.

Caribbean cuisine also makes use of tiny, dried peppers, sometimes called bird peppers. As with many other foods, pepper nomenclature varies, depending on where you live. Giving cookbook directions for hot peppers is a tricky thing. It's difficult to gauge the heat intensity of any one, given pepper. Even the same variety will not always produce the exact same results. Their flavor and heat will vary based on size, seeds, how old they are, and where they were grown. To compensate for some of these variations, occasionally I call for a minced, measured amount of pepper, rather than a pepper quantity such as 1 or 2.

Pepper Sherry

Sherry, just like rum, is a great conduit for hot peppers. It readily absorbs the heat of the peppers, and with its own sweet flavor added, makes a handy shake-on condiment. Add it to soups or stews, and other dishes that cook for a long time, so it can marry and mingle with the other ingredients. I consider it essential to a good Picadillo (page 233) and also use it, as a last-minute seasoning, on steamed vegetables, as well as on rice and beans. And, I promise, you'll never drink a bloody mary again without it. It can be made two ways: with very dry, golden sherry or with a red, tawny port. If you have neither of those, grab the rum instead.

¹/₂ cup very dry sherry or tawny port

¹/₂ Scotch bonnet pepper, seeded and cut into slices

Combine the two ingredients in a clean glass jar or bottle with a lid. Let the mixture sit at room temperature for at least 1 week before using. It keeps indefinitely at room temperature or refrigerated.

Makes ¹/₂ cup

Per Teaspoon: Calories: 5; Fat, Cholesterol, and Sodium: 0; No other significant nutritional value

Sour Orange Mix

Sour oranges—wrinkly, bumpy, but juicy oranges—are commonly used in Latin cooking. Since these are not eating oranges, their juice is the thing. And there's no better way to marinate pork than to use sour oranges in a marinade base, as they are in Garlic Mojo (page 32) and in Pineapple, Pork, and Boniato Stew (page 211). You'll recognize sour oranges in your produce section because they are the ugliest-looking oranges around. If you can't find them, this recipe makes an ideal substitution, by combining orange juice and fresh lime juice to duplicate the slightly tart, sour flavor. Mix up a batch and keep it in the refrigerator for no more than 7–10 days. As a cooking condiment, it adds a nice bit of Vitamin C to your daily diet.

¹/₂ cup orange juice   *¹/₂ cup fresh lime juice*

Combine the juices in a clean glass jar or bottle with a lid. Cover and refrigerate. Use to marinate pork or chicken, and occasionally turn the meat. I don't recommend this mix for fish, as the high acid content will literally cook the seafood, ceviche-style. For a little added flavor interest try substituting it in any recipe where you might usually use orange juice.

Makes 1 cup

Per Tablespoon: Calories: 5; Fat, Cholesterol, and Sodium: 0; % Daily Value: Vitamin C 10%

Smokin' Rub

This is a dry spice rub that I like to use when smoking pork, beef, chicken, or turkey. The brown sugar creates a mahogany-colored, caramelized crust on the outside of the meat, the kind you might expect if you had basted with oil or butter, only this stuff has absolutely no fat. The sugar also tones down the heat of the black and cayenne peppers, nicely balancing the sweet-hot tastes. This recipe makes enough to coat about a 5-pound piece of meat. Double or triple the amounts to make enough for whatever you're smoking.

2 tablespoons dark or light brown sugar

2 teaspoons ground thyme

2 teaspoons salt

1 teaspoon ground dry mustard

1 teaspoon black pepper

1 teaspoon cayenne pepper

Combine all ingredients. Cover, and store at room temperature.

Makes ½ cup

Per Tablespoon: Calories: 15; Fat and Cholesterol: 0; Sodium: 535 mg; No other significant nutritional value

The Journey of Jerk

Any discussion of jerk, Jamaica's namesake dish, is bound to cause a stir. It's like talking about the best way to make an Italian red sauce, which my family wouldn't dare call sauce—but call it "making gravy." Everyone has an opinion about what's the best recipe, and sometimes even the name is disputed.

Having researched many jerk recipes, I found that the ones I like best all have one thing in common: They cause a flavor explosion in your mouth. While I don't mean to imply that jerk is the beginning and end of Jamaican cuisine, because Jamaican cooking is much more varied than that, jerk may be one of the few Caribbean dishes that most Americans have eaten.

Jerking is a method of cooking, as well as a flavor profile. It's a low-, slow-heat cooking method, a combination of smoking and barbecuing. In Jamaican jerk huts, seasoned beef, pork, or chicken is wrapped in foil and cooked over smoldering coals in an enclosed grill for several hours. The meats are then unwrapped and finished directly on the grill for a crispy exterior. Whole fish can also be done this way, but cooked for a shorter time. This procedure can be closely simulated in your own backyard by using a closed grill or smoker and cooking on the top rack, over low heat.

The flavoring aspect of jerk is not quite so cut and dried. Everyone seems to have a special ingredient that makes his jerk better than the next guy's. There's a wide assortment of jerk sauces, pastes, and rubs on the market today, and many are terrific products. But if you have a hankering to make your own, there are a few key ingredients you must use so as not to commit jerk heresy.

The heat is supplied by Scotch bonnets with a sweet contrast from allspice. These two ingredients are the backbone of any jerk recipe. Jerk's aim is not simply to blow your head off with the heat, but to be a flavorful seasoning, as well. Toward this end, I think adding a fruit, such as mango, adds more depth to the flavor. The beauty of all of this is that you wind up with an extremely big-flavored cooking condiment without any added fat.

Jolly Mon Jerk Paste

Pastes are like rubs in that they are flavor enhancers added during the cooking process. While rubs are dry, pastes have moisture. In this case the moisture comes from the mango, yielding an easy, slathered-on consistency. In addition, the sweetness of the mango plays against the heat of the Scotch bonnets. If time permits, let the paste permeate the meat for several hours before cooking. Try it on skinless chicken, pork loin, or even a whole turkey. As with all chile pepper recipes, you control the heat level with the amount of peppers used. To reduce the fire, you can remove the seeds, since they contain a good bit of heat.

1 cup quartered onion

¹/₂ cup chopped scallion

1 tablespoon ground allspice

1 tablespoon ground thyme

¹/₂ teaspoon freshly grated nutmeg

¹/₄ teaspoon salt

1 teaspoon minced Scotch bonnet pepper, with seeds

³/₄ cup (1 small fruit) ripe, cubed mango

1. Combine all the ingredients except the mango in a food processor. Process on medium speed for 1–2 minutes, until there are no chunks left, and you get a pasty consistency that somewhat holds together. Add the mango and pulse a few times, just enough to incorporate the fruit into a smooth consistency. Slather this all over whatever food you're jerking. Refrigerate for as long as possible; at least a few hours.

2. When it comes time to grill or bake, to keep the paste from sticking to the grill rack or the pan, use a nonstick cooking spray. You should also use low heat. For grilling purposes, I start off by cooking the food on a shallow, aluminum baking sheet, or on tin foil. This buffers the heat, helps the paste to adhere to the

meat, not the grill rack, and makes for easier cleanup. After 45 minutes or so, transfer the food directly to the grill rack and continue cooking until done. If cooking in the oven, set the temperature at 250 degrees, and bake in the pan for about $1^1/2$ hours.

Makes about 1 cup, or enough to cover $1^1/2$–2 pounds of meat

Per $^1/4$ cup: Calories: 70; Fat and Cholesterol: 0; Sodium: 140 mg;
% Daily Value: Vitamin C 51%, Vitamin A 25%

Hot Zone: Rating the Peppers

The heat level of peppers is measured in something called a Scoville unit. If you think of how we measure temperature (in degrees), then Scoville units (SU) make sense. The following chart makes it quite apparent that Scotch bonnets are the hottest on the chile scale. So if you're a little timid about jumping right in, substitute a milder pepper.

HEAT BAROMETER

Green or Red Bell Peppers	0 SU
Cherry Peppers	100–500 SU
Ancho or Poblano	1,000–1,500 SU
Jalapeño	2,500–5,000 SU
Serrano	5,000–15,000 SU
Cayenne	30,000–50,000 SU
Bird or Thai	50,000–100,000 SU
Scotch Bonnet or Habanero	150,000–300,000 SU

Jerk Rub

Aspice or herb rub, in my opinion, is one of the most convenient tools of tasty, low-fat cooking. A rub will adhere to many different cuts of beef, pork, poultry, or fish, without requiring any oil. I call this a jerk rub because the combination of seasonings is similar to those you would find in a jerk paste or sauce. While this recipe yields just 3 tablespoons, you will find it goes a long way. A light dusting on both sides of the food, before grilling, baking, or broiling, makes for a quick flavor hit.

1 tablespoon onion powder

1¹/₂ teaspoons ground allspice

1 teaspoon ground thyme

¹/₂ teaspoon ground ginger

¹/₂ teaspoon cinnamon

¹/₂ teaspoon cayenne pepper

¹/₄ teaspoon freshly ground nutmeg

¹/₄ teaspoon garlic powder

¹/₄ teaspoon salt

Combine all ingredients. Cover, and store at room temperature. A tablespoon will properly season 5–6 pork chops or chicken breasts.

Makes 3 tablespoons

Per Tablespoon: Calories, Fat, Cholesterol: 0; Sodium: 200 mg; No other significant nutritional value

Seasoning-Up

Seasoning-up is a Caribbean cooking term used to describe a kind of herb marinade. There is absolutely no hard and fast rule about what goes into this concoction, but, generally speaking, it's a mixture of fresh herbs, as opposed to dry. Used to season meat and chicken, the blend should be scraped off for browning, then added to the pan to flavor the stock, water, or whatever liquid you might be using to make a gravy. A simple but delicious meal can be had by seasoning-up boneless pork loin medallions, then pan-sautéing them. Remove them from the pan, and use chicken stock thickened with arrowroot, and the seasoning-up blend, to make a light brown sauce for pouring over the meat and accompanying rice.

¹/₄ cup minced onion

2 tablespoons minced fresh chives

2 tablespoons minced fresh curly leaf parsley, stems included

2 tablespoons minced fresh marjoram, stems included

1 tablespoon fresh lime juice

1 tablespoon soy sauce

1 teaspoon minced fresh thyme, stems included

¹/₂ teaspoon dried oregano leaves

¹/₂ teaspoon ground turmeric

¹/₄ teaspoon salt

¹/₈ teaspoon crushed red pepper flakes

3 garlic cloves, smashed

In a mortar and pestle, or in a small bowl, mash the ingredients together with the pestle or the back of a wooden spoon. The mixture will be slightly damp and loosely held together. Spread it all over what-

(Seasoning-Up continued from page 25)

ever you're seasoning-up, and let it sit for about 1 hour at room temperature. Transform your favorite recipe by using the seasoning-up to flavor pot roasts, beef stew, chicken and wine dishes, braised pork dishes, and roasts.

Makes a heaping ½ cup, enough to season-up 1 pound of meat

Per ¼ of the recipe (assuming 4 servings per 1 pound meat): Calories: 15; Fat and Cholesterol: 0;
Sodium: 300 mg; % Daily Value: Vitamin C 10%

Jump-Up

Jump-ups are Caribbean street parties that, luckily, are held on an ongoing basis. Usually on weekends, locals and tourists alike party to music, food, and drink. When vacationing in the islands, ask around to find out when and where the weekly Jump-up is occurring.

St. Lucia is one island that has Jump-ups every Friday night in the northern village of Gros Islet. If you don't make it to a Jump-up, there are other fun events on the island that offer an opportunity to check the local food. In Ausut there's Market Feast, hosted by vendors at the Castries market, where the emphasis is on music and specially prepared local dishes. If you're going to St. Lucia in November, look for the International Food Fair. This annual charity event, at Pointe Seraphine, will provide one-stop eating for a cross section of food from St. Lucia's many cultures. And should you visit in December, Annou Tjuit Sent Lisi is the annual culinary competition for island chefs, whose winner goes on to represent St. Lucia at the larger Caribbean-wide competition.

Mint and White Dressing & Marinade

Mint is an herb commonly used in Caribbean cooking. And while plain mint is just fine for this recipe, there are over thirty species cultivated worldwide, such as orange mint, apple mint, pineapple mint, and even chocolate mint. Whenever you're cooking with mint, make sure the leaves are not wilted, and that it looks perky and fresh. Its flavor is compatible with a light style of cooking, and it's a good accent for sweet, fruit-based dishes as well as savory recipes, such as marinades and dressings. One of the challenges in making a good-tasting, low-fat vinaigrette is replacing the viscosity that is lost when the oil is reduced. In this recipe, I've used white bread to perform that function. This helps to thicken up the dressing without added fat calories. If you're using this as a marinade, not a salad dressing, for chicken or fish, boil what's left over, or give it a quick zap in the microwave, and use it for a last-minute brushing.

$^1/_4$ *cup white wine*

$^1/_4$ *cup fresh mint leaves, stems removed*

$^1/_2$ *slice white bread, crust removed*

2 tablespoons olive oil

2 tablespoons chopped fresh curly-leaf parsley, stems removed

1 tablespoon minced shallots

1 teaspoon honey

$^1/_4$ *teaspoon salt*

$^1/_8$ *teaspoon ground black pepper*

In a blender, combine all the ingredients and puree until smooth. Taste the vinaigrette before pouring it from the blender. It may look smooth, but if it doesn't taste smooth, and you sense tiny bread particles on your tongue, process again until it tastes as smooth as it looks. If using it as a marinade, count on this recipe being enough for 4 (4–6-ounce) boneless chicken breasts or fish fillets.

Makes a scant ½ cup

Per Tablespoon: Calories: 45; Fat: 3 g; Cholesterol: 0; Sodium: 75 mg; No other significant nutritional value

Spanish Olive and Molasses Spread

Similar to tapenade, a Mediterranean olive paste, this spread works not only as a cooking condiment but also as a snack spread on crispy flat bread or plain, unsalted crackers. The salty, intense flavor of the pimento-stuffed green Spanish olives is offset by the addition of molasses. And since molasses comes from sugar cane, it seems like an ideal Caribbean ingredient to use in a nontraditional way. Normally, olive spreads contain a fair amount of oil, but the syrupy consistency of molasses makes a perfect substitute liquid. A small amount of bread crumbs also helps to increase the volume without adding any more fat. Use this spread on fish fillets and chicken, wrap in a foil pouch, then grill. The green-and-red-flecked spread looks particularly pretty over a pink salmon fillet.

1 cup small Spanish pimento-stuffed
  olives
2 tablespoons fresh bread crumbs
1 tablespoon capers, drained

2 garlic cloves, coarsely chopped
1 teaspoon molasses
Coarsely ground black pepper, to taste

1. In a blender or food processor, process the olives, bread crumbs, capers, and garlic on low speed until coarsely pulverized into a mixture that loosely holds together. Do not puree.

2. Transfer to a bowl, and stir in the molasses and pepper.

Makes 8 servings

Per Serving: Calories: 30; Fat: 2 g; Cholesterol: 0; Sodium: 240 mg; No other significant nutritional value

Annatto Oil

This red-orange oil is created by using the annatto seed, something the Caribbean Indians used to make body dye. History says that painting their skin red with this natural dye provided protection from the sun as well as insects. But, lucky for us, annatto is also used for cooking, where it lends a mild flavor but a bold color. You may see it called by its Spanish name, *achiote,* as a key ingredient in many Puerto Rican dishes. It also goes by the name *rou cou* on Trinidad, Martinique, and Guadeloupe. Annatto seeds look like tiny, red-brown pebbles, and are sold with other spices. There are several recipes throughout the book that call for annatto oil, or you may use it in place of your regular sautéing oil. One thing to remember: The color will lighten the longer it cooks, so don't let it sit on the heat too long.

¹/₂ cup corn oil   *¹/₄ cup annatto (achiote) seeds*

In a small saucepan, over very low heat, combine the oil and seeds. Heat for 5 minutes, or until the oil takes on a deep orange color. Remove from the heat, cool, and strain. Store in a clean glass jar or bottle with a lid. It keeps indefinitely at room temperature or refrigerated. This is used so sparingly that this ¹/₂ cup recipe will last quite a while.

Per Teaspoon: Calories: 40; Fat: 5 g; Cholesterol and Sodium: 0; No other significant nutritional value

Garlic Mojo

Mojo is a classic Cuban cooking condiment. This garlic and citrus blend is used as a marinade for Cuban Roast Pork (page 216), or with any meats, for that matter. It's also a drizzle-on condiment for boiled yuca, steamed vegetables, and mashed or boiled potatoes, and it's a great sour cream alternative for baked potatoes. It's like a vinaigrette, the difference being that mojo is lightly heated. Mojo recipes normally call for lots more oil than you find in this version. To pick up the necessary volume, I've added white wine and water. Consider it an all-around cooking marinade.

3 tablespoons olive oil

6–8 garlic cloves, minced

¹/₂ teaspoon dried oregano leaves

¹/₂ teaspoon salt

¹/₄ teaspoon black pepper

¹/₂ cup Sour Orange Mix (page 18)

¹/₄ cup white wine

¹/₄ cup water

1. In a small saucepan, over low heat, warm the olive oil for 3 minutes.

2. In a small bowl, combine the remaining ingredients, then stir them into the warm oil, and heat for another 2 minutes. Cool slightly before using. Store in a clean glass jar or bottle with a lid, and refrigerate. This keeps only a day or two in the refrigerator.

Makes 1 cup

Per Tablespoon: Calories: 30; Fat: 3 g; Cholesterol: 0; Sodium: 70 mg; No other significant nutritional value

How to Iron a Cuban Sandwich

There are some traditional and classic elements to Cuban cuisine, like mojo, café con leche, and pressed sandwiches. All Cuban sandwiches, no matter what's between the bread, look like they've been sent out to the cleaners for a pressing.

This is possible because Cuban bread does not have the crunch and crust of Italian or French breads, but is a relatively soft-crusted loaf. The heated, pressed sandwiches are done on a little tabletop piece of equipment that looks like a waffle iron with flat top and bottom surfaces. There isn't a Cuban lunch counter or coffee stand that doesn't have one of these presses heated and busy all the time.

No matter what time of day, all sandwiches get pressed. In the morning, it may be a simple Cuban toast, cheese bread (American cheese slices between the bread), or an egg and cheese sandwich. Once breakfast is over, out come the roast pork sandwiches, thinly sliced, with onions, or a Cuban mix; a hodgepodge combination of ham, pork, cheese, pickle, lettuce, tomato, mustard, and mayo. These, too, are pressed, yielding a crispy exterior and a slightly warmed center. The handheld delight is then wrapped in a square of waxed paper and cut in half. While Cuban sandwiches can't be considered low calorie, they are a good value for the money, costing no more than $4.00.

To duplicate this idea at home with more nutritionally sound sandwich fillings, I heat my largest heavy, cast-iron skillet. The sandwich of choice, made with soft-crusted loaf bread, is then wrapped in foil and placed in the skillet, with an iron or a smaller cast-iron skillet sitting on top. Anything with some weight, like a brick, will do fine. Heat on low for 5 minutes, turn, and repeat. Turn the radio to a salsa music station, get into a Latin state of mind, and enjoy your Cubano-style sandwich.

Sofrito

Sofrito is the basic starting point for many Cuban, Puerto Rican, and Spanish dishes. It's the equivalent of the French mirepoix, the onion, carrot, and celery trio used as a flavoring for many dishes. The literal translation of sofrito is "lightly fried," and that's just what we're doing with this seasoning. The requisite components include garlic, onion, and green bell pepper. From there, the personal touch takes over but sofrito often will include tomato, ham, herbs, and spices. For an extra-flavor bump, I also added cilantro and capers.

This is the type of item you want to prepare in a batch, then have on hand for future use. Freeze it in ice cube trays or Ziploc bags, in 2-tablespoon portions, enough for flavoring a soup, stew, rice, gravy, or beans. Once thawed, complete the sofrito by adding the tomato and ham. While old-time cooks did not have the luxury of a food processor, I find it's quick, easy, and doesn't compromise the end product. Otherwise, do it the old-fashioned way with a mortar and pestle or a very sharp knife.

1 cup coarsely chopped onion

1 cup coarsely chopped green bell pepper

¼ cup fresh flat-leaf parsley, stems removed

¼ cup cilantro, stems removed

2 tablespoons chopped garlic

1 tablespoon capers, drained

2 teaspoons dried oregano leaves

½ teaspoon salt

1 tablespoon olive oil

FOR EVERY 2 TABLESPOONS OF THE ABOVE, USE:

1 ounce lean ham, finely minced

1 plum tomato, finely minced

1. Combine all ingredients except the ham and tomato in a food processor. Process, on low speed for 1 minute, scraping down the sides at least once. You want a pulverized consistency, but not a puree, meaning you should still see teeny, tiny pieces of food. Freeze in 2-tablespoon portions (see Headnote above).

2. When ready to cook, thaw the sofrito. One portion is enough for a soup, stew, or rice that will serve four. Using whatever pan you'll be cooking in, over medium-low heat, cook the ham 3 minutes, until lightly browned. Add the tomato and the sofrito. Cook over low heat for 5–10 minutes, stirring occasionally, until the tomato starts to brown. Your sofrito is now complete, and you can continue with your recipe.

Makes about 4 cups, enough to season about 7 recipes

Per 1 finished sofrito recipe: Calories: 100; Fat: 3 g; Cholesterol: 15 mg; Sodium: 510 mg;
% Daily Value: Vitamin C 107%, Thiamine 27%, Vitamin B$_6$ 18%

Island Shrimp Stock

Abeef or veal stock made from scratch can take up to 12–18 hours. Not so with seafood stocks, especially shrimp stock. You can do a fine job of extracting the flavor from shrimp shells in less than 1 hour, start to finish. If I'm using peeled shrimp in a recipe, I always save the shells, and freeze them in a Ziploc bag. The shells can then go directly from the freezer into the stockpot when I need to whip up a quick stock. When available, I buy shrimp with the heads on, and add the heads to the shells to really enhance the flavor of the stock. This shrimp stock is an excellent, low-fat way to start a tomato-based seafood sauce, a bouillabaisse, or a white clam sauce for linguine. It also can be used as a simple poaching broth for fish fillets. So, don't be put off by the notion of making a stock from scratch. It's really not that time-consuming, nor is it difficult.

1 tablespoon olive oil　　　　　　*¹/₂ teaspoon salt*
1 medium onion, coarsely chopped　*8 whole peppercorns*
1 large carrot, coarsely chopped　*8 whole coriander seeds*
2 celery stalks, coarsely chopped　*1 bay leaf*
Heads and shells from 1 pound shrimp　*3 cups water*
1 cup white wine

1. In a 4-quart pan, over medium heat, warm the oil. Add the onion, carrot, celery, shrimp heads, and shells. Cook for 10 minutes, stirring occasionally, until the vegetables soften.

2. Increase the heat to high, add all the remaining ingredients except the water, and cook for another 10 minutes, until the wine is reduced by half.

3. Add the water, and bring the mixture to a boil. Reduce the heat to medium, and simmer for 30 minutes. When it looks as though you have about 2 cups of liquid left in the pot, strain it through a fine mesh strainer or cheesecloth. You want the stock as clear as possible, so strain again, if necessary. Your final yield should be pretty close to 2 cups, although this is not an exact science. Freeze any that you won't use immediately.

Makes about 2 cups

Per ¹/₂ cup: Calories: 75; Fat: 3 g; Cholesterol: 3 mg; Sodium: 140 mg; No other significant nutritional value

Shell Shocked

Making seafood stocks from crustacean shells, fish heads, and skeletons should not be a shocking thought to you. For some people, cooking with cracked crab claws and shrimp heads is an icky idea, but recycling this stuff not only produces delicious, low-fat stocks, it keeps the trash can from smelling until garbage day arrives.

Seafood stocks can be made while making or cleaning up from dinner; otherwise the shells get put in the fridge, and you never get around to it. Once a stock has been made, it can be frozen (1 cup increments are handy), then thawed for future use. If using cooked crab claws, lobster shells, and fish bones, rinse them first, to keep the finished broth as clear as possible and to minimize straining.

Jolly Mon Bubba Barbecue Sauce

There are a million different kinds of barbecue sauces sitting on grocery shelves, so why would you bother to make your own? Because this sauce has an unusual flavor, slightly sweet yet slightly hot, that you won't find in a bottle. It's got a bit of a Jamaican jerk twist to it, because some of the ingredients are very similar to what's in jerk sauce: onion, scallion, allspice, thyme, and Scotch bonnet peppers. But the tomato sauce, brown sugar, and vinegar give it that all-American barbecue touch. There's not a speck of oil in this recipe, making it a fat-free, big-flavored cooking sauce. Use it on anything that goes on the grill, as well as the Down Island Smoked Pulled Pork (page 218).

$^1/_3$ cup minced onion

2 tablespoons minced scallion

1 (15-ounce) can tomato sauce

3 tablespoons dark brown sugar

2 tablespoons cider vinegar

$1^1/_2$ teaspoons ground thyme

1 teaspoon minced Scotch bonnet pepper

1 teaspoon ground allspice

1 teaspoon ground dry mustard

$^1/_4$ teaspoon salt

$^1/_4$ teaspoon black pepper

1. In a medium saucepan over medium heat, cook the onion and scallion for 5 minutes, until soft but not browned.

2. Add the remaining ingredients; bring to a boil, reduce the heat, partially cover, and simmer for 20 minutes. Remove from the heat and cool. The sauce will thicken as it cools, making for a substantial sauce consistency that stays on a basting brush. To store, cover and refrigerate or freeze.

Makes 1½ cups

Per 2 Tablespoons: Calories: 30; Fat and Cholesterol: 0; Sodium: 225 mg;
No other significant nutritional value

Big-Flavor
Accompaniments

■ ■ ■ ■ ■ ■ ■ ■ ■ ■ ■

Accompaniments are little bundles of flavor that are scooped or poured on at the table. What separates accompaniments from the recipes in the preceding chapter is that they make their appearance on the plate, while cooking condiments work their magic in the kitchen, among the pots and pans.

Caribbeans have been spicing up their meals with accompaniments for centuries. Hot sauces and mango chutney are pantry staples in island kitchens across the region. Keeping these items on hand adds zest to island diets, which in years past, often included poorer quality meats and limited variety. A syrup, a sauce, a salsa, or a relish can add that same lively zest to your dinner plate, whether you live in New York or New Mexico.

Most of these selections are newly created dishes using typical Caribbean ingredients and seasonings as their anchor. Calling on tropical fruits and their juices, and an explosive use of spices, these big-flavored accompaniments are all that you need to complete exciting, healthy meals. No lengthy sauces to make, or complex cooking methods. These recipes are quick and to the point. If you've spent any time in the kitchen trying to cut calories and reduce fat, you know that delicious food is created, not by eliminating ingredients but by adding in as many big flavors as possible. What easier way to do that than with these intensively flavored accompaniments.

Small Bad Sauce

I derived the name "small bad sauce" from the recipe's original Haitian French name, *ti-malice. Ti* is a Creole shortcut for *petit,* and the Latin root of malice means bad. A bad sauce, indeed, it's spicy, vinegary, but not a sauce in the traditional sense. It's more like a finely grated, marinated slaw. An intensely flavored accompaniment, it's used in small quantities to top plainly cooked chicken, pork, or fish. Scoop it on with a fork or slotted spoon, draining off the marinade.

1/2 cup finely shredded green cabbage
1/4 cup finely shredded carrot
1/4 cup finely shredded radish
1/4 cup finely shredded onion
2 garlic cloves, minced
1/4 cup cider vinegar

1 tablespoon fresh lime juice
1 tablespoon olive oil
1/4 teaspoon salt
1 dried 3-inch chile pepper, with seeds,
    finely minced

Combine all the ingredients in a medium bowl. Toss and let sit at room temperature for at least 1 hour before serving.

Makes 6 servings

Per Serving: Calories: 30; Fat: 2 g; Cholesterol: 0; Sodium: 100 mg; % Daily Value: Vitamin C 10%

Caribbean Ranch Dressing

This dressing is not based on anything authentic, but is my island interpretation of a creamy-style salad dressing. And when my husband, Taster Ted, tried it, he said, "Caribbean ranch dressing, right?" It seemed like a perfect name to me. While this is not a low-fat dressing, it's an extremely flavorful one, with the island touch coming from tamarind paste and fresh lime juice. This recipe makes enough to dress five side salads, but can easily be doubled to make more. To control salad dressing calories, dress and toss the salad in a large bowl, then serve it. This method coats the lettuce much better, using less dressing than when people do it themselves.

2 tablespoons peanut oil

2 tablespoons orange juice

1 tablespoon low-fat cottage cheese

1 tablespoon fresh lime juice

1 tablespoon cider vinegar

1 tablespoon water

2 teaspoons unsweetened tamarind paste

   (see page 45)

¹/₂ teaspoon sugar

¹/₄ teaspoon salt

Coarsely ground black pepper, to taste

In a blender, combine all the ingredients except the pepper. Puree on medium speed for 1 minute, until smooth and creamy. Stir in the coarsely ground black pepper.

Makes about ¹/₃ cup

Per Tablespoon: Calories: 60; Fat: 5 g; Cholesterol: 0; Sodium: 200 mg; No other significant nutritional value

The Tale of Tamarind

Sometimes called an Indian date, tamarind, used in many dishes and drinks, is an important ingredient in Caribbean, Indian, and Middle Eastern cuisine. This is not a fruit you eat right from the tree, but it's the sour, sticky pulp, available in various forms, that is a versatile flavoring ingredient.

Tamarinds hang off a large tree, and have an outer shell, about 6 inches long, that houses the seeds and the datelike pulp. They remind me of a dark brown, flattened cigar, or a huge Tootsie Roll. I've had a lot of time to examine tamarinds, because a huge tamarind tree took up the entire backyard at my previous home. I was constantly sweeping up the brown pods, as the tree dropped more than I could possibly use.

Since most folks don't have the luxury of fresh tamarind in the backyard, there are several ways to buy the product, usually available at ethnic or specialty markets. It comes as: pressed pulp with the seeds, pureed frozen pulp, sweetened or unsweetened paste, nectar, and syrup. You will find several recipes, throughout the book (Tamarind Scallion Chicken Bundles, page 197, Grilled Beef with Spicy Tamarind Sauce, page 235, Tamarind Soda, page 293), that call for tamarind in one of these forms. Because tamarind has a sour taste, except for the sweetened paste and nectar, most recipes call for some type of sweetener.

Parsley Dill Chimichurri

This pesto-like condiment originates in South and Central America, where it's typically smeared on grilled steaks. Although this is usually made with lots of olive oil, I obtain the right consistency by using just a little oil, plus some tomato and onion for added moisture. Fresh dill added to the classic parsley version makes for a more complex flavor, in my opinion. This recipe makes enough to top 4 servings of grilled flank steak, pork tenderloin, or firm fish such as tuna and swordfish. While preparing test batches for this book, I discovered it's also delicious as a salsa snack, served with baked tortilla chips.

1 cup fresh curly parsley, stems removed

$^{1}/_{4}$ cup fresh dill, stems removed

$1^{1}/_{2}$ tablespoons olive oil

1 tablespoon finely diced onion

1 tablespoon fresh lime juice

1 plum tomato, finely chopped

2 garlic cloves, minced

$^{1}/_{4}$ teaspoon salt

$^{1}/_{8}$ teaspoon black pepper

In a food processor, combine all ingredients, using 1 tablespoon of the oil. Puree on high for 30 seconds; scraping down the sides once. Process again for an additional 30–45 seconds while drizzling in the remaining $^{1}/_{2}$ tablespoon of oil. The mixture will be smooth, with tiny, visible, red tomato flecks. Use it immediately, or cover and refrigerate. A small amount of liquid will accumulate after it sits, so stir before using.

Makes $^{1}/_{2}$ cup

Per Tablespoon: Calories: 30; Fat: 3 g; Cholesterol: 0; Sodium: 70 mg; % Daily Value: Vitamin C 23 %

Grapefruit, Corn, and Candied Ginger Relish

Candied ginger, sold in specialty stores and well-stocked supermarkets, adds an interesting flavor dimension to whatever dish you're using it in. It's part spicy ginger and part sugar sweet. Ginger itself, widely used in island cooking, is a throwback to East Indian and oriental influences. The other thing this relish has going for it is its colors. Nothing could be prettier than pink grapefruit, yellow corn, green scallions, and flecks of candied ginger. Not a speck of oil is used, and you couldn't ask for more flavor.

*1¹/₂ cups (1 large fruit) fresh pink
grapefruit sections cut into ¹/₂-inch
pieces, membranes removed and juice
reserved*

1 cup drained canned corn

*¹/₄ cup finely sliced scallions, green part
only*

*3 tablespoons candied ginger cut into
paper-thin strips*

¹/₄ teaspoon salt

1 dried bird pepper, minced

In a medium bowl, combine all the ingredients. Cover, and refrigerate for at least 30 minutes. I find relishes, chutneys, and salsas taste better when they're not ice cold, so serve this at room temperature.

Makes 4 servings

*Per Serving: Calories: 100; Fat and Cholesterol: 0; Sodium: 140 mg;
% Daily Value: Vitamin C 68%, Iron 14%, Potassium 13%*

Sorry, Not a Love Fruit

Even though passion fruit won't change your love life, it's still a wonderful tropical fruit, whose juice has an intense flavor and aroma.

Good thing it's got a great name and tastes delicious, because passion fruit itself is nothing much to look at. It's a small, purple-brownish, egg-shaped fruit that is wrinkled when it's ripe. And inside isn't much prettier. A yellow, almost jelly-like pulp is intermingled with a mass of black seeds, reminiscent of a pomegranate interior. It's this seedy pulp, when strained, that yields the aromatic passion fruit juice. Although this description is less than glowing, don't let it dissuade you from buying the fruit when you see it in the market. If you're using frozen pulp or canned or frozen juice, you will need only a small amount. This is high-flavor stuff.

So where *did* the name come from? The plant's intricate flower, when in bloom, is supposedly named after the Passion of Christ, representing the wound, crucifixion nails, crown of thorns, and the Apostles. Who dreamed that one up?

Passionate Salad Dressing

I would describe the flavor of passion fruit as perfumey, tart, and heavenly. These small, wrinkled, egg-shaped fruits are difficult even for me to find, and I live in the subtropics. More reliable to locate, and just as delicious, is frozen passion fruit pulp. Like the orange juice concentrate in this recipe, the pulp lends viscosity, eliminating the need for lots of oil. There should be little else to compete with passion fruit's unique flavor, so this is a fairly simple recipe.

¹⁄₄ cup frozen passion fruit pulp, thawed
   (see page 48)
¹⁄₄ cup frozen orange juice concentrate,
   thawed
2 tablespoons white wine vinegar

2 tablespoons water
2 teaspoons honey
1¹⁄₄ teaspoons ground ginger
Coarsely ground black pepper, to taste

Combine all the ingredients in a jar and shake. Dress the salad greens in a large bowl, tossing to coat thoroughly.

Makes ¹⁄₂ cup

Per 2 Tablespoons: Calories: 25; Fat, Cholesterol, and Sodium: 0; % Daily Value: Vitamin C 23%

Mango, Tomato, and Coconut Mix

This accompaniment requires using a mango that's just turning ripe, something with a little solid texture to it. A very ripe mango will be difficult to dice fine without turning it into pulp (a good thing for some recipes, but not this one). You'll also need unsweetened shredded coconut, usually located in the baking aisle, different from the sweet variety you may be accustomed to using for baking. Use this mix with grilled, baked, broiled, or roasted entrees. Or as a snack, on top of reduced-fat cream cheese and crackers. The ever-so-slight coconut flavor, mingled with the other savory ingredients, will be a pleasant surprise to your taste buds.

1 cup moderately ripe, peeled, finely diced mango

1/2 cup seeded, finely diced tomato

2 tablespoons finely sliced scallion, green part only

2 tablespoons finely chopped cilantro

1 tablespoon finely chopped red onion

1 tablespoon shredded, unsweetened coconut

1 tablespoon fresh lime juice

1/8 teaspoon salt

1 small bird pepper, minced

In a medium bowl, gently toss all ingredients until well combined. Cover, and refrigerate for at least 1 hour, to allow the flavors to blend. There shouldn't be much liquid in the bottom of the bowl, just whatever has come from the mango and tomatoes. If the mixture appears too runny, drain off some of the liquid, leaving just enough to keep it moist. Serve at room temperature.

Makes 4 servings

Per Serving: Calories: 50; Fat and Cholesterol: 0; Sodium: 70 mg;
% Daily Value: Vitamin C 39%, Vitamin A 23%

Mad for Mangoes

For most people, mangoes are probably the most readily available tropical fruit. Mango drinks and desserts are popular, but my goal, in this book, is to present them in different and diverse ways (Jolly Mon Jerk Paste Sauce, page 22, Shrimp and Mango–Stuffed Yellowtail, page 164, Veal with Sweet Potatoes, Mangoes, and Plantain Chips, page 241).

The majority of mangoes sold in U.S. supermarkets are grown in Mexico, Central America, and Florida. Their growing season extends from June to September, when they are most plentiful and least expensive. During the summer months, I often get my supply from neighboring trees, waiting for the ripe ones to fall and scarfing them up before someone else does. When selecting a mango in the market, a ripe fruit will be soft to the touch, with a yellow-orange or red-blushed skin. If it's still hard, let it sit at room temperature for further ripening.

While there are many different varieties of mango, they all should have a fragrant aroma when ripe. I've heard their flavor described as a peach and pineapple combo. I disagree; I think a mango tastes like a mango, and nothing else is quite like it. A good-quality, ripe mango is juicy, wet, and sloppy to eat, especially if you're scraping your teeth over the skin, artichoke-style, to get that last bit of fruit. Dental floss nearby might also be a good idea, as some varieties are quite fibrous.

This is the easiest way, I've found, to remove the mango fruit from the flat, stonelike seed and skin.

How to Cut a Mango

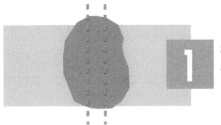

1 Stand the fruit on one end, and skimming alongside the pit, cut off two sides.

2 Make a series of crisscross slits, based on the desired cube size, taking care not to cut through the skin.

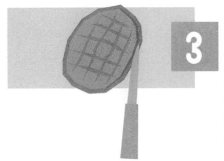

3 Slide the knife along the underside of the fruit, releasing it from the skin. With a paring knife, trim around the pit, to obtain whatever fruit is still clinging. No matter how good you are at this, there will invariably be some fruit remaining on the skin and seed. Lean over the sink and eat what's left, artichoke style.

Mango Hot Sauce

This is one of my favorite all-around recipes. It's made with two staple Caribbean ingredients, mango and Scotch bonnet pepper. It's slightly sweet because of the mango, and definitely hot because of the Scotch bonnet. Although I like spicy food, I don't really consider this a blow-your-head-off sauce. It should be treated as an all-purpose tabletop condiment, a dipping sauce for raw oysters, or an add-in for meat loaf, beef stew, or bread stuffing. Try to store it in a small glass bottle, like the kind steak sauce comes in. That way, it's easier to shake out. It makes a perfect hostess gift, with its brilliant coral color and a bright ribbon tied around the bottle neck.

1 cup very ripe, peeled, cubed mango

1/3 cup water

2 tablespoons cider vinegar

3 garlic cloves, smashed

1/2 Scotch bonnet pepper, finely minced

1/2 teaspoon turmeric

1/2 teaspoon ground dry mustard

1/2 teaspoon sugar

1/4 teaspoon salt

In a small saucepan, combine all the ingredients. Cover, and simmer for 1/2 hour. Pour into a food processor or blender, and process until smooth. The amount of time this takes will vary based on the equipment you're using, but either way, you need to achieve a pourable consistency. Cool to room temperature before storing in a clean, dry bottle or jar with a tight-fitting lid. This keeps in the refrigerator for a few months, although mine never lasts that long.

Makes about 1 cup

Per Tablespoon: Calories: 15; Fat and Cholesterol: 0; Sodium: 35 mg; % Daily Value: Vitamin C 10%

Who's Who in Caribbean Sauces

The choice in hot sauces is staggering. Not only are there tons to choose from but they're sold everywhere—in airport shops, upscale boutiques, and stores devoted to nothing but hot sauces. These little jars of fire come from every corner of the world, and the Caribbean is well represented. Island-made sauces tend to use Scotch bonnet peppers for fire, while other ingredients often include vegetables, tropical fruits, mustard, vinegar, and assorted spices and herbs. For experienced, traveling hotheads, there's nothing more fun than coming home from vacation with an obscure, no-one-has-ever-seen-it sauce under your arm.

Caribbean sauces, with their weirdly shaped bottles and oddball names, are fun additions to a low-fat pantry. Once you start seasoning with these lively sauces, you'll never again consider butter or oil a must-have ingredient. Here's a list, culled from Jenifer Trainer Thompson's, *The Great Hot Sauce Book,* of Caribbean-made sauces. Though it's not an exhaustive list, you might want to check out these products the next time you're traveling to the islands, or in a supermarket aisle. There are many other Caribbean-style sauces made in the States that are not included here.

BRAND NAME/SAUCE NAME	ISLAND
A Taste of Caribbean Sunshine	St. John
Baron West Indian Hot Sauce	St. Lucia
Blazin' Saddle Habanero Pepper Extra-Hot Sauce (imported by D. L. Jardine, Texas)	Belize
Bush Browne's Pukka Hot Pepper Sauce and Bush Browne's Spicy Jerk Sauce	Jamaica
Chief Trinidad Hot Sauce	Trinidad

Country Home Hot Pepper Sauce	Barbados
Edun's Caribbean Pepper Sauce	Puerto Rico
Erica's Country-Style Pepper Sauce	St. Vincent
Eve's Pepper Sauce	Tobago
Forbes Ground Red Peppers	Costa Rica
Grand Anse Moko Jumbie Grill Sauce	St. Thomas
Gray's Hot Pepper Sauce	Jamaica
Grenfruit Hot Sauce	Grenada
Gunsam's Hot Sauce	St. Vincent
Heatwave North Side Hot Sauce and Heatwave North Side Mango Sauce	St. Thomas
Hecho En Casa Pique Criollo	Puerto Rico
Island Heat Scotch Bonnet Pepper Sauce	Costa Rica
Isla Vieques Mountain Herb Hot Sauce, 3-Pepper Hot Sauce, Pique, and several other varieties	Vieques
Lottie's Bajan-Cajun Premium Hot Pepper Sauce	Barbados
Marie Sharp's Habanero Pepper Sauce	Belize
Marinda's West Indian Hot Sauce	St. Vincent
Matouk's Hot Sauce	Trinidad
Melinda's Hot Sauce	Costa Rica
Miss V's Caribbean Hot Sauce	St. Croix
Nel's Old Time Scotch Bonnet Hot Sauce	Jamaica
Pickapeppa Pepper Sauce	Jamaica
Pirates Blend Caribbean Condiment	Costa Rica

Rica Red Habanero Banana Jama Sauce	Costa Rica
Sunny Caribbee Hot Sauce, and other island seasonings and condiments	Tortola
Susie's Original Hot Sauce	Antigua
Uncle Willie's Hibiscus Vinegar, Uncle Willie's Mangos Jammin' Hot Sauce, and other varieties	St. Thomas
Virgin Fire Dragon's Breath, and other varieties	St. John
Walker's Wood Jonkanoo Pepper Sauce, and others	Jamaica
West Indies Creole Classic Red Pepper Sauce	Dominica
Westlow's Bonney Pepper Sauce	Barbados

Orange Marmalade Lime Glaze

Neither oranges nor limes are indigenous to the Caribbean, but were brought by Columbus himself, and eventually became prolific throughout the region. Spain's famous Seville orange marmalade is a tasty reminder that oranges are a European, not a New World, food. Considered the gold standard, Seville marmalade, or another high-quality type, is an excellent choice for this recipe. Let this dish do its simmering while you're getting dinner together, or doing something else. I like to use it as a glaze for ham, turkey, pork, and fish. It's also perfectly at home on morning toast and English muffins.

*1/2 cup Seville or other high-quality
    orange marmalade*
*1 tablespoon lime zest cut into paper-
    thin, 1/2-inch-long strips*

*2 teaspoons peeled fresh ginger cut into
    paper-thin, 1/2-inch strips*
2 teaspoons fresh lime juice
6 whole cloves

In a small saucepan, combine all ingredients. Cover, and cook over very low heat for about an hour. If the mixture is bubbling, reduce the heat, or move the pan partially off the burner. Test for doneness by tasting the lime zest and ginger; if it's a pleasure to chew, and very soft, it's done. Remove the cloves before using the glaze.

It's best to use this warm, as it thickens when it cools, making it harder to spread with a pastry brush. To keep a supply on hand, double the recipe, store it in a tightly covered jar, and refrigerate. It will keep for two weeks. When ready, heat it gently on the stove top or microwave it for 20–30 seconds to thin it down.

Makes 1/2 cup, or enough to glaze about 4 pork chops, fish fillets, or chicken breasts

Per Tablespoon: Calories: 50; Fat, Cholesterol, Sodium: 0; No other significant nutritional value

Nutmeg Syrup

Nutmeg is a spice that most of us reach for only when baking. But in fact, all over the islands, it's used in many other, more versatile ways. While you will find numerous savory recipes that use nutmeg throughout this book, a nutmeg-flavored syrup is a fun, sweet addition to your condiment shelf. The basic rule of thumb when making syrup is this: The longer you heat the sugar-water mixture, the more the liquid evaporates, the thicker, more concentrated the syrup. There is a point of no return, however, when you end up with hard, brittle, pseudo candy, so don't walk away from the stove when preparing this. If you want a really dark-colored syrup, use dark brown sugar; for a golden, maple syrup shade, use light brown sugar. Warm nutmeg syrup tastes good drizzled over frozen vanilla yogurt, Cashew Waffles (page 279), or as a sweet antidote to a chile pepper hot sauce.

2 cups water   *3 nutmegs, cut in half*
1 cup dark or light brown sugar

1. In a small saucepan over medium-high heat, combine all ingredients. Bring the mixture to a light boil, then reduce the heat just enough to keep it at a full simmer. Keep small, gentle bubbles breaking the surface, not a rolling boil. Simmer for 30 minutes, until the syrup is thick enough to coat the back of a spoon.

2. Remove from the heat; the syrup thickens as it cools. When cool, store in the refrigerator in a clean glass jar or bottle with a lid, or a plastic squirt bottle. I leave the nutmegs in because they look nice and add more flavor during storage.

Makes about 1 cup

Per Tablespoon: Calories: 50; Fat and Cholesterol: 0; Sodium: 5 mg; No other significant nutritional value

Two Peas in a Pod

Most people don't realize how efficient the nutmeg is, yielding not only nutmeg but also mace. As the nut ripens, on 70–90-foot-tall trees, a spongy outer coating splits open, allowing the mace-covered nut to drop from the tree. I have bought whole nutmeg in island markets that still has the red mace overlay on it, which is somewhat pliable and can be peeled off with your hands. For commercial production, the mace is removed, dried, cured, and graded, turning it into a golden-colored spice in its own right. Its flavor is stronger and less sweet than that of nutmeg, and it takes about 6 pounds of nutmeg to produce 1 pound of mace.

The whole nutmeg is also graded and sorted by size and oil content. Most of us buy packaged ground nutmeg, but you will never again want to use that, once you've tasted it freshly grated. Fresh nutmeg is the only way to go, and, with very few exceptions, makes all the difference in a recipe. It's like comparing freshly grated Parmesan cheese with the prepackaged grated variety; there is no comparison. Whole nutmeg is inexpensive, keeps for a long time, and requires only a small, metal nutmeg grater.

Grenada, often referred to as the Spice Island, is a major player in worldwide nutmeg production, as well as many nutmeg-related products, such as jams, jellies, and syrup. These make terrific gifts to bring home from a vacation. If you are planning to visit Grenada, inquire about their late June celebration, which showcases spice products, culinary arts, culture, music, as well as local arts and crafts.

Grilled Tomatillo Sauce

Tomatillos belong to the same family as tomatoes, and, in fact, look like small, hard green tomatoes with a paper wrapper. But that's where the similarity ends. Tomatillos are used green, and have a somewhat tart, lemony flavor. Common to the cuisine of coastal Mexico, which is considered part of Caribbean rim cuisine, tomatillos form the base for many Mexican green sauces. Available in the produce section of many U.S. markets, they have the added feature of a fairly long shelf life, about 3–4 weeks refrigerated. Grilling all the vegetables in this recipe has a two-fold purpose. It makes them soft enough to puree, and it adds a wonderful, smoky, grilled flavor. Just a small amount of oil helps hold it all together, for a virtually fat-free accompaniment, served warm or room temperature, alongside simply broiled or grilled meats and fish.

5 tomatillos, paper husks removed
¹⁄₂ medium red bell pepper
¹⁄₂ medium red onion, cut into thick
  slices
2 garlic cloves, peeled

¹⁄₄ Scotch bonnet pepper, seeded
¹⁄₂ cup reduced-sodium chicken stock
¹⁄₄ cup chopped cilantro
¹⁄₄ teaspoon salt

1. Coat the grill rack or grill tray with nonstick cooking spray. Grill the tomatillos, red pepper, onion, garlic, and Scotch bonnet (the last two skewered together so you don't lose them) over medium heat for 15 minutes, turning once, until all the vegetables are soft and charred. Once the tomatillos are soft and mushy, remove them from the grill until the pepper and onion are tender. Remove everything to a plate, and let them sit until cool enough to handle. The dish can be prepared in advance up to this point.

2. Transfer all the grilled items, including any juices that may have accumulated in the plate, to a food processor. The charred tomatillo and red pepper skins will pulverize just fine, so there's no need to peel them. Add the remaining ingredients and process on high for 2 minutes, until the mixture is smooth, with no visible chunks. Use as is, or warm slightly before serving. This keeps well in the refrigerator for a few days.

Makes 1 cup

Per 2 Tablespoons: Calories: 25; Fat and Cholesterol: 0; Sodium: 95 mg; % Daily Value: Vitamin C 59 %

Pimento and Roasted Garlic Sauce

Fashioned after a traditional Puerto Rican sauce, this gorgeous, burnt orange sauce is fabulous over chicken or fish, and would make a good dipping sauce for grilled shrimp, too. This version is spicy, and while it tastes almost overwhelming in the pan, its intensity is quickly diffused when soaked up by chicken or rice. The olive oil lends some body, while the texture of the sauce is really supplied by the Vitamin C–rich pimento. While the sauce is not low-fat by itself, when put into the context of an entree, it works out quite well.

6 garlic cloves
1 (6¹/₂-ounce) jar whole pimentos, with
    their liquid
3 tablespoons olive oil
1 tablespoon fresh lime juice

1 tablespoon red wine vinegar
¹/₄ teaspoon salt
1 (3-inch) dried chile pepper, minced
Coarsely ground black pepper, to taste

1. Preheat the oven to 350 degrees. Wrap the garlic in aluminum foil and place it on the oven rack. Cook for 30 minutes, until squishy soft. When cool enough to handle, peel the cloves.

2. In a blender, combine the remaining ingredients and the roasted garlic. Puree on high speed for 30 seconds, until the mixture is smooth and the chili pepper is well blended. Transfer to a small saucepan, and, over low heat, warm and serve.

Makes 5 servings

Per Serving: Calories: 90; Fat: 8 g; Cholesterol: 0; Sodium: 125 mg;
% Daily Value: Vitamin C 55%, Vitamin A 17%

Madras Creole Sauce

Tomato-based Creole sauces are either cooked or raw, not too unlike a salsa. Tomato, bell pepper, and celery are usually the three required ingredients, and after that, it's open for interpretation. I chose to use red bell pepper rather than the traditional green, and got the green highlights from the celery, scallion, and basil-parsley herb blend. While most Creole sauces use an acid, such as vinegar or lime juice, I went with the French style of flavoring, and call for white wine. The sauce derives its name from the traditional "madwas" headgear sometimes worn by French West Indies women, particularly at holiday festivals or special events. When you see the finished sauce, you'll agree that it has a bit of a red and green madras look.

2 teaspoons olive oil

¼ cup finely chopped red bell pepper

¼ cup finely chopped onion

2 tablespoons finely chopped scallion

¼ teaspoon minced Scotch bonnet pepper

2 tablespoons finely chopped celery

2 garlic cloves, minced

¼ teaspoon salt

1 cup (2 medium) peeled, seeded, finely diced tomatoes

2 tablespoons dry white wine

1 tablespoons minced fresh flat-leaf parsley

1 teaspoon minced fresh basil

1. In a small skillet, over low heat, warm the oil. Add the pepper, onion, scallion, celery, Scotch bonnet, garlic, and salt. Cook for 10 minutes, until the vegetables are soft but not browned.

(Madras Creole Sauce continued from page 63)

2. Increase the heat to medium and add the tomatoes. Cook for 10 minutes, stirring occasionally, until the mixture is thick and pulpy. Stir in the wine, parsley, and basil. Serve immediately. It's a lovely sauce served over shrimp, fish, pork chops, chicken, or an omelet.

Makes 4 servings

Per Serving: Calories: 50; Fat: 2 g; Cholesterol: 0; Sodium: 140 mg;
% Daily Value: Vitamin C 75%, Vitamin A 14%

Creole Cooking

Creole cooking is a hard thing to define. I'm not even sure there is any one explanation, except to say, "It's cooking that's all mixed up."

Creole, and in Spanish, *criolla,* is a word most of us equate with Louisiana cooking. But long before Louisiana, Creole was born in the islands. As the Caribbean was being settled during the late 1500s and 1600s, cooking techniques and ingredients from France, Spain, and Africa meshed together to create a new cuisine, called Creole, a synonym for Caribbean cuisine. Creole is a fusion of different culinary influences that have evolved over the years. Yet today the term "Creole" is more often used to describe the bold, big flavors of the French West Indies, particularly Guadeloupe and Martinique.

Creole-style recipes will most often include tomatoes, sweet and hot peppers, onions, and usually celery. But then again, a dish cooked in the "Creole style," such as Crab Farcis (page 99) may not have all those ingredients. This just goes to show, there may be guidelines for Creole cooking, but no hard, fast rules.

Eggplant and Chayote Chutney

Chayote, or, as it's known in the French Caribbean, christophene, is a pale apple-green, pear-shaped vegetable. Its flesh tastes similar to summer squash and surrounds a big center seed. Chayotes can be lightly cooked, as in this recipe, to retain their nutrients, crisp texture, and delicate flavor. Like eggplant, chayote readily absorbs other flavors, making it a good sponge for the sweet-sour combination. Chayote has become widely available, and you should have no problem finding it in the produce section of your supermarket.

2 teaspoons olive oil

2 cups unpeeled, julienned eggplant

1 cup peeled, julienned chayote

1 cup julienned carrots

1/2 cup thinly sliced onion

1/4 cup cider vinegar

1/4 cup water

1 tablespoon dark brown sugar

1/4 teaspoon salt

1 tiny bird pepper, minced

5 whole cloves

1. In a large skillet, over high heat, warm the oil. Add the eggplant, chayote, carrot, and onion; stir and cook for 2 minutes.

2. Add the remaining ingredients, reduce the heat to medium, and cook for an additional 5–7 minutes, until the eggplant and chayote are soft and the carrot still has a little crunch. The texture contrast is one of the things that makes this an interesting chutney, so don't cook everything to mush. Pour the mixture into a bowl and cool it to room temperature before serving.

Makes 4 servings

Per Serving: Calories: 75; Fat: 3 g; Cholesterol: 0; Sodium: 145 mg;
% Daily Value: Vitamin A 77%, Vitamin C 14%

Grilled Pepper and Banana Salsa

This may seem like a strange combination, but believe me, the pepper and banana work well together. That roasted, grilled flavor cuts the sweetness of the banana, resulting in a Vitamin C–packed salsa. Make sure the tomatoes are at room temperature (they should never be refrigerated anyway) because the whole dish tastes best served slightly warm or at room temperature. This is not a soupy, wet salsa, but is moistened only by the tomatoes, vinegar, and a small bit of olive oil. Definitely a low-calorie flavor hit!

1 red bell pepper, halved and seeded

1 green bell pepper, halved and seeded

1 large ripe, firm banana, unpeeled and
     cut in half lengthwise

2¹/₄ teaspoons olive oil

1 tablespoon balsamic vinegar

¹/₄ teaspoon salt

Coarsely ground black pepper, to taste

2 tablespoons finely chopped, mixed fresh
     herbs (parsley, thyme, marjoram,
     oregano, whatever you have)

1. Coat the grill rack or grill tray with nonstick cooking spray. Grill the peppers over high heat, on both sides, for a total of 10 minutes, until soft and charred. Rub the cut side of the banana with ¹/₄ teaspoon of the oil; lay it cut side down, and grill on a slightly cooler part of the grill, for 2–3 minutes, until lightly charred. Turn and grill an additional 2 minutes. Set everything aside until cool enough to handle.

2. Peel the skin from the peppers, and remove the banana peel. Dice the peppers and banana into ¼-inch pieces, and place them in a shallow bowl.

3. Combine the remaining olive oil, the vinegar, and the salt in a cup; pour over the salsa and toss. Season with black pepper, and gently stir in the fresh herbs.

Makes 4 servings

Per Serving: Calories: 75; Fat: 3 g; Cholesterol: 0; Sodium: 135 mg;
% Daily Value: Vitamin C 250%, Vitamin A 38%

Grilling Fruit

Grilling peppers, onions, eggplant, zucchini, and mushrooms is something we all do. But what about fruit? It takes no time at all, and is a dynamite, low-fat way to add a contrasting sweet touch to salads, accompaniments, and main dishes. The slightly smoky flavor of grilling adds another dimension to the natural sweetness of pineapple, mango, or papaya. Beyond the tropical fruit basket, there are lots of other moist yet sturdy fruits to grill, such as peaches, nectarines, plums, figs, and oranges. Coat a grill tray, or the grill rack (if skewering the fruits) with nonstick cooking spray. Larger fruits, like peaches, should be cut in half, then grilled. Grill over medium heat for just a few minutes, long enough to get some grill marks on both sides and thoroughly warm the fruit. Use as ingredients in Grilled Pepper and Banana Salsa (page 66), or simply serve as a "mixed grill" with any meat or poultry.

Peach Compote in Honeydew Syrup

Technically speaking, a compote is fresh or dried fruit that's been slowly cooked in a flavored sugar syrup. I've used both fresh and dried fruits as the compote base but do not put them through the slow cooking process. The "syrup," to save calories, is cooked down, pureed honeydew melon. This tastes great next to sautéed, boneless chicken breasts or roasted pork loin.

2 tablespoons dark brown sugar

1 teaspoon Worcestershire sauce

1 teaspoon Rose's lime juice; or fresh lime juice and $^1/_2$ teaspoon sugar

2 garlic cloves, minced

$^2/_3$ cup pureed (about $1^1/_2$ cups diced fruit) honeydew melon

1 teaspoon cider vinegar

1 cup peeled, finely diced fresh peaches

$^1/_4$ cup finely diced dried papaya

$^1/_4$ cup finely diced dried mango

1 tablespoon thinly sliced scallion, green part only

1. In a small saucepan, over low heat, cook the sugar, Worcestershire sauce, lime juice, and garlic for 5 minutes, until the sugar melts, the garlic is softened, and you have a thick, dark brown syrup.

2. Pour the mixture into a blender and add the honeydew puree and vinegar. Puree on high speed for 1 minute, until smooth. Return the mixture to the pan and, over very low heat, cook it for 15 minutes, un-

til slightly thickened. Stir in the peaches, papaya, and mango. Remove from the heat, garnish with scallions, and serve.

Makes 4 servings

Per Serving: Calories: 95; Fat and Cholesterol: 0; Sodium: 20 mg;
% Daily Value: Vitamin C 66%, Vitamin A 16%, Potassium 11%

Little Tastes
& Mini Meals

These are the hors d'oeuvres, the tapas, the appetizers of the Caribbean. Use them as handheld bites, on small plates for a cocktail party, or as one of many dishes on a buffet table. But don't think for a minute that this is strictly party food. I would just as quickly use some of these in place of dinner, when a light nibble will hit the spot. Or put a few together, and you do have dinner.

Several recipes in this chapter are based on authentic, namesake dishes you will find when traveling through the Caribbean. Empanadas, escovitch, conch salad, crab farcis, and rotis are standard fare in the Caribbean rim. Yet other recipes are new inventions, using a lighter hand with native ingredients, such as smoked fish, yuca, and stone crabs.

Watching portion sizes, as any student of healthy eating knows, is key to calorie control. Having a repertoire of small plates, or little meals, fits right in with lighter eating. I often find grazing, and ordering a few appetizers instead of an entree, a more interesting, and satisfying way to dine out. Eating small portions of different foods provides more variety for the taste buds and eliminates any possibility of that dreaded word, deprivation. You'll use these recipes because they taste terrific; the fact that they're lighter is a secondary benefit.

Garlic-Stuffed Chorizo Dates

This is the simplest of hors d'oeuvres, and reminds me of the one-bite, toothpick-skewered tapas you find scattered on the bar tops of Spain. The idea was adapted from a popular appetizer served at Key Bosh, a world cuisine restaurant here in Key West. Dates are associated more with the Mediterranean than with the Caribbean, but I've added the island touch by using chorizo sausage, common in the Spanish islands. It's the sweetness of the dates combined with the salty, spicy sausage that makes these taste so good. They're quickly baked, allowing just enough time to take the bite out of the garlic and for the chorizo to crisp up. A Garlic Mojo (page 32) dipping sauce is a nice addition, but not a necessity. For party purposes, simply make these ahead and bake as needed.

3 garlic cloves, cut into slivers

18 pitted dates

1 ounce chorizo, cut into 18 pieces

¼ cup Garlic Mojo (page 32), optional

Preheat the oven to 375°. Stuff a piece of garlic into the center of each date. Thread the date and a slice of chorizo onto a toothpick. Place on a baking sheet and bake for 10 minutes. Serve immediately, with Garlic Mojo, if you like.

Makes 18 pieces

Per Piece: Calories: 30; Fat and Cholesterol: 0; Sodium: 20 mg; No other significant nutritional value

A Big-Flavor Ingredient

Many ingredients have suitable substitutes. Not so, chorizo. This slightly spicy, garlic-seasoned dried pork sausage is an integral ingredient in many Spanish dishes. Perhaps the most well known is paella, one of Spain's national dishes, and one I love so much it was served at my wedding. Chorizo comfortably made the leap from Old World to New World kitchen because of Spain's early dominance of Caribbean exploration. It is used in many shrimp, chicken, and rice combination dishes, acting more as a flavoring agent than a main-stay meat ingredient.

Chorizo is becoming more readily available in mainstream supermarkets, packaged in shelf-stable plastic, and sold by Goya and other regional producers. The paper-thin skin covering the sausage should be removed prior to cooking, making it easier to slice. While it is, indeed, a high-fat sausage, a small amount brings big flavor results. For most brands, a $1^1/_2$-ounce link has about 130 calories and 8 grams of fat. Divide this among several servings, and you really haven't done any major damage. Whatever fat or calories chorizo contributes are well worth the taste.

Pineapple on Fire

This is another one of those three-way flavor combinations that may sound weird but meshes together quite nicely. Exciting the palate is what low-fat cooking is all about, and your taste buds will stand at attention when you bite into this pineapple. Sweet, juicy pineapple, tart lime juice, and spicy peppercorns contrast *and* complement each other for a real flavor explosion. Serve it as an hors d'oeuvre at a cocktail or buffet party, or as a side item for barbecued meats. It's important that the pepper be coarsely ground, providing a nice texture contrast. If you like less heat, reduce the amount of pepper.

1 pound (about ¹/₂ whole fruit) peeled fresh pineapple, cut into 8 half-moon slices

¹/₄ cup fresh lime juice
2 teaspoons coarsely ground black pepper

Dip the pineapple in the lime juice, and grind the pepper onto both sides of the fruit. Grill the pineapple, over medium heat, on both sides, for a total of 5–7 minutes, or until it softens slightly and is lightly charred. If using this as an hors d'oeuvre, cut each slice into three or four pieces after grilling, and have toothpicks on hand.

Makes 8 servings

Per Serving: Calories: 30; Fat, Cholesterol, and Sodium: 0; % Daily Value: Vitamin C 20%

Antigua's Black Pineapple

Antigua's fresh fruits and vegetables are similar to those found on other islands, with one exception: the black pineapple. Originally introduced by the Arawak Indians, it was believed to be food for the gods, and hardly a bit of it went to waste. The thorny leaves were used for making twine and cloth, while the juice of the fruit was for medicinal purposes, and to produce wine. Smaller than most commercial pineapples, the fruit looks black when young, then turns into the more traditional golden pineapple color as it ripens.

If you're interested in checking out the black pineapple, as well as Antigua's other culinary delights, head on down to the island during the last week in April, for the now legendary Sailing Week. Going strong for thirty years now, this is one of the world's biggest annual regattas and certainly the largest in the Caribbean. Some two hundred sailing vessels, of all types and from all parts of the world, participate in five days of racing, a must-see spectator event for anyone who loves sailboats. It's also a big party week, so be prepared for a jumpin' good time.

Smoked Fish
and Horseradish Dip

Before the days of refrigeration, smoking was an ideal way for islanders to preserve seafood. Today, we eat smoked fish because it tastes good, and because this ancient technique is still one of the most flavorful, non-fat cooking methods. If you choose to smoke your own fish for this recipe, follow the guidelines described in Smoking Basics (page 220). If not, walk down to your local fish counter, where there is bound to be an assortment of smoked fish to choose from. Any type will do, and if saltwater varieties are not available, then something like smoked trout would be okay, too. This is a good party recipe because it can be made ahead and keeps well in the refrigerator. It's a nice item to bring to a party too, because it doesn't spill or slosh around in transit.

1 pound boneless smoked fish
¹/₂ cup (1 medium) peeled, seeded, finely
*   diced tomato*
¹/₃ cup finely sliced scallions, green
*   part only*

¹/₃ cup peeled, finely grated fresh
*   horseradish*
¹/₄ cup reduced-fat sour cream
¹/₄ cup reduced-fat mayonnaise
¹/₄ cup fresh lime juice

1. Remove any skin from the fish. In a medium bowl, crumble the fish into small pieces.

(Smoked Fish and Horseradish Dip continued from page 77)

2. In a small bowl, thoroughly combine the remaining ingredients. Using a fork, stir this mixture into the fish, for a chunky spread-like texture. Cover and refrigerate at least a few hours, so the flavors mingle together. Serve with plain melba toast, or unflavored stoned-wheat thin crackers.

Makes about 3 cups

Per $1/4$ cup: Calories: 70; Fat: 3 g; Cholesterol: 12 mg; Sodium: 310 mg;
% Daily Value: Vitamin B$_{12}$ 20%, Vitamin C 14%

Bahama Man Conch Salad

Conch (pronounced konk) is a mollusk that lives in a spiral-shaped pink shell. You may have seen the shells sold at Caribbean souvenir stands. Perhaps you've also eaten conch chowder, fritters, or salad, but never attempted to cook them. Well, this is a simple way to try your hand at conch. Because the mollusk is a tough one, it must be pounded, ground, or tenderized in some way before eating. Many fish markets now carry conch, and if you can buy it already ground, do so. If not, tenderize the muscle by pounding it with a mallet before dicing it. In this recipe, the conch is "cooked" seviche-style by the acidic action of the lime juice. On a trip to the Bahamas, I had my very own dockside-prepared conch salad. While a local fisherman diced the freshly caught conch, he sent me across the street to the open-air market to buy the other ingredients. It's his simple recipe, with clean, uncomplicated flavors, that I present here.

1/2 pound conch, finely diced

1/4 cup ground or finely diced green bell pepper

1/4 cup finely diced red bell pepper

1/4 cup finely diced celery

1/4 cup fresh lime juice

2 tablespoons finely diced onion

1/4 teaspoon seeded, finely minced Scotch bonnet pepper

1/4 teaspoon salt

In a medium bowl, combine all the ingredients. Cover and refrigerate for at least 3 hours to allow the flavors to develop. This is typically served with saltines; no fancy gourmet crackers, please.

Makes 4 servings

Per Serving: Calories: 75; Fat: 0; Cholesterol: 50 mg; Sodium: 310 mg; % Daily Value: Vitamin C 83%, Pantothenic Acid 17%

Outlaw Conch

Here in the Conch Republic, also known as Key West, the conch's pretty pink shell is somewhat of a national logo. Yet all the conch fritters and conch chowder served in this town, and throughout south Florida, are made with imported conch. Years ago, conch harvesting, along with sponging, was a major industry throughout the Florida Keys. Commercial and recreational conch harvesting in Florida waters was outlawed in 1985 to help preserve the dwindling supply. The warm Florida waters are the primary U.S. source of conch, so if you're eating conch in the United States today, it's coming from the Bahamas and other off-shore locations, where it's alive, well, and for sale. Although still a protected species, the ban has been beneficial, with local conch numbers now on the upswing. However, it may not be too long before farm-raised conch will provide another consistent, high-quality supply for the American marketplace.

When perusing Caribbean recipes and menus, bear in mind that the Carib name for conch is *lambi* or lambie, and is often used in English and French island cuisines. The Spanish name is *concha,* while the French word is *conque,* the latter pronounced the same as conch in English.

Empanaditas

Empanadas are handheld meat pies, eaten as a snack on many different islands but originating in Central and South America. These baked turnovers usually have a savory filling, or a guava paste and cheese filling. They're sold in bakeries, sandwich shops, and anywhere you might stop for a quick snack. Often eaten as a quick breakfast or a midday munch, they also make fine hors d'oeuvres. Because the typical pastry dough has a fair amount of fat, I've used cake/pastry flour, which has less gluten and requires less fat to make a tender crust. The recipe that follows is for the empanada dough. For fillings, I suggest traditional Picadillo (page 233), Grilled Tomatillo Sauce (page 60), or a small smear of light cream cheese flavored with Pickapeppa Pepper Sauce (page 55). No matter what filling you choose, make sure there's minimal moisture, otherwise you will have a soggy turnover. Because these are mini-size empanadas (empanaditas), you'll need only a teaspoon of filling for each.

2 cups plus 2 tablespoons cake flour, and
additional 1/4 cup reserved for rolling
1 teaspoon salt
5 tablespoons very cold margarine

1 egg
6 tablespoons cold water
1 egg white, beaten

1. Preheat the oven to 450°. Coat two baking sheets with nonstick cooking spray. In a large bowl, combine the 2 cups flour and salt. Cut the margarine into the flour with a pastry blender or two knives until the mixture resembles small, crumbly little pebbles.

(Empanaditas continued from page 81)

2. Make a well in the center of the flour; add the egg and water. Stir until the mixture is well moistened and holds together in a non-sticky ball, adding some reserved flour, if necessary. Divide the dough into two balls.

3. Flour your work surface, and roll out one ball to a circle 12 inches in diameter, about $\frac{1}{8}$ inch thick. Cut out 12 (3-inch) circles using a cutter or the open end of a jar. Lay the dough circles on the baking sheets, and place a teaspoon of filling in the center of each. Fold them in half and press down with the tines of a fork to close the pocket. Brush the egg white over the tops to help browning. Flouring the work surface again, repeat this process with the remaining dough. At this point, you may freeze the empanaditas in Ziploc bags for up to two weeks.

4. Bake for 7–8 minutes, until lightly browned. Serve immediately, with hot pepper sauce or Mango Hot Sauce (page 53) for dipping.

Makes 24

Per 2 Empanaditas: Calories: 120; Fat: 5 g; Cholesterol: 20 mg; Sodium: 230 mg;
% Daily Value: Thiamine 12%, Vitamin E 11%

Escovitch

As with many island preparations, there can be several different names for the same dish, depending on where you're eating it. In Jamaica, this dish is called escovitch, the literal translation being "pickled." On Spanish islands, escabeche is the term used for seafood or poultry that has been cooked, then marinated. This dish is an ideal example of how an authentic preparation is inherently low in fat. Because of the intense vinegar marinade, this tastes best when eaten in small portions, as an hors d'oeuvre or as part of a buffet.

¹/₂ pound boneless, semifirm, white-
   fleshed fish fillets, such as grouper
¹/₂ teaspoon salt
¹/₄ teaspoon black pepper
2 teaspoons corn oil
¹/₂ medium red bell pepper, sliced
¹/₂ medium green bell pepper, sliced

¹/₂ medium onion, sliced
¹/₂ cup distilled white vinegar
¹/₂ cup water
1 bay leaf
5–6 black peppercorns
Pinch of ground cloves

1. Pat the fish dry. Make a few slits on both sides of the fillets, and season both sides with ¹/₄ teaspoon of the salt and the pepper.

2. In a large, heavy (preferably cast-iron) skillet, over high heat, warm 1 teaspoon of the oil, until it starts to smoke. Add the fish and cook on both sides, a total of 7–10 minutes, until lightly browned and no longer translucent in the center. Reduce the heat if the fish appears to be burning before the center is cooked. Transfer the fish to a shallow dish, just large enough to hold it.

(Escovitch continued from page 83)

3. In the same skillet, over medium-high heat, heat the remaining 1 teaspoon of oil. Add the peppers and onion. Cook for 5–7 minutes, until the vegetables are slightly soft and lightly browned. Pour in the vinegar; this will cause a lot of sizzle and a puff of smoke. Reduce the heat to medium-low, add the water, bay leaf, peppercorns, cloves, and the remaining ¼ teaspoon of salt. Sweat for 3 minutes, until the vegetables are fork-tender. Pour the entire mixture over the fish.

4. Cover, and let the escovitch sit at room temperature for 30 minutes, then refrigerate it overnight. Bring to room temperature before serving, or gently warm it. Be sure to remove bay leaf and include some marinade with each portion, or have it nearby for dipping.

Makes 4 servings

Per Serving: Calories: 100; Fat: 3 g; Cholesterol: 40 mg; Sodium: 315 mg;
% Daily Value: Vitamin C 150%, Vitamin A 19%

Sweaty Fish

Escovitch or escabeche? The direction of the trade winds will determine which name you use. As you sail westerly, in Jamaica's direction, the name switches to escovitch. Toward Puerto Rico and the Dominican Republic, the dish is called escabeche. No matter what you call it, this is a do-ahead, low-cal way to prepare any type of fish fillets, poultry, or game.

Sweating (yes, it's a real cooking term) usually refers to cooking vegetables in a small amount of fat in a covered pan. It's a way to soften the food, and create moisture, and it's the method that both cooks the vegetables and allows the warm fish to readily absorb the flavorful vinegar marinade. Make sure the fish or chicken is patted dry before it goes into the hot pan, so you can get a lightly browned exterior. The simple flavors that mingle and marry in the covered dish evolve into a complex taste combination.

Shrimp and Grits

Grits were brought to both the American South and the Caribbean by African slaves. Used for brunch, or as a small meal, shrimp and grits get a Spanish flair from the addition of chorizo, which tastes terrific blended with shrimp. Cheddar cheese is often melted into the grits, but to spare calories, fat, and cholesterol, I've left it out. There's so much flavor going on in this recipe that you won't even miss the cheese.

1 ounce chorizo sausage, peeled and
  diced
1/2 cup diced green bell pepper
1/2 cup diced red bell pepper
1/4 cup diced onion
1 teaspoon minced Scotch bonnet pepper
1/4 cup water
1/4 teaspoon salt

1 (14 1/2-ounce) can reduced-sodium
  chicken broth
1 1/4 cups skim milk
1 cup quick-cooking grits
1/2 pound small, peeled shrimp
1/2 teaspoon arrowroot
1/2 cup beer
Hot sauce, to taste

1. In a large skillet over medium-low heat, cook the chorizo for 3 minutes, until it is lightly browned and the bottom of the pan gets coated with the oil released by the sausage. Cook the green and red peppers, onion, and Scotch bonnet pepper for 5 minutes, or until tender. Add to the chorizo. Add the water and salt, scraping up any browned bits from the bottom of the pan.

2. Meanwhile, in a medium saucepan, heat the chicken broth and milk to a boil. Stir in the grits, bring to a boil again, cover, and reduce the heat. Cook, stirring occasionally, for 5 minutes.

3. When the liquid is absorbed, the grits are just about ready; add the shrimp to the skillet with the veg-

etables, and cook for 1–2 minutes, until pink and no longer translucent. In a cup, stir the arrowroot into the beer, then stir this mixture into the skillet. Heat for 1–2 minutes, stirring constantly, until slightly thickened. Season with hot sauce, if desired. To serve, spoon the grits into individual shallow bowls, and spoon on the shrimp and sauce.

Makes 4 servings

Per Serving: Calories: 290; Fat: 4 g; Cholesterol: 90 mg; Sodium: 395 mg; % Daily Value: Vitamin C 150%, Vitamin A 24%, Niacin 22%, Iron 20%, Thiamine 20%, Riboflavin 19%

Drunken Shrimp

Cooking with white or red wine is second nature to many cooks, but most people wouldn't give rum a second thought. What a pity, because rum is as useful in cooking as it is in a cocktail. The most commonly drunk liquor throughout the islands, rum adds a rich, complex flavor to many dishes. For most recipes, I favor using amber or dark rum, as opposed to clear, light rum, for the flavor and color it provides.

The guava nectar used in this recipe is readily available in small cans, and is sold either in the juice aisle, or with other Hispanic products. Ground thyme lends a flavor and appearance similar to those found in New Orleans-style barbecued shrimp dishes, which, although delicious, are swimming in a high-fat, butter/oil–based sauce. Have plenty of crusty bread on hand because this is definitely sauce for dunking.

¹/₂ cup guava nectar

¹/₄ cup orange juice, preferably the pulpy
   home-style type

2 tablespoons dark rum

2 teaspoons peanut oil

¹/₂ teaspoon ground thyme

¹/₂ teaspoon ground allspice

¹/₄ teaspoon turmeric

¹/₄ teaspoon curry powder

Scant ¹/₄ teaspoon dried red pepper flakes
   or ¹/₂ small bird pepper, minced

1 pound medium, peeled, deveined
   shrimp, tails on

1. In a wide, shallow dish big enough to accommodate the shrimp without stacking them, combine all the ingredients. Toss to coat the shrimp, cover, and refrigerate at least 1 hour.

2. Coat a grilling tray with nonstick cooking spray, and lay the shrimp out flat (no crowding), reserving the marinade. If you don't have a grill tray, skewer the shrimp, and spray the grill rack. Grill over

medium heat on both sides for a total of 3–5 minutes, until pink, no longer translucent, and with light grill marks.

3. Meanwhile, in a small saucepan, bring the marinade to a boil for 2 minutes, then pour it into a shallow serving bowl. Remove the shrimp from the grill and toss to coat thoroughly in the heated marinade. Use these as an appetizer for a dinner party, or make a bigger batch and leave it out, buffet-style, for guests to help themselves.

Makes 4 servings

Per Serving: Calories: 150; Fat: 3 g; Cholesterol: 175 mg; Sodium: 200 mg; % Daily Value: Vitamin B$_{12}$ 21%, Vitamin C 18%, Iron 17%

Cooking with Alcohol

Many culinary studies have been conducted, over the years, to determine just how much alcohol, and calories, remain after food has been cooked. Estimates can be made, although there's no such thing as a precise answer, because of all the variables. The amount of alcohol left behind will be influenced by the method of heat (simmering versus flaming) and the length of heating. Long, slow simmering, such as in braised chicken and wine sauce, will eliminate more alcohol than the quick, high heat used to flame a liqueur-based dessert sauce. The final alcohol content of the chicken dish will also depend on when the wine was added—at the beginning or toward the end of the cooking process. For alcohol-flavored dishes that are not heated, there will still be some, but not as much, alcohol loss. A cordial poured over fresh fruit will lose some of its potency, as the result of evaporation, especially if the food is left uncovered.

When doing the nutrition analysis for the recipes in this book that use rum, sherry, or wine, judgment calls had to be made. How long was the food marinating, was the marinade heated and used as a finishing sauce, and how long did it cook? All these questions factored into my estimate of how much alcohol was probably left.

None of this should make you paranoid about using alcohol in cooking, because it can be a tremendous flavor asset. Just evaluate each recipe and be realistic about the resulting calories and alcohol.

Yuca and Sweet Onion Crab Cakes

Yuca, also known as cassava, is grown throughout South America and the Caribbean. It's a narrow tuber with a beige-brown bark and a hard, white, coconut-looking flesh. In fact, the white flesh is used to make tapioca, a familiar thickening agent. This starchy, potato-like vegetable doesn't have much flavor to call its own, so it readily absorbs any others it comes into contact with. It's often cubed or sliced for use in stews and soups. Because the flesh is so hard, it's also good for grating, which is what I've done with it in this recipe. Instead of frying or pan-sautéing these crab cakes, I've quickly baked them in a very hot oven to crisp the bottom, then broiled them for top browning. Once out of the oven, I dab on, (as though applying expensive perfume) a small bit of oil, for a little glisten. Since this recipe makes quite a few crab cakes, try them as finger food for your next party.

1 medium (12 ounces) yuca (about 2 cups grated)
1¹/₂ cups grated sweet Vidalia onions
¹/₂ pound shredded crabmeat or surimi
¹/₂ cup chopped fresh flat-leaf parsley
¹/₂ cup chopped cilantro
¹/₂ cup fine bread crumbs

2 eggs
6 tablespoons fresh lime juice
2 tablespoons grated fresh ginger
2 teaspoons minced garlic
1 teaspoon salt
12 drops hot sauce
1 tablespoon peanut oil

1. Preheat the oven to 550°. Coat a baking sheet with nonstick cooking spray. To peel the yuca, make a lengthwise slit just through the outer bark. With a paring knife, remove the bark, and the pale

(Yuca and Sweet Onion Crab Cakes continued from page 91)

pink skin underneath. Using the grater disk of a food processor, or a hand grater, grate the yuca to yield about 2 cups.

2. In a large bowl, combine the grated yuca, onions, and all remaining ingredients except the peanut oil until the mixture holds together in your hand.

3. To form the crab cakes, measure a heaping tablespoon and place it on the baking sheet. With the palm of your hand, press it down to a 2-inch diameter (these will be irregular shapes, not perfect rounds). Bake for 5 minutes, checking the bottom for burning and reducing the heat slightly if necessary. When crisped on the bottom, change the oven setting to broil, move the baking sheet 8–10 inches from the broiler, and broil for 2–3 minutes, until lightly browned. Remove from the oven, and, dipping your finger in the oil, moisten the top of each cake. Or, in place of the oil, try a light touch of Orange Marmalade Lime Glaze (page 57). Continue with remaining mixture, covering cooked cakes with aluminum foil to keep warm, until they're all ready. Serve immediately.

Makes 32–34 crab cakes

Per 3 Cakes: Calories: 100; Fat: 3 g; Cholesterol: 60 mg; Sodium: 310 mg;
% Daily Value: Vitamin B$_{12}$ 26%, Vitamin C 14%

A Carib Leftover

Cassava bread is one of the few foods originally eaten by Carib Indians that is still produced and enjoyed throughout the islands. Cassava, also known as yuca or manioc, is boiled, then ground into meal for bread-making. Cassava bread, usually baked in round, flat loaves, is available in many Latin and Caribbean markets throughout the United States. Just as wheat, and thus bread, has been considered modern man's "staff of life," so was cassava bread to the Indian culture.

Yet, ironically, cassava could take away life. There are actually two types of cassava, sweet and bitter. The juice of the bitter variety contains poisonous prussic acid, which is removed by processing before the vegetable is made into tapioca. But the Indians used this root juice to commit suicide, rather than live as slaves of the Spanish. It's this same juice that forms the base of cassareep, a flavoring ingredient used in West Indian pepper pot stew.

Stone Crab Claw Pasta Salad

While pasta is not indigenous to island menus, it seemed like a good fit with stone crab claws. Here in Florida waters, stone crabs are caught only during the winter months, making them a seasonal item in the fish markets. Mother nature was very efficient with the stone crab, because it recycles itself. Once the crabs are caught (and this is done in traps) the claws are broken off and the body is thrown back into the ocean, where it regenerates a new set of claws. This process is repeated at least a few times before a stone crab kicks the bucket.

Delicious and mild-tasting, crab claw meat can be pricey. If your budget can't handle it, by all means substitute another type of lump crabmeat (none of which are cheap), or go for scallops. The traditional dip used when eating stone crab claws is a simple mixture of mayonnaise and Dijon mustard. I've taken that basic dip, extended and lightened it with nonfat plain yogurt, and turned it into a pasta dressing. There are few other ingredients in this dish, so the mild crabmeat is not overpowered. Because the pasta quickly soaks up any dressing, it's at its creamy best when the dressing is added just prior to serving. The yield from this recipe is large, making it a great choice for parties or buffets.

12 ounces uncooked medium shell pasta
½ cup plain nonfat yogurt
¼ cup reduced-fat mayonnaise
2½ tablespoons Dijon mustard

2 cups (12 ounces) cooked stone crab
  claw meat (in small chunks)
2 cups unpeeled, diced tomatoes
½ cup sliced scallions

1. Cook the pasta according to package directions. Drain, rinse with cool water, and drain again. Transfer to a large serving bowl.

2. To make the dressing, in a small bowl, combine the yogurt, mayonnaise, and mustard.

3. Toss the crabmeat, tomatoes, and scallions with the pasta. The dish can be made in advance up to this point. Cover and refrigerate until ready to use. When ready, thoroughly combine the dressing with the salad, then serve immediately.

Makes 20 servings

Per Serving: Calories: 95; Fat: 1 g; Cholesterol: 10 mg; Sodium: 250 mg; % Daily Value: Zinc 10%

Seafood Rundown

Rundown is a Jamaican dish that gets its name from cooking, or running, down the coconut milk. On other islands, such as Barbados, it's called oil down, not a very appetizing name. In this recipe, a lower-calorie version is made possible by using "lite" coconut milk. Running down is similar to "reducing" an ingredient to achieve a more concentrated flavor. Rundown is often made with salted codfish, but using smoked fish is easier because it doesn't need to be soaked, and adds a nice smoky flavor to the completed dish. Vegetables can be assorted, although sturdy root veggies such as yuca, turnips, rutabaga, and carrots work best. Once the tomatoes are added, the white coconut milk sauce turns a lovely shade of pale pink-orange. Serve this as a first course or a part of a buffet table.

1 (14-ounce) can "lite" coconut milk
1 cup peeled, ¹/₂-inch diced malanga (see page 98)
¹/₂ cup finely diced onion
3 garlic cloves, minced
5–6 sprigs fresh thyme

¹/₂ Scotch bonnet pepper, seeded
1¹/₂ cups diced tomatoes
¹/₂ pound assorted smoked fish, cut into ¹/₂-inch pieces
1 large, semiripe plantain, sliced
¹/₄ teaspoon salt

1. In a large skillet over medium heat, cook the coconut milk at a full simmer for 10–15 minutes, until it appears slightly thickened.

2. Add the malanga, onion, garlic, thyme, and Scotch bonnet. Cook another 15 minutes, until the malanga is almost tender.

3. Add the tomatoes, fish, plantain, and salt. Reduce the heat to low, cover, and cook 5–10 minutes, until the malanga is tender and all ingredients are thoroughly hot. Remove the Scotch bonnet and thyme before serving.

Makes 6 first course servings

Per Serving: Calories: 170; Fat: 5 g; Cholesterol: 40 mg; Sodium: 280 mg; % Daily Value: Vitamin C 47%, Niacin 28%, Vitamin B$_{12}$ 21%, Vitamin A 19%, Vitamin B$_6$ 15%, Magnesium 10%

Malanga Is Not a Dance

Malanga sounds as though it should be a Latin dance, like the rhumba and merengue. But it's less glamorous than that. Malanga is one of the several, workhorse starchy tubers used in Caribbean cooking. Shaped like a long sweet potato, it has a dark brown, patchy skin and a hard white- or pale peach-colored flesh. Once peeled, it can be kept submerged in cold water. I find it works best as a potato substitute when diced and added to stews (as in Two Potato and Malanga Beef Stew, page 227), or cooked in liquid of some sort. As it cooks, its starch is released and will naturally thicken whatever it is you're making. Although not a low-fat option, it is often thinly sliced and deep-fried as malanga chips.

Walk Through Peppers

Seafood Rundown (page 96) uses an island technique for cooking with hot pepper known as walking through. For dishes where you want the heat of the Scotch bonnet but not the actual pieces of it, you simply walk the pepper through the dish. It might sit in the dish during the entire cooking process, or walk through for just a few minutes. This is an excellent technique for those who want to ease their way into Scotch bonnets before taking the full-fledged plunge. Regardless of your method, it should always be removed from the dish before serving.

Crab Farcis
(Stuffed Crabs)

Stuffed crabs are a signature of Creole cuisine, and you will find them served often in Guadeloupe and Martinique. On these islands of the French West Indies, the meat is taken from land crabs (something we don't readily have), made into a seasoned mixture, and tucked back into the shell for baking. This recipe uses any type of water crabmeat, and streamlines the process for busy cooks. If you can buy clean crab or scallop shells, for stuffing, by all means, do so. If not, 4- or 6-ounce ramekins will also work. This is a recipe where allspice works its magic in savory ways, and a small drizzle of melted butter, much less than original recipes call for, lends an illusion of decadence.

10 ounces fresh or frozen crabmeat,
   preferably blue crab or dungeness
   crab
1/2 cup fresh bread crumbs
1/2 cup finely diced mushrooms
2 tablespoons finely chopped flat-leaf
   parsley
2 tablespoons dark rum

1 tablespoon fresh lime juice
3 garlic cloves, minced
1/2 teaspoon finely minced Scotch bonnet
   pepper
1/2 teaspoon ground allspice
1/4 teaspoon salt
1 tablespoon butter, melted
1 tablespoon minced chives

1. Preheat the oven to 350°. Coat four crab shells or small ramekins with nonstick cooking spray.

(Crab Farcis continued from page 99)

2. In a large bowl, combine all the ingredients except the butter and chives. Spoon the mixture into the ramekins and drizzle the melted butter over each. Bake for 20 minutes, then broil for 1–2 minutes, until lightly browned. Remove from the oven, and garnish with chives.

Makes 4 servings

Per Serving: Calories: 140; Fat: 4 g; Cholesterol: 80 mg; Sodium: 400 mg; % Daily Value: Vitamin B_{12} 86%, Vitamin E 21%, Niacin 14%, Vitamin C 13%, Folic Acid 10%

Hot Clams Shiitake

In warm Caribbean waters, it's not unusual to find clams measuring just a $1/2$ inch across. Do the best you can at your seafood market, and buy the tiniest, most tender clams you can find. Shiitake mushrooms, originally from Japan but now cultivated throughout the United States, seemed to be the ideal complement, without overpowering the clams. The grapefruit juice adds a refreshing tartness to the white wine broth, giving this a beachside flair. The tasty, practically fat-free broth is fired up (and I mean fired up a notch) with finely minced Scotch bonnet. If you want something tamer, reduce the amount of pepper by half. As always, if the clams don't open when heated, don't use them. To compensate for that possibility, always buy a few extra. And make sure you have lots of crusty bread for mopping up the juice.

$1/2$ teaspoon sesame oil
$3/4$ cup thinly sliced shiitake mushrooms,
    stems removed
1 teaspoon freshly grated ginger
$1/2$ teaspoon seeded, finely minced Scotch
    bonnet pepper
4 garlic cloves, minced
$1/4$ teaspoon salt

1 cup dry white wine
$1/2$ cup grapefruit juice
4–6 sprigs fresh thyme
$2^1/2$ dozen cherrystone clams, or
    the smallest available clams,
    rinsed clean
1 tablespoon minced chives

1. In a large skillet over low heat, warm the oil. Cook the mushrooms, ginger, pepper, garlic, and salt, for 5–7 minutes.

(Hot Clams Shiitake continued from page 101)

2. Add the white wine, grapefruit juice, and thyme. Increase the heat to medium, bring to a light boil, and add the clams. Reduce the heat to low, cover, and cook for 8–10 minutes, or until the clams open. Don't overcook them, as they'll toughen up.

3. To serve, spoon 6 clams and some broth into each of four shallow soup bowls. Garnish with the chives.

Makes 4 servings

Per Serving: Calories: 115; Fat: 1 g; Cholesterol: 20 mg; Sodium: 170 mg; % Daily Value: Vitamin B$_{12}$ 482%, Iron 48%, Vitamin C 31%, Riboflavin 10%

Why Indian Food in the Caribbean?

Unless you understand the history of the Caribbean, curry and flat bread seem unlikely foods to find halfway around the globe from their homeland. The answer lies with the emancipation of slaves. Around 1850, slaves were finally set free, although grudgingly so, by the French and British. Sugar plantations were in full swing, and owners no longer had a captive workforce. The solution was to import servants from India and China, and with them came curries, flat bread, and rice. On islands like Hispaniola (Dominican Republic and Haiti) and Puerto Rico, where there were few slaves, Indian and Chinese food influences are practically nonexistent.

For visitors who want to experience Trinidad's Indian-style food, there's no better time than during February Carnival. Considered one of the Caribbean's biggest parties, this pre-Lenten event is packed with costumes, parades, dancing, and, of course, lots of hand-held street food. From the makeshift food stalls, meat pies and rotis, stuffed with all sorts of curries, are sold as quickly as they're made. Deep-fried fritters made of chickpea or split pea batter, are also proudly churned out by the women who set up for this event. Spicy beef stew or grilled chicken, washed down with a beer or sorrel rum punch, will put a smile on your face and your tummy.

Vegetable Curry Roti

Roti actually has two meanings. It's the Indian flat bread commonly eaten in the West Indies, especially Trinidad. And when the flat bread is wrapped up with a beef, chicken, or vegetable curry filling and eaten as a handheld snack, that too, is a roti. Like a Caribbean burrito, the roti bread is a soft, pliable wrapper for savory fillings. This particular filling is vegetarian, but diced, cooked chicken or beef can easily be added to it. The flat bread itself is cooked on a griddle or in a heavy, cast-iron frying pan. My version requires just a teeny bit of oil, hand-rubbed over the bread, making this a very low-fat little meal. If you're serving these at a party, have the dough already prepared, then let guests take over from there. Cooking the dough, and assembling the rotis, is great hands-on fun for guests. Both flat bread and filling proportions can be doubled, although the proportion of water to flour might vary slightly, and should be dictated by achieving a firm, pliable dough. As with any bread-making, it's got to feel right.

FLAT BREAD
2 1/4 *cups all-purpose flour*
1/4 *teaspoon baking soda*
1/4 *teaspoon salt*
1/2 *cup water*
2 *teaspoons vegetable oil*

FILLING
1 *teaspoon vegetable oil*
2 *garlic cloves, minced*

1/4 *teaspoon fennel seeds, crushed*
1 *tablespoon curry powder*
1 *cup finely diced cauliflower*
1/2 *cup peeled, finely diced potato*
1/4 *cup finely diced carrot*
2 *tablespoons finely chopped scallion*
2 *tablespoons reduced-sodium chicken or*
    vegetable broth
1/4 *teaspoon salt*
1/4 *cup finely diced tomato*

1. To make the flat breads, in a large bowl, combine 2 cups of the flour, the baking soda, and the salt. Add the water, 2 tablespoons at a time, stirring with a wooden spoon until the dough starts forming a ball and pulls away from the sides of the bowl. You will need a nonsticky dough, suitable for kneading and rolling.

2. Flour your work surface with some of the remaining ¼ cup, and knead the dough for 2–3 minutes, until it becomes smooth and elastic. Cut the dough into six pieces, and roll each into a 5–6-inch circle, ¼ inch thick. With your fingers, lightly rub 1 teaspoon of the oil over both sides of the dough. Roll each into a ball, and let them sit for 15 minutes.

3. While the dough is resting, prepare the filling. In a medium saucepan over low heat, warm the oil, and cook the garlic and fennel seeds for 3 minutes. Stir in the curry powder and cook for 1 minute. Add all the remaining ingredients except the tomato. Cover and cook over low heat for 10 minutes, until the vegetables are tender but not mushy. Remove from the heat and keep covered until ready to use.

4. Dust your work surface again with remaining flour, and roll the balls of dough into six equal-size circles. Heat a griddle or cast-iron frying pan (minimum 8-inch diameter) until very hot. When a drop of water immediately sizzles and sputters, it's hot enough. One at a time, lay a flat bread in the pan, and cook it for about 1 minute. The bread will quickly puff up in spots, and lightly brown on the bottom.

With your fingers, use the remaining teaspoon of oil to rub on the top side of the flat breads. Turn and cook the other side for 1 minute. Remove from the pan and slap or clap the bread between your hands. If you have asbestos hands as I do, this is not a problem. If not, hold a dish towel between your hands, and clap. This helps make the bread soft and pliable, suitable for encasing a filling. While repeating the process with the remaining dough, keep the flat breads warm in a very low oven.

5. To serve, put the filling down the middle of the flat bread, roll it up, and enjoy.

Makes 6 rotis

Per Roti: Calories: 225; Fat: 3 g; Cholesterol: 0; Sodium: 240 mg; % Daily Value: Thiamine 27%, Vitamin C 22%, Niacin 16%, Iron 15%, Vitamin A 14%

Mambo Chicken Pot Pie

I don't know about you, but I'm always looking for a new leftover chicken idea. Pot pies are a great way to use leftover chicken, but the thick gravy and double pastry crusts can pack a lot of fat grams. Not your typical pot pie filling, this one is like a picadillo, but uses chicken instead of ground beef. Rather than make a crust from scratch, I opt for a boxed pie crust mix, and slightly alter the proportions. To further save calories, I use just a top crust, which still gives the feeling that this is a pot pie. Cubanelle peppers have no fire to them. They are similar in appearance to green bell peppers, but are a much lighter shade of green and slightly skinnier. If necessary, substitute bell peppers. If you're really in a time crunch for mid-week dinners, make the filling and put it into the pan the night before. When you walk in the door, just roll the crust, and 15 minutes later you're eating.

1 teaspoon olive oil

²/₃ cup finely diced onion

¹/₂ cup finely diced celery

¹/₂ cup finely diced cubanelle peppers

4 garlic cloves, minced

1 (14¹/₂-ounce) can whole tomatoes, juice reserved

1 (2-ounce) jar chopped pimentos

3 tablespoons pitted, chopped Spanish olives

1 tablespoon drained capers

1 teaspoon dried thyme leaves

1 teaspoon dried oregano leaves

¹/₂ teaspoon salt

¹/₂ teaspoon black pepper

¹/₂ pound (about 2 cups) cooked, finely diced, skinless white and dark chicken meat

2 tablespoons cold water

1 cup pie crust mix

1 tablespoon flour for dusting

1. In a large skillet over medium heat, warm the oil. Cook the onion, celery, peppers, and garlic for 10 minutes, or until soft. Add the tomatoes, pimentos, olives, capers, thyme, oregano, salt, and pepper. Reduce the heat to medium-low, and cook for 5 minutes. Add the chicken and the reserved tomato juice a little at a time, until the mixture is moist but there is no liquid in the bottom of the pan. Pour this into a 9-inch deep-dish pie plate.

2. Preheat the oven to 450°. In a small bowl, using a fork, mix the water with the pie crust mix until it forms a soft, pliable ball. Flour your work surface and roll the dough into a 10-inch round. Carefully pick it up, and drape it over the chicken filling. Crimp the edges and make two small slits on top. Bake for 12–15 minutes, until golden brown.

3. To serve, cut into six wedges, and remove with a spatula.

Makes 6 servings

Per Serving: Calories: 220; Fat: 11 g; Cholesterol: 30 mg; Sodium: 650 mg; % Daily Value: Vitamin C 63%, Niacin 18%, Vitamin B$_6$ 14%, Iron 12%

Caribbean Carbos

Vegetables, beans, peas, and rice have always taken center stage in Caribbean cuisine. One-pot meals, fish soups, rice and beans in their infinite variations, and starchy tubers are the ingredients island cooking is made of. Peasant-style dishes, hearty and filling, these foods are extremely nutritious. This chapter includes some of the most nutrient-dense recipes in the book, rich in fiber, complex carbohydrates, protein, folic acid, Vitamins A and C, as well as a wide array of minerals and other micronutrients. Translated, this means you get more nutritional bang for your calorie buck.

On the island table, animal protein is more the exception than the rule. Instead, locally grown, inexpensive root vegetables and other plant staples form the base of most meals. Some dishes are totally vegetarian, while others use small amounts of fish and ham as an adjunct flavoring, a built-in control for fat and cholesterol. As in the previous chapter, some of these selections are lighter interpretations of traditional dishes, such as Calypso Callaloo (page 114) and Pepper Pot Soup (page 116). Other recipes fuse Caribbean ingredients with new executions, but always with an eye on nutritional value.

You may choose to use the soups, stews, and the rice and bean dishes as main courses, just as islanders do. Or work them in as first courses, or side dishes to create an eclectic menu. Regardless of how you use them, they add soul-satisfying substance to any dish. Chances are they'll make your belly smile.

St. Thomas Fish Soup

While visiting St. Thomas, my friend Mary and I stumbled onto the Snapper Restaurant, located a few streets from the main tourist thoroughfare. We foodie types quickly realized this was where the locals ate. When you order something called "fish soup" in a local joint, you're never quite sure what's going to come out. In this case, it was a winner. I asked the proprietor how she made it, and tried to duplicate it from her vague directions, with a few intentional changes. I purposely did not thicken with flour, but opted for a clear broth. As with most island cooking, what goes into the pot depends on what's available that day. So, in true island style, feel free to improvise by using other root vegetables, such as rutabaga or parsnips, which might be more readily available. This is a quick, simple, light soup, suitable as a first course for dinner or an ample lunch. Its bumper Vitamin A content comes from the sweet potatoes and calabaza. And don't forget some crusty bread for sopping up the tasty broth.

2 cups Island Shrimp Stock (page 36)

²/₃ cup unpeeled white potatoes cut into ¹/₂-inch cubes

¹/₂ cup peeled turnips cut into ¹/₂-inch cubes

¹/₃ cup unpeeled sweet potatoes cut into ¹/₂-inch cubes

1 teaspoon dried thyme leaves

¹/₃ cup peeled, grated calabaza or pumpkin

1 tablespoon finely sliced scallion, green part only

¹/₂ teaspoon minced Scotch bonnet pepper

6 ounces grouper, cobia, monkfish, or other semifirm white fish, cut into ¹/₂-inch cubes

2 teaspoons cider vinegar

(St. Thomas Fish Soup continued from page 111)

1. In a 2- or 3-quart saucepan with a lid, bring the shrimp stock to a boil. Add the white potatoes, turnips, sweet potatoes, and thyme. Reduce the heat to medium, cover, and simmer for 5–8 minutes, or until the vegetables are tender.

2. Add the calabaza, scallion, and Scotch bonnet, cover and heat for 2 minutes. Add the fish and vinegar, and turn off the heat. Let the soup sit, covered, for 3–5 minutes, until the fish is thoroughly cooked. Serve immediately.

Makes 4 servings

Per Serving: Calories: 165; Fat: 4 g; Cholesterol: 15 mg; Sodium: 165 mg;
% Daily Value: Vitamin A 40%, Vitamin C 21%

Front Porch Cooking

Throughout the Caribbean, women are head chefs not only in their homes but also in restaurant kitchens, which might be no farther away than the front porch. Some women cook on a daily basis, with closing time dictated by when the food runs out. Others set up shop in their front yard only for special festival events. Arriving in Portsmouth, Dominica, at night, without any local currency, I stumbled onto one of these eateries. Walking up the front steps, I called out, only to have the proprietor peek out from the adjoining, curtained room. Since there's no menu in this type of place, there are few decisions to make. She told me what was on the stove, and the Callaloo sounded good. Not only was it delicious, but she waited to be paid until the next morning when I could ante up in local Eastern Caribbean (EC) dollars.

Calypso Callaloo

This is one-pot Caribbean comfort food at its best. Callaloo, the name of this soup, is also the name of the leafy green vegetable that goes into it. These leafy greens are also known as taro leaves, look like big elephant ears, and have an edible root called dasheen. How's that for food confusion? African slaves can be credited with bringing callaloo (the vegetable), along with okra, to the New World. Within the Caribbean, Trinidad is usually considered the home of callaloo, although it's prepared in various ways in Jamaica, Haiti, Guadeloupe, and other islands. Unfortunately, callaloo greens are not readily available here in the States, but spinach or Swiss chard makes a suitable substitute, and I like using a combination of the two. Though recipes vary, callaloo often contains salt pork, okra, coconut milk, and crabmeat. To lighten up the dish, I've replaced the salt pork with bacon, used "lite" coconut milk, and deleted the crabmeat (although you could add 8 ounces, if using this as a main-course soup). Somehow the odd-sounding combination of bacon and coconut milk, a salty and sweet flavor contrast, works to create a delicious taste. If you're just not an okra person, leave it out. You can see from the analysis how incredibly nutritious this soup is, a result primarily of the leafy greens.

6 slices bacon

*1 1/2 pounds mixed, torn spinach and
    Swiss chard leaves*

5 cups water

*1 (14-ounce) can reduced-sodium chicken
    broth*

1 cup chopped onion

2 scallions, sliced

1/4 pound okra, sliced

2 garlic cloves, minced

6 sprigs fresh thyme

1/2 teaspoon salt

Coarsely ground black pepper, to taste

1/2 cup "lite" coconut milk

1. In an 8-quart saucepan with a lid, brown the bacon until crisp. Remove the bacon, crumble it, and set aside. Pour off any excess fat from the pan. Add all the remaining ingredients except the coconut milk to the pan. Bring to a boil, reduce the heat to medium, cover, and cook for 30 minutes, until the greens are tender.

2. Add the coconut milk and crumbled bacon to the pan. Remove from the heat, cover, and let it sit for 5 minutes. The broth will look cloudy from the coconut milk, so just give it a stir before ladling the soup into bowls.

Makes 6 servings

Per Serving: Calories: 100; Fat: 5 g; Cholesterol: 0; Sodium: 425 mg; % Daily Value: Vitamin A 64%, Vitamin C 59%, Folic Acid 40%, Magnesium 27%, Iron 18%, Dietary Fiber 13%

Pepper Pot Soup

There are two pepper pots roaming around the Caribbean. One is a Trinidadian stew, the other is a soup. Pepper pot stew originated with the island Indians, and can be distinguished from the soup because it contains only meat, no vegetables, and cassareep, an unusual-tasting juice derived from the cassava root. Pepper pot soup, prepared in Antigua, Jamaica, and many other islands, is a thick, dark green soup, hearty enough to be a main dish. Pepper pot soup, like the Callaloo recipe, would also call for callaloo greens, but I've found that collard greens work just as well. At first, you may not be crazy about the soup's appearance; it's a dark, murky green color. But get beyond that, and you'll love the savory flavor. Start this the day before you plan to eat it, or at least leave a few hours, so there's time for chilling and removing the congealed surface fat. This step makes for a fairly low-fat, main dish that gives the impression of being rich and high-calorie.

2 pounds beef chuck blade roast, bone-in

7–8 cups water

1 pound collard greens, coarsely chopped
    and stems removed

1 cup unpeeled, thinly sliced sweet
    potatoes, cut in half

1 cup diced onion

1/2 cup peeled, grated yuca

1/2 cup sliced scallions

1/2 cup diced green bell pepper

3 garlic cloves, minced

1 1/2 teaspoons salt

1 teaspoon minced Scotch bonnet pepper

1 teaspoon dried thyme leaves

1 cup "lite" coconut milk

4 ounces small, peeled shrimp

1. Heat an 8-quart saucepan with a lid over high heat, for 2 minutes. Add the meat, and brown it on all sides for a total of 10 minutes. Add 6 cups of the water, bring it to a boil, cover, and reduce the heat to

low. Simmer for 45 minutes, or until the meat is pretty tender, almost the way you'd want to eat it. As the meat is cooking, skim and remove any surface scum. This is a tough cut of meat, so you need to cook the heck out of it. When it's fork-tender, remove the meat, and strain the broth.

2. Refrigerate the broth for at least 2 hours, until the surface fat hardens so that you can remove it. When the meat is cool enough to handle, cut or shred it into small pieces. There's nothing fancy about this technique; just get it off the bone. Although you started with a 2-pound piece of meat, once you trim the gristle, and remove the bone, you should have about 6 ounces. The dish can be made in advance up to this point.

3. In the same saucepan, heat the defatted broth to a boil, and add the collard greens. Cover and cook over medium-high heat for 20 minutes. Working in batches, scoop the greens, with a little of their broth, into a blender. Pulse 6–8 times on high until you get a thick yet still pulpy mixture, not a totally smooth puree. Return all the batches to the pan.

4. Bring the mixture to a boil and add the sweet potatoes, onion, yuca, scallions, green pepper, garlic, salt, Scotch bonnet, thyme, and the meat. Add enough water (about 1–2 cups) to just cover all the ingredients. Bring to a boil again, cover, and reduce the heat to medium-low. Simmer for 15 minutes, or until the sweet potatoes are tender. The onion will probably still have a little crunch, which is fine.

5. Stir in the coconut milk and shrimp; heat for 1 minute. This is a thick soup with lots of stuff in it, and whether you consider it a soup or a stew is just a matter of semantics.

Makes 8 servings

Per Serving: Calories: 140; Fat: 4 g; Cholesterol: 45 mg; Sodium: 450 mg; % Daily Value: Vitamin A 62%, Vitamin C 44%, Zinc 17%, Iron 10%

Black Bean and Olive Soup

No Caribbean cookbook is complete without a black bean soup. Black beans, *frijoles negros,* typical of Cuban cuisine, also go by the name turtle beans. Most black bean soup recipes call for starting with a sofrito, and this one is no exception. I've expanded the basic sofrito by adding more vegetables to it. Doing this gives the soup more flavor, varied textures, and a nutritional boost. Beans need a strong flavor hit, and Spanish olives provide the kick. Crushed salad olives are less expensive than whole olives and work just fine since they'll be chopped up anyway. The splash of red wine vinegar at the end of cooking further heightens the flavor without adding too much salt. This is a good dish to make the day before you need it, as it seems to taste better the longer it sits.

14 ounces dried black beans

7 cups plus 1–2 tablespoons (optional) water

1 (14¹/₂-ounce) can reduced-sodium chicken broth

SOFRITO

1 tablespoon olive oil

1 cup finely chopped green bell pepper

1 cup finely chopped onion

³/₄ cup Spanish salad olives plus 2 tablespoons brine

¹/₂ cup finely chopped carrot

¹/₄ cup finely chopped celery

5 garlic cloves, minced

2 teaspoons dried thyme leaves

¹/₄ teaspoon salt

2 tablespoons red wine vinegar

1. Rinse and drain the beans. In an 8-quart saucepan with a lid, bring the beans and 7 cups of water to a boil for 2 minutes. Remove the pan from the heat, cover, and let it sit for 1 hour. The dish may be pre-

pared in advance up to this point. To continue, add the chicken broth to the pan, cover, and bring it to a boil. Reduce the heat, and keep at a full simmer for approximately 3 hours, or until the beans are tender.

2. While the beans are cooking, start the sofrito by heating the oil in a large skillet. Add all the remaining ingredients, except the vinegar. Cook over low heat, stirring occasionally, for 1 hour, until the mixture is very soft. Don't brown this, but slowly cook it down into a soft mush, adjusting the heat as needed. Add a tablespoon or two of water if the mixture starts to stick.

3. When the beans and sofrito are done, stir the sofrito into the beans. Scoop out 1 cup, and puree in a blender. Return the puree to the pan, cover, and, over low heat, cook an additional 30 minutes. Stir in the vinegar 5 minutes before serving.

Makes 9 servings

Per Serving: Calories: 200; Fat: 4 g; Cholesterol: 0; Sodium: 315 mg; % Daily Value: Folic Acid 51%, Vitamin C 41%, Potassium 22%, Iron 17%

Ignatius's Stew

This is adapted from a recipe I have enjoyed many times. It was told to me by my friend Ignatius, an elderly Spanish man who does tile and stucco work at my home. We now routinely trade recipes and share whatever's growing in our gardens. Since Ignatius originally hails from the Canary Islands, this dish calls for red beans, commonly used in Spanish cuisine. I've eliminated Ignatius's use of salt pork, to save on calories, fat, and sodium, but kept the chorizo sausage, a critical ingredient. It may seem weird using bananas (his version called for plantains), but their slight sweetness, contrasted with the salty, flavorful chorizo, really tastes wonderful. And the stew is even better on the second and third day—that is, if there's still any left.

1 pound dried red kidney beans

1 cup chopped onion

1 cup chopped green bell pepper

*1 cup (about 2 [3-inch] links) thinly
 sliced chorizo sausage, cut lengthwise
 first*

6 garlic cloves, smashed

1/2 cup tomato sauce

1/2 teaspoon salt

1/2 teaspoon pepper

2 bay leaves

4 cups water

1 cup peeled, diced potato

*1 cup semiripe, sliced banana, cut
 1/2 inch thick*

1. Rinse and drain the beans. In an 8-quart saucepan with a lid, cover the beans with 3 inches of fresh water, and bring to a boil for 2 minutes. Remove the pan from the heat, cover, and let it sit for 1 hour. Pour the beans and cooking water into a bowl, and set it aside.

2. In the same pan, over medium-high heat, cook the onion, pepper, chorizo, and garlic for 5–7 minutes, until the onion and pepper soften. The chorizo should release enough fat to prevent sticking. Stir in the tomato sauce, salt, pepper, bay leaves, and beans with their cooking water. Add 3 more cups of water. Bring it to a boil, cover, and reduce the heat to medium. Keep at a full simmer for 1^{1}/$_{2}$ hours.

3. Add the potato and the remaining 1 cup of water. Cover and cook over medium-low heat for 45 minutes. Add the banana, cover, and cook an additional 20 minutes, or until the beans and potatoes are tender. You will find that the potatoes and banana help to thicken the liquid, resulting in a thick, deep red-brown broth. If time permits, cover and refrigerate overnight to let the flavors develop more fully. The next day reheat, covered, over low heat for 10–15 minutes, until warmed through. Remove bay leaf before serving.

Makes 10 servings

Per Serving: Calories: 210; Fat: 5 g; Cholesterol: 5 mg; Sodium: 195 mg; % Daily Values: Folic Acid 48%, Vitamin C 47%, Vitamin B$_6$ 24%, Iron 23%

A Legume Lesson

Throughout the islands, beans and peas are words that are used interchangeably. They refer to both fresh and dried legumes, which are high in complex carbohydrates, rich in soluble fiber, packed with protein, and an excellent source of folic acid, magnesium, iron, zinc, as well as other micronutrients. With a nutritional profile like that, why aren't we eating more of them? Culturally speaking, peas and beans have been considered peasant food, something to fill the belly when one could not afford meat. But thanks to the growing popularity cuisines, such as Mexican, Mediterranean, and Caribbean, that rely heavily on legumes, Americans are realizing the versatility and nutritional value these foods can offer, although, except for vegetarians, most Americans don't yet consider a bowl of rice and beans as their dinner.

In the Caribbean, legumes go by different names, depending on the island's heritage. Cuban menus refer to black beans as *frijoles,* while the Puerto Rican and Dominican term is *habichuelas,* usually some type of red bean. In the Bahamas, pigeon peas and rice is an everyday dish, made with a small, round, green legume, known as a pigeon pea. Their Spanish name is *gandules.* Yet in Jamaica, if you find peas on the menu, it's probably kidney beans. Then, of course, there's the French term *pois* (literal translation is peas), which may refer to dried beans. And to add further confusion to the bean pot, Trinidadians often call regular green peas, pigeon peas. So when dining in the Caribbean, bone up on your p's and q's before ordering your peas and beans.

New Year's Black-Eyed Peas

There's a Southern U.S. tradition of eating black-eyed peas on New Year's Day to guarantee good luck for the coming year. It was the African slaves who brought black-eyed peas to the American South as well as to the Caribbean. This recipe doesn't have the traditional salt pork or fat back, but uses smoked ham shanks and "lite" coconut milk for flavoring. This past New Year's Day, with company lounging around the house, I served this recipe with Down Island Smoked Pulled Pork sandwiches (page 218), for a high-fiber side dish. If you're not serving a crowd, portion it out and freeze the rest for future use.

3/4 pound dried black-eyed peas

3/4 pound trimmed, smoked ham shanks, center slices

1 cup finely chopped mushrooms

1/2 cup finely chopped onion

4 garlic cloves, minced

1 teaspoon dried oregano leaves

1 teaspoon black pepper

2 bay leaves

2 tablespoons red wine vinegar

3/4 teaspoon salt

1/2 cup "lite" coconut milk

1. Rinse and drain the peas. In a 4-quart saucepan with a lid, cover the peas with 2 inches of water and bring to a boil for 2 minutes. Remove the pan from the heat, cover, and let it sit for 1 hour. The dish may be prepared in advance up to this point.

2. Add the ham shanks, mushrooms, onion, garlic, oregano, pepper, and bay leaves to the saucepan. Partially cover, and cook over medium heat, at a full simmer, for about 2 hours. Don't bring this to a full boil because the skins on the peas will break and it won't look as nice. If necessary, remove the cover com-

(New Year's Black-Eyed Peas continued from page 123)

pletely to allow more liquid to evaporate. When done, the beans should be soft, with most of the liquid evaporated, as though to eat them, either a fork or a spoon would do. Remove the ham shanks, and, when cool enough to handle, cut or shred the meat.

3. Add the vinegar, salt, coconut milk, and the ham to the beans. Heat for 2 minutes. Discard the bay leaves. This will be moist enough so that serving it in little bowls or ramekins is a good idea.

Makes 12 servings

Per Serving: Calories: 140; Fat: 2 g; Cholesterol: 5 mg; Sodium: 380 mg; % Daily Value: Dietary Fiber 31%, Thiamine 31%, Iron 15%, Vitamin C 12%, Zinc 10%

Holiday Cheer . . . Island-Style

While we're chilling the champagne and cooking up a batch of black-eyed peas to ring in the New Year, island locals are busy making their own merriment. In Martinique, where French holiday traditions mix with Creole, the New Year's *le réveillon,* a late night feast, often centers around a roast pork, smoked ham, or a fruit-studded turkey or chicken. Side dishes might include raw oysters, warm pâtés, yams, a pork ragout with congo peas, and boudin Creole, a spicy West Indian sausage. At Christmas dinner, a similar meal would have been topped off with a bûche de Noël, the traditional yule log dessert.

Pigeon Peas and Rice

This Bahamian staple, often seasoned with a small piece of meat, is eaten as a main or side dish. Just about every island has its own version of peas and rice, and the Bahamians often use salted pig's tail for flavoring. I think we'll use something more common, like smoked ham. For islanders, who do not eat a lot of animal protein, the rice and bean combination makes a complete protein, helping to ensure a nutritious diet. Pigeon peas, also called congo peas or *gandules,* are a dried legume, sold in small bags or in bulk along with other dried peas and beans. In this recipe, I use the same water for soaking and cooking, which preserves nutrients and happens to be easy, too.

¹/₄ pound dried pigeon peas

3 cups water

¹/₄ pound lean smoked ham, diced

¹/₂ cup finely diced onion

¹/₂ cup finely diced green bell pepper

2 peeled, seeded, diced plum tomatoes

3 garlic cloves, minced

1¹/₂ teaspoons dried thyme leaves

¹/₂ teaspoon minced Scotch bonnet pepper

¹/₂ teaspoon salt

1 cup uncooked long-grain rice

1 cup reduced-sodium chicken broth

1. Rinse and drain the peas. In a 4-quart saucepan with a lid, bring the peas and 3 cups of water to a boil for 2 minutes. Remove the pan from the heat and let it sit for 1 hour. The dish may be prepared in advance up to this point.

2. Add the ham, onion, green pepper, tomatoes, garlic, thyme, Scotch bonnet, and salt to the pan. Cover, and bring to a boil. Reduce the heat to medium-low and cook for 30 minutes, until beans are tender but not mushy.

(Pigeon Peas and Rice continued from page 125)

3. Stir in the rice and broth and bring it to a boil. Cover, reduce the heat, and cook an additional 20–25 minutes, until the liquid is absorbed and the rice is tender.

Makes 8 servings

Per Serving: Calories: 170; Fat: 1 g; Cholesterol: 10 mg; Sodium: 300 mg; % Daily Value: Vitamin C 38%, Thiamine 24%, Folic Acid 19%

Coo-Coo

Coo-coo, meaning a "cooked side dish," can best be described as the Caribbean version of polenta, the popular Mediterranean cornmeal side dish. This African-influenced, starchy dish turns up on many different island menus. In Barbados, it's usually made with okra, while in the Virgin Islands and other locations, you will see it minus the okra, when its name changes to fungi or funchi. There are also sweet, dessert versions made with coconut milk, and wedges that have been fried in butter or oil. The small amount of butter in this recipe is okay to use and delivers only 1 gram of fat per serving. While coo-coo can be served warm or cold, I like it much better served immediately out of the pan. It should really be the last item put on the table, cut into wedges, and served piping hot.

1½ cups water

¾ teaspoon salt

½ (10-ounce) box frozen or thawed cut okra

1 cup cornmeal

1 teaspoon butter

1 tablespoon sliced pimento

1. In a 3-quart saucepan, bring the water and salt to a boil. Add the okra and cook 2–3 minutes. If the okra is still frozen, cook it for 6–7 minutes.

2. Slowly add the cornmeal, stirring constantly until all the water is absorbed, about 5 minutes. Stir in the butter and pimento. The finished mixture should pull away from the sides of the pan and practically stand up by itself. Immediately spread the mixture onto a flat plate, forming an 8-inch-diameter circle. Cut it into wedges and serve.

Makes 6 servings

Per Serving: Calories: 85; Fat: 1 g; Cholesterol: 2 mg; Sodium: 280 mg; % Daily Value: Dietary Fiber 13%

"Lite" Coconut Milk

Coconut milk, a staple ingredient in Caribbean, Thai, and Indian dishes, is high in fat and calories (11 grams of fat, and 110 calories per ¼ cup). But with the advent of "lite" coconut milk, you can get real coconut flavor for only 3 grams of fat and 35 calories in ¼ cup. Manufacturers accomplish this by boiling and pressing the coconut, which skims off the fat. The differences in flavor among various brands depend on whether or not the coconut milk is canned from the first pressing, a concept similar to the most flavorful olive oil being obtained from the first pressing. A more watered-down, less flavorful coconut milk is the result of multiple steamings, boilings, and pressings.

Coconut Rice

Coconut is a flavor most of us associate with sweet things, but in Caribbean cooking, it's more often used in savory ways: for curries, soups, and rice dishes. Coconut and coconut milk are high-fat and saturated-fat ingredients. But "lite" coconut milk delivers the essence of coconut without busting the nutritional budget. Some dishes hit you over the head with a dominant flavor, while others, like this one, are more subtle in their approach. In fact, if this recipe had a different name, you might not be able to put your finger on the specific flavor, but would only know it tasted good.

1 cup water	*2 tablespoons minced scallion, green part*
1 cup "lite" coconut milk	* only*
Pinch of saffron	*1 garlic clove, minced*
1 cup uncooked long-grain rice	*¹/₄ teaspoon salt*

In a medium saucepan with a lid, bring the water, "lite" coconut milk, and saffron to a boil. Stir in the rice and bring to a boil again. Reduce the heat to medium-low, cover, and cook for 15–20 minutes, until the liquid has been absorbed and the rice is tender. Stir in the scallion, garlic, and salt. Serve immediately.

Makes 4 servings

Per Serving: Calories: 210; Fat: 3 g; Cholesterol: 0; Sodium: 135 mg;
% Daily Value: Thiamine 18%, Iron 11%

Avocado Panzanella Bread Salad

This is one of the times when an Old World recipe meets New World ingredients. Panzanella is a Mediterranean salad made with stale bread, tomatoes, capers, maybe cucumbers, and a few other seasonings. I've given it an island twist by using avocados, which, yes, are high in fat, particularly monounsaturated fat. The good news is that a small amount is all that's necessary. The salad's other tropical variation comes from using a lime vinaigrette dressing in place of the traditional balsamic or red wine version. This recipe is a good example of how you can indulge judiciously in high-calorie, high-fat ingredients while keeping the finished dish within dietary guidelines.

2 cups (2 ounces) stale, 1/4-inch, Italian or French bread cubes

1/2 cup diced tomato

1/4 medium avocado, peeled and cut into 1/4-inch cubes, reserving 1 tablespoon mashed

2 tablespoons finely diced red onion

2 tablespoons finely chopped fresh mint

2 tablespoons fresh lime juice

2 tablespoons water

2 teaspoons peanut oil

1/4 teaspoon salt

Coarsely ground black pepper to taste

1. In a shallow serving dish, combine the bread, tomato, cubed avocado, onion, and mint. The dish can be prepared in advance up to this point. If so, refrigerate, then bring it to room temperature before serving.

2. To make the dressing, in a small jar combine the remaining ingredients, including the reserved mashed avocado. Shake well, and toss thoroughly with the salad.

Makes 4 servings

Per Serving: Calories: 90; Fat: 5 g; Cholesterol: 0; Sodium: 220 mg; % Daily Value: Vitamin C 16%

Florida versus California Avocados

Florida avocados are the larger of the two types, and are wrapped in a bright green, shiny skin. Those grown in California, sometimes labeled Haas, are small, dark green to almost brown, with a nubby, bumpy peel. When you have both varieties in front of you at the produce section, there will be no problem making the distinction. Their looks are not the only difference. The calorie and fat content in $3^1/2$ ounces of a California avocado weigh in at about 175 calories and 17 grams of fat. The same amount of a Florida avocado yields approximately 110 calories and 9 grams of fat. Need I say more about which kind you'll want to use if you're counting fat grams?

A ripe avocado should be soft to the finger touch, although if you buy one rock-hard, it will ripen at room temperature in a few days. Once ripe, the pulp will be creamy and spoon-scooping soft. The pale yellow-green flesh starts to discolor as soon as it's exposed to air. This discoloration can be forestalled by sprinkling with something acidic, such as lemon or lime juice, or even vinegar. All avocados are rich in Vitamin A and potassium, while their fat content is primarily monounsaturated, which is considered a good type of fat for blood cholesterol levels.

Hot 'n Sour Mushroom and Cucumber Salad

This is a takeoff on the hot bacon and spinach salads that were so popular back in the eighties. The chorizo and olive oil are so flavorful that only a small amount of each is needed. And, luckily, mushrooms and cucumbers take on flavor easily, so they don't require much dressing.

1 1/2 cups sliced mushrooms, stems removed

1 cup halved, sliced cucumbers

1 ounce (about half a 3-inch link) chorizo sausage, cut in half lengthwise and thinly sliced

1/4 cup thinly sliced red onion

2 tablespoons cider vinegar

2 tablespoons water

1 1/2 tablespoons sugar

1 teaspoon olive oil

1/8 teaspoon salt

1. In a medium bowl, combine the mushrooms and cucumbers, which should be of similar size. Refrigerate while preparing the dressing.

2. Heat a small skillet over medium heat, add the chorizo, and cook for 3–5 minutes, until crispy. Remove the sausage from the pan and add the onion. Cook for 5–7 minutes, until soft. The small amount of oil left in the pan from the chorizo will prevent the onion from sticking. Stir in the vinegar, water, sugar, oil, and salt. Bring it to a light simmer, and add the chorizo.

3. Pour the hot dressing over the mushrooms and cucumbers. Toss to coat, and serve immediately.

Makes 4 servings

Per Serving: Calories: 75; Fat: 4 g; Cholesterol: 5 mg; Sodium: 160 mg; No other significant nutritional value

Cooking Contrasts at Work

The use of hot and sour, or sweet and sour flavors isn't a new idea at all. Think about Chinese hot 'n sour soup, traditional sweet and sour meatballs, chutney, and pickled condiments. They all use sugar and acid to achieve their unique flavor balance. This basic concept can be transferred to other ingredient combinations, as a means of achieving low-fat, big-flavor dishes.

It's this sweet and sour contrast that's at work in the Hot 'n Sour Mushroom and Cucumber Salad. The flavors of two fairly bland vegetables are heightened not only by sugar and vinegar, but also by the chorizo, which adds another spicy, salty flavor to the mix. But let's not stop there. Temperature contrasts also come into play by pouring a warm dressing over chilled vegetables. To add more complexity to what seems like a simple dish, there's texture contrast, too. Crisp cucumbers and soft mushrooms make the chew in your mouth a little more interesting.

Cooking healthy doesn't necessarily mean relying just on reduced-fat ingredients or complicated recipes. By using the principles of contrast cooking, critical to all good cooking, you can create food that excites all of your culinary senses.

Chayote Slaw

This Caribbean-style coleslaw is a mixture of the tried and true red cabbage, with something new and different, chayote squash. Because the chayote is lightly cooked, it's texture will be a bit softer than that of the raw cabbage, creating a pleasant texture contrast. There's no high-fat, mayo dressing used here, but rather a small amount of an intensely flavored, mustard-based mixture. Once the dressing is tossed in, it makes the red cabbage bleed, creating a pretty, pale pink salad. Definitely not the typical coleslaw!

*1 pound (about 2 medium) chayote,
    quartered*
1 cup shredded red cabbage
¼ cup grated onion
1 tablespoon minced flat-leaf parsley
3 tablespoons fresh lime juice
1½ tablespoons water
2 teaspoons vegetable oil

1½ teaspoons sugar
*1½ teaspoons prepared yellow mustard
    (commercial, nothing fancy)*
½ teaspoon fennel seeds
½ teaspoon salt
⅛ teaspoon onion powder
Coarsely ground black pepper, to taste

1. In a 3-quart saucepan, bring 1 inch of water to a boil. Add the chayote, cover, and steam over medium heat for 5 minutes, until the chayote is tender enough to pierce with a knife but still has some firmness, suitable for grating. Drain, rinse, and, when cool enough to handle, peel off the skin. The little almond-shaped seeds in the center are delicious, and a nice tidbit to snack on as you're cooking. Grate the chayote to yield 2 cups, and, in a large bowl, combine it with the cabbage, onion, and parsley.

2. To make the dressing, in a small bowl, combine all the remaining ingredients. This will look like a small amount, and you'll swear you've done something wrong. You haven't. The lime juice and mustard are strong flavors and a little goes a long way. Toss the dressing into the salad to thoroughly coat. Serve immediately, or cover and refrigerate until ready to use. Bring to room temperature before serving.

Makes 4 servings

Per Serving: Calories: 70; Fat: 3 g; Cholesterol: 0; Sodium: 295 mg; % Daily Value: Vitamin C 39%

Christophene,
the West Indies Squash

In our markets, it's called a chayote; in the West Indies, it goes by christophene. The taste of this pear-shaped vegetable seems to be a cross between summer squash and cucumber, and can pinch hit for either in a recipe.

It's a bit of a funny-looking vegetable in that one side is tucked in, making it look like a mouth without its false teeth in place. The outside is the color of a Granny Smith apple, while the interior is a bland beige. To my mind, it's easier to peel before cooking, since removing the skin afterward gets to be a slippery affair. Christophene can be quickly blanched for grating in salads or slaw, lightly steamed for stuffing, or boiled to a soft consistency for pureeing in soups. In the islands, christophene is sometimes used in place of apples for making pie or sauce. At only 20 calories for $1/2$ cup, you can well afford to add some sugar to the pie.

Christophene "Applesauce"

Christophene (chayote) can amazingly be transformed into "applesauce" when cooked down and properly seasoned. I promise you, people will not be able to tell that it's made of anything other than apples. This same mock applesauce can be created by using pawpaw, which is unripe papaya. It's a simple dish to make, and tastes best when served warm. For an extra flavor bump, you might try stirring in a bit of rum before serving.

2 cups peeled, diced christophene

2 cups water

1/4 cup fresh lime juice

3 tablespoons sugar

6 whole cloves

1 cinnamon stick

1 (2-inch) piece vanilla bean

Cinnamon, for garnish

1. In a medium saucepan over high heat, bring all the ingredients except the cinnamon to a boil. Reduce the heat to medium, cover, and cook for 20 minutes. Partially uncover, and cook an additional 20–25 minutes, until the christophene is very soft.

2. Remove the cloves, cinnamon stick, and vanilla bean. Using a slotted spoon, drain the christophene, keeping the liquid in reserve, and transfer the christophene to a blender or food processor. Pulse a few times, just until smooth. Add some of the cooking liquid only if needed to thin out the consistency. Pour the "applesauce" into a bowl, dust with cinnamon, and serve immediately.

Makes 6 servings

Per Serving: Calories: 40; Fat, Cholesterol, and Sodium: 0; % Daily Value: Vitamin C 11%

Marinated Palm Hearts

$\mathcal{Y}$es, these are exactly what they sound like. You might think that a vegetable taken from the inner core of a palm tree would be tough and stringy, but these are creamy smooth and fork-tender. They remind me of white asparagus with no tips. Fresh palm hearts are served in the Caribbean and in some old Florida-style restaurants, but at home, you'll need to rely on palm hearts packed in cans or jars and sold with the canned vegetables or in the gourmet product aisle. Because they are so tender, treat them with care, otherwise you'll have mush on your hands. This is a simple dish that can lend a tropical touch to any menu.

1 (8-ounce) can hearts of palm, drained	*2 teaspoons cider vinegar*
20 fresh chives	*¹/₄ teaspoon salt*
1 (2-ounce) jar minced pimento, drained	*¹/₈ teaspoon black pepper*
1¹/₂ tablespoons olive oil	*2 teaspoons fresh thyme leaves*
1 tablespoon water	

1. Slice the palm hearts lengthwise into four pieces. Slice the chives lengthwise into four pieces, the same length as the palm hearts. Place both in a wide, shallow dish so that they're lying flat, not stacked on top of each other. Sprinkle the pimento on top.

2. In a small jar, combine the oil, water, vinegar, salt, and pepper. Shake and pour over the palm hearts. Sprinkle the thyme over the top. If time permits, refrigerate for a few hours to allow the flavors to develop, then bring to room temperature before serving.

Makes 4 servings

Per Serving: Calories: 110; Fat: 5 g; Cholesterol: 0; Sodium: 145 mg; % Daily Value: Vitamin C 27%

Stewed Calabaza and Leeks

Calabaza is the Caribbean pumpkin, a variety of squash. One-pot stewing, typical of island home-cooking, requires minimal cleanup, needs no added fat, and preserves nutrients. Mashing a small amount of the pumpkin into the broth thickens the entire dish, creating a richer consistency. While calabaza is readily available in the produce section of most major supermarkets, Hubbard or butternut squash are both suitable substitutes. The whole family of orange-yellow squash is a tremendous source of Vitamin A.

*3 cups peeled, seeded, 1-inch cubes
    calabaza*
1 cup sliced leeks, white part only
1 cup reduced-sodium chicken broth
*3/4 cup coarsely chopped green bell
    pepper*

8 thin slices peeled fresh ginger
1/4 teaspoon curry powder
1/4 teaspoon salt
1/8 teaspoon black pepper
2 tablespoons chopped cilantro

1. In a 4-quart saucepan, combine all ingredients except the cilantro. Bring to a boil over medium heat, cover, and cook for 10 minutes, until the calabaza is easily pierced with a fork.

2. Reduce the heat to low, remove 4–5 calabaza cubes, and thoroughly mash them with a fork. Stir them back into the pan and heat for 3–5 minutes. Add the cilantro, and serve. There's enough liquid in this dish for it to be served over white rice, if desired, or portioned into individual ramekins or small bowls.

Makes 6 servings

*Per Serving: Calories: 40; Fat and Cholesterol: 0; Sodium: 100 mg;
% Daily Value: Vitamin C 27%, Vitamin A 11%*

A Calabash Kitchen

Calabaza and calabash sound almost alike, but the calabash is used as a kitchen utensil rather than an edible ingredient. Originally used by the Carib and Arawak Indians, the hard, durable shell of the calabash gourd continues to serve as spoon, ladle, plate, and bowl in rural island households. There are quite a few cottage industries throughout the islands that produce and sell products made from these hard-shelled gourds. Ideal take-home gifts for tourists, the outsides are sometimes etched and decorated with native designs and motifs. While shopping in Roseau, the capital of Dominica, I purchased a few kitchen items, as well as a had-to-have small purse. I realize now that the sturdy gourd purse can also serve as a weapon, should I ever need to whack someone on the head.

Grilled and Spiced
Sweet Potatoes

The story of yams and sweet potatoes is thoroughly explained in Potato Confusion (page 143). This recipe uses American-style, orange sweet potatoes, but gets its seasoning from a peppery-allspice blend. While many island potato recipes call for deep-frying the tubers, this low-fat version gets its crispness and smoky flavor from the grill.

2 medium sweet potatoes

2 teaspoons hazelnut oil

½ teaspoon dried thyme leaves

¼ teaspoon ground allspice

¼ teaspoon salt

⅛ teaspoon cayenne pepper

1. Preheat oven to 350°. Scrub the potatoes clean and dry them. Place them on the oven rack and bake for 45 minutes, until easily pierced with a fork. Remove from the oven, and slice in half lengthwise.

2. Using your fingers, coat the cut sides of the potatoes with the oil. In a small dish, combine all the remaining ingredients, and sprinkle the spice mixture over the oiled potato halves.

3. Grill the potatoes over high heat, cut side down, for 5–10 minutes, until the surface is crisped and light grill marks appear. If they're starting to char, reduce the heat, or move them to a cooler area of the grill. Serve cut side up.

Makes 4 servings

Per Serving: Calories: 120; Fat: 2 g; Cholesterol: 0; Sodium: 140 mg;
% Daily Value: Vitamin C 17%, Potassium 16%

Baked Boniato
with Creamy Rum Dressing

The best part of a baked boniato, the Caribbean white-fleshed sweet potato, is its crusty skin. This is a potato with plenty of chew on the outside and a fluffy texture on the inside. Because the flesh is somewhat drier than that of a regular baked potato, it needs a little moisture, which it gets from the rum dressing. Depending on its size, one potato might be enough for 2 to 4 servings.

2 pounds boniato
3 tablespoons "lite" cream cheese,
   softened
2 tablespoons plain nonfat yogurt

1¹/₂ tablespoons dark rum
¹/₂ tablespoon honey
Freshly grated nutmeg, for garnish

1. Preheat the oven to 400°. Wash and dry the potatoes. Place them on the oven rack and bake for 1 hour, until easily pierced with a fork. An 8- to 12-ounce potato will take about 1 hour, while a 1¹/₂–2-pound potato can take up to 2 hours.

2. Meanwhile, to make the dressing, in a small bowl, whisk together all the remaining ingredients except the nutmeg, and let the mixture sit at room temperature.

3. When the potatoes are done, cut them into four equal portions. Slit them across the top, and fluff up the inside, then drizzle on the dressing. Sprinkle the nutmeg on top and serve immediately.

Makes 4 servings

Per Serving: Calories: 220; Fat: 2 g; Cholesterol: 5 mg; Sodium: 80 mg; % Daily Value: Vitamin A 377%,
Vitamin C 70%, Vitamin E 26%, Dietary Fiber 20%

Potato Confusion

Caribbean potatoes are caught up in a real identity crisis; so let's try and sort out the difference between yams and sweet potatoes.

The orange-fleshed potatoes we sometimes call yams are not really yams at all but sweet potatoes. True, these two names are often used interchangeably, but yams, or ñame, are something altogether different. Yams are an important, worldwide crop, grown throughout the subtropics and tropics. They are rather unattractive-looking, shaggy brown specimens, not at all sweet, but with a bland, starchy taste, suitable for heavy flavoring.

When shopping for yams in the produce department, look for an irregularly shaped, hairy, dark brown tuber. They resemble deformed rocks, with pale yellow or off-white flesh. Often deep-fried (not a good choice for us), they can also be peeled, diced, and boiled, as an add-in to soups, or eaten as a side vegetable drizzled with a Garlic Mojo (page 32). They're rich in potassium, folic acid, and zinc, and a good calorie buy at about 80 calories per 1/2 cup.

Now to make the potato story even more confusing, in most of the world, a sweet potato is not the orange, sweet-tasting potato we are accustomed to eating here in America. Rather, it's a white-fleshed, slightly sweet, red, bumpy-skinned tuber. In the Caribbean, it goes by the name boniato, and is a delightful way to start incorporating a tropical touch into your diet.

With a slightly dry, chestnut-like quality, boniato is great baked or boiled, when it must stay covered with liquid so the peeled flesh doesn't discolor. Although 115 calories per 1/2 cup, I'd consider these nutritionally dense, since they're an excellent source of Vitamin A and potassium, and fairly rich in protein and Vitamin C.

Sweet Potato, Boniato, and Plantain Mash

I created this recipe for Christmas dinner last year, and it was a wonderful blend of a traditional food with a Caribbean influence. Because these ingredients are all mashed together, it's a great way to introduce new items, without their staring you in the face. Each of the three tubers, plus the roasted garlic, brings a distinctive flavor to the finished dish, with no one overpowering the other. Using a small amount of butter adds a finished creaminess and a touch of indulgence. If you have any leftovers, dig in with a spoon and enjoy them cold, too. We're talking a very nutritious carbohydrate-rich dish here, loaded with Vitamin A and fiber.

8 garlic cloves, unpeeled
6 cups (6–7 small) peeled, 1-inch cubes sweet potatoes
2 cups (1 medium) peeled, 1-inch cubes boniato
1 cup (1 medium) black-ripe, peeled, sliced plantain cut ¹/₂ inch thick

8 cups water
1¹/₂ cups skim milk
1¹/₂ tablespoons butter
³/₄ teaspoon salt
Freshly grated nutmeg, for garnish

1. Preheat the oven to 350°. Wrap the garlic in an aluminum foil pouch, place it on the oven rack, and bake it for 30 minutes, until it's squishy soft. Set aside until cool enough to handle, then peel.

2. In an 8-quart saucepan, over high heat, bring the sweet potatoes, boniato, plantain, and 8 cups of

water (or enough to adequately cover everything) to a boil. Cover and boil for 20 minutes, until all three items are soft enough to whip with a beater. Drain, and keep the vegetables in the pan.

3. Using an electric beater, whip on high speed, gradually adding the milk, butter, roasted, peeled garlic, and salt, until creamy. Transfer to a serving bowl, and garnish with nutmeg.

Makes 10 servings

Per Serving: Calories: 165; Fat: 2 g; Cholesterol: 5 mg; Sodium: 200 mg; % Daily Value: Vitamin A 155%, Vitamin C 41%, Potassium 15%, Dietary Fiber 12%

Fins
'n Things

◻ ◻ ◻ ◻ ◻ ◻ ◻ ◻ ◻ ◻ ◻

You would expect that, surrounded by water, Caribbean cooks would have a wealth of seafood at their fingertips. And they do, to a certain extent. For those who make their living as fishermen, there is plenty to feed family and friends. But chefs in large resorts and restaurants, who require large volume and consistent quality, find they can't always rely on the local catch. That's why a great deal of seafood from south Florida and even points farther north, is routinely air-shipped to the Caribbean.

This chapter includes several different kinds of snapper, conch, grouper, sea bass, dolphinfish, salmon, tuna, shark, lobster, shrimp, crabs, and clams—all species that are readily available at most quality seafood markets around the country. Some seafood, such as flying fish, the national dish of Barbados, are good eating, but are just not available here in the States. So, with a concession to practicality, such items have not been included. When you can't find a particular type of fish, don't fret. Just substitute something similar. After all, if you were on an island, you would simply make do with what was plucked from the ocean.

Seafood is the perfect choice for healthful entrees: low in fat and mild enough to readily absorb other flavors. Even higher-fat varieties, such as tuna, can be used in moderate portion sizes. And speaking of portion sizes, you will note that many of these dishes use 6 ounces of fish per person. Any recipe can be made lighter by simply cutting back on the portion size. That's taking the easy way out, so I've made a real effort to ensure these recipes provide ample servings. Shrimp, lobster, and crab are no longer considered off lim-

its, as they once were, because of their cholesterol content; a little bit of everything is perfectly okay. While most people love to order seafood at a restaurant, many hesitate to prepare it at home. I think they're intimidated by cooking it, for fear of overcooking, undercooking, or smelling up the house. These recipes use easy, low-fat preparation methods so that grilled, baked, poached, crusted, stuffed, curried, and glazed seafood dishes just couldn't get any easier to make.

Anise-Rubbed Tuna Medallions with Grilled Asparagus and Honey Vinaigrette

My husband, Ted, always says tuna is like eating steak. And he's right. It has a dense, meaty texture, a dark color, and a flavor that can stand up to strong seasonings. Because of the natural shape of the fish, you can get medallion-like slices, similar to a beef tenderloin. While not strictly a warm-water fish, tuna comes in a few varieties—most common are black fin and yellow fin. Anise is grown and used in Caribbean cooking, and, in this rub, it provides a nice balance to the black pepper. This recipe is super-simple because the rub and dressing can be made in advance. Tuna and asparagus both cook on the grill in just a matter of minutes, saving on time and cleanup. Calories are spared by finishing off the dish with a reduced-oil vinaigrette.

ANISE RUB
1 tablespoon coarsely ground black
  pepper
2 teaspoons anise seeds
1 1/2 teaspoons ground allspice
1 teaspoon ground ginger
1/2 teaspoon garlic powder

HONEY VINAIGRETTE
2 1/2 tablespoons hazelnut oil

1 1/2 tablespoons honey
1 tablespoon balsamic vinegar
1/4 teaspoon dry mustard
1/4 teaspoon salt

1 pound fresh tuna, cut into 4 (1/2-inch-
  thick) medallions
1/2 pound fresh asparagus, trimmed

1. Combine the rub ingredients in a mortar and pestle. Combine the vinaigrette ingredients in a small jar. Both of these can be prepared in advance and set aside.

2. Coat the grill rack with nonstick cooking spray. Coat both sides of the tuna with the rub. Grill the tuna over medium heat, turning it once, for a total of 8–12 minutes, until the fish flakes easily when tested with a fork. When the tuna is halfway done, add the asparagus to the grill, turning it once and cooking it for a total of 5 minutes, until just lightly browned and tender.

3. To serve, place a few asparagus on a plate, top them with a medallion, and drizzle a portion of the vinaigrette over both.

Makes 4 servings

Per Serving: Calories: 250; Fat: 10 g; Cholesterol: 50 mg; Sodium: 180 mg; % Daily Value: Niacin 55%, Thiamine 34%, Folic Acid 19%

Blaff

This dish derives its funny name from the sound (blaff, or perhaps splash) of freshly caught fish being tossed into a pot of hot stock. It's a simple, regional dish of the French West Indies, often cooked on the beach, requiring only fresh fish and few other ingredients. In its simplest terms, blaff is poached fish in an herb broth. I've used salmon for this recipe because the pink color stands out beautifully in a clear broth, but any other semifirm fish fillet would also be perfect. Salmon is slightly higher in fat, especially the heart-healthy omega-3 fatty acids, than many other fish. But without a speck of added fat in the recipe, the nutritional bottom line looks just fine.

5 cups water

¹/₄ cup fresh lime juice

1 teaspoon salt

4 (6-ounce) salmon fillets

4 scallions, cut into 1-inch pieces

¹/₄ cup fresh curly-leaf parsley, stems
*   removed*

3 teaspoons minced garlic

¹/₂ teaspoon dried thyme leaves

6 whole cloves

6 whole allspice berries

1 tiny bird pepper, cut in half

1. In a shallow dish, combine 2 cups of the water, 3 tablespoons of the lime juice, and ¹/₄ teaspoon of the salt. Stir to dissolve the salt, and add the salmon. Refrigerate for 1 hour, turning once. Drain the fish, and discard the marinade.

2. In a large skillet with a tight-fitting lid, bring the remaining 3 cups of water to a boil, add all other ingredients except the remaining lime juice and the remaining ³/₄ teaspoon of salt. Cover and heat for 5 minutes.

3. Reduce the heat to medium-low, add the salmon, cover, and poach for 10 minutes, until the fish flakes easily when tested with a fork. While poaching, you want just tiny bubbles breaking the surface. If the heat is too high and the broth boils, the fish will toughen up.

4. To serve, portion the salmon into shallow soup bowls. Pick the cloves and allspice out of the broth, if you wish, but I don't bother. Add the remaining 1 tablespoon of lime juice to the broth, then ladle the broth over the fish. Serve immediately.

Makes 4 servings

Per Serving: Calories: 205; Fat: 6 g; Cholesterol: 85 mg; Sodium: 560 mg; % Daily Value: Vitamin C 25%, Potassium 17%, Vitamin A 10%, Iron 10%

Another Kind of Court Bouillon

The court bouillon served on French West Indies islands such as Martinique, Guadeloupe, and St. Bart's is not the classical French poaching liquid used for cooking seafood or vegetables. It does, however, make a delicious French Creole dish very similar to Blaff. Sometimes the terms are even used interchangeably, but more often court bouillon requires sautéing the fresh and dried ingredients in a little oil before adding the fish to the liquid.

Cashew and Papaya—Crusted Snapper

I created this dish as a way to use tropical fruit in a nontraditional manner. And because, let's face it, fish needs window dressing. The papaya lends a beautiful coral color to the basic bread coating, which blankets the fillets and keeps them moist. Cashews are also an island contribution, a fact many people don't realize, as they grow from the base of the cashew apple, a tropical fruit not generally imported in the United States. Mixing cashews into the coating adds some crunch, providing a texture contrast for the soft fish underneath. Because this whole dish can be prepared in advance, it's perfect for company. It looks so impressive on the plate, your guests will think you really knocked yourself out in the kitchen. The Vitamin C and potassium content are courtesy of the papaya.

MARINADE

3 tablespoons fresh lemon juice

2 tablespoons dark rum

1 tablespoon soy sauce

1 teaspoon hazelnut or peanut oil

3 garlic cloves, minced

4 (5-ounce) snapper fillets, no more than
* $^1/_2$ inch thick*

2 cups (2 ounces) stale Italian or French
*   bread cubes*

$1^1/_2$ cups cubed papaya

$^1/_2$ teaspoon curry powder

$^1/_4$ teaspoon salt

1 garlic clove, minced

$1^1/_2$ ounces roasted unsalted cashews

4 tablespoons chopped, mixed fresh herbs
*   (basil, oregano, thyme, marjoram)*

1. In a shallow dish, combine all the marinade ingredients. Add the fish fillets, turning to coat them. Cover and refrigerate, turning once, for 30 minutes.

2. Meanwhile, in a food processor, process the bread cubes on high speed for 1 minute, until they're crumbly but not totally fine. Add the papaya, curry powder, salt, and garlic. Pulse on low speed 15–20 times, until the papaya has been thoroughly incorporated into the bread. You should have coral-colored bread with tiny bits of fruit throughout. Coarsely chop 1 ounce of the cashews, then stir the coarsely chopped nuts and herbs into the bread coating.

3. Preheat the oven to broil. Coat a baking sheet with nonstick cooking spray. Remove the fillets from the marinade, and place them on the baking sheet. Discard the marinade. Using a spoon or knife, cover the top and sides of the fillets with the coating. Finely chop the remaining $1/2$ ounce of cashews and sprinkle them over the top of the coated fish.

4. Broil for 5 minutes, until the bread and cashews start to brown and get a crusty look. Reduce the heat to 500°, and bake an additional 3–5 minutes, until the fish flakes easily with a fork. Use a spatula to remove the fish from the baking sheet. The pretty pink color of this entree looks great when served next to black beans and rice.

Makes 4 servings

Per Serving: Calories: 275; Fat: 8 g; Cholesterol: 50 mg; Sodium: 365 mg; % Daily Value: Vitamin C 57%, Potassium 23%, Magnesium 20%

Papaya Perfect

The papaya is a chameleon. When unripe, it is used like a vegetable; ripened it is a richly colored, sweet fruit. In the islands, pawpaw, another name for unripe papaya, is often grated and made into chutneys, hot sauce condiments, or used as an apple replacement. Most of us, however, are accustomed to eating ripe papaya, in blended drinks, sliced for a fruit plate, or diced and pureed in desserts. Consider also using ripe papaya as a hot sauce base, for a fish coating, or as a salsa ingredient.

The papayas sold in the supermarket are often quite large, much bigger than any of us need. If you're forced to buy such a large specimen, and can't possibly use all the fruit at once, puree part of it and freeze it for later use. To make sure it's ripe, look for a yellow skin and a soft feel. When fully ripe, the fruit will be buttery soft, without any of the fiber that accompanies many mango varieties. When cut open, you'll encounter the caviar-looking seeds. Some people like their peppery flavor, but they are not one of my favorites.

Papaya is a low-calorie blessing too, with only about 55 calories per cup, and lots of Vitamin C and potassium. The coral sunset color of the fruit means it's an ideal high-visibility ingredient, so use it where you can see it.

Suds 'n Snapper

Using beer as a poaching liquid lends flavor, but not much in the way of calories, and certainly no fat. If you want the island touch, use a Caribbean beer. Check the listing on page 159, and see if you can find one of these brands. I would avoid the stouts, as well as European imports, which have a distinctive flavor that might overpower the fish. When poaching, it's important to keep the liquid at a light simmer, with bubbles just breaking the surface. A more intense heat will make the fish protein tighten up and resemble rubber. This is a dressed-up version of the humble poached fish dishes commonly prepared in the islands, where a pot, a fish, water, and a few herbs are all that's needed to create a heavenly supper.

1 (12-ounce) bottle beer
1/2 cup reduced-sodium chicken broth
1/2 cup chopped cilantro
2 tablespoons minced green bell pepper
2 tablespoons minced shallots
1 tablespoon honey

1/4 heaping teaspoon salt
4 (6-ounce) gray or red snapper fish
*   fillets*
1 1/2 teaspoons dry mustard
1 teaspoon arrowroot

1. Combine the beer, 1/4 cup of the chicken broth, the cilantro, green pepper, shallots, honey, and salt in a shallow dish. Add the fish, turn it once, and refrigerate for at least 1 hour.

2. Remove the fish and pour the marinade into a large shallow pan with a tight-fitting lid. Over low heat, bring the marinade to a light simmer. Add the fish, cover, and poach for 3–4 minutes. Turn, cover,

(Suds 'n Snapper continued from page 157)

and cook an additional 3–4 minutes, until the fish flakes easily when tested with a fork. Remove the fish from the pan with a spatula, but keep the heat on.

3. In a small bowl, mix the remaining chicken broth, the mustard, and the arrowroot. Stir this into the marinade and bring to a boil until slightly thickened. Pour the suds sauce over the fillets and serve immediately.

Makes 4 servings

Per Serving: Calories: 240; Fat: 3 g; Cholesterol: 60 mg; Sodium: 250 mg; % Daily Value: Potassium 22%, Vitamin C 14%, Magnesium 14%

Caribbean Brews

In addition to their own local brands, some islands are licensed to brew and sell European brand beers. You will find Heineken produced in Costa Rica and Guinness Stout brewed in Jamaica. This beer tour of the Caribbean was part of a three-segment story, published in *Bahama Breeze,* Darden Restaurants' monthly newspaper, a customer service for its Bahama Breeze restaurant in Orlando. It's reprinted here with their permission.

Barbados	Banks: smooth, lager/Banks Extra Strong; higher alcohol content
Belize	Crown Lager: light, highly carbonated
Costa Rica	Imperial: mild and fizzy
Cuba (sort of)	Hatuey: full-bodied lager, actually brewed in Baltimore by Bacardi, it was originally brewed in Cuba
Dominican Republic	Presidente: mild pilsner
Haiti	Prestige Stout: dark, heavy, higher alcohol content than most beers
Honduras	Port Royal Export: mild pilsner
Jamaica	Red Stripe: probably one of best-known Caribbean beers sold in the United States
	Dragon Stout: dark, heavy, strong flavor
Mexico	Corona: everyone knows this one; considered watered-down by some
	Modelo: lager; Negro Modelo: dark ale
	Dos Equis: amber lager
	Sol: similar to Corona

(Caribbean Brews continued from page 159)

	Noche Buena: strong winter brew
	Carta Blanca: light flavor
	Bohemia: mild pilsner
	Tecate: strong flavor
Puerto Rico	India: light flavor
Trinidad	Royal Extra Stout: dark, strong, slightly sweet

Sour Sop Snapper

Sour sop, which also goes by the name guanábana, is a prickly green, football-shaped fruit with a unique sweet and sour flavor. It's not a fruit you readily find in the States, but Goya produces guanábana nectar, available in small cans, that delivers the unusual flavor in this recipe. Because the juice is a rather unappealing milky-white color, I've used turmeric to color it a beautiful shade of pumpkin. And when mixed with pink grapefruit and pineapple juice, the resulting colors are as stunning as the taste. Arrowroot is the preferred thickener, creating a translucent, nonpasty sauce. While I use the little lane snappers we catch here in the back country of Key West, any mild-tasting white fish will do.

¹/₄ teaspoon salt

4 (6-ounce) lane snapper fillets

2 (7-ounce) cans guanábana nectar

¹/₂ teaspoon turmeric

1¹/₂ teaspoons arrowroot

3 tablespoons evaporated skim milk

¹/₂ cup finely diced fresh pineapple

¹/₂ cup finely diced fresh pink grapefruit
*   sections, membrane and pith removed*

¹/₄ cup minced scallions, green part only

Coarsely ground black pepper

1. Coat the grill rack or a grill tray with nonstick cooking spray. Salt both sides of the fillets, and grill them over medium heat, on both sides, for a total of 10 minutes, until the fish flakes easily when tested with a fork. If using the oven broiler, coat the broiler with nonstick cooking spray. Broil fish 6 inches from heat on both sides for a total cooking time of 8–10 minutes, until fish flakes easily with a fork.

2. Meanwhile, in a small saucepan, bring the guanabana nectar and turmeric to a boil. In a small cup, stir the arrowroot into the evaporated skim milk until dissolved. Reduce the heat to low and stirring con-

(Sour Sop Snapper continued from page 161)

stantly, add the arrowroot mixture. Heat until slightly thickened, about 5 minutes, keeping in mind that arrowroot reaches its maximum thickening power just prior to boiling.

3. To serve, put a small amount of sauce on the bottom of each plate. Add a fillet, then top with the pineapple and grapefruit. Drizzle a little more sauce over the fruit, scatter the scallions around the plate, and garnish with the pepper. The yellow, orange, and pink colors in this dish will remind you of an oceanside sunset—just beautiful!

Makes 4 servings

Per Serving: Calories: 270; Fat: 3 g; Cholesterol: 60 mg; Sodium: 235 mg; % Daily Value: Vitamin C 59%, Potassium 31%, Magnesium 19%, Calcium 11%

Arrowroot from St. Vincent's

St. Vincent's, the largest of the thirty-two Grenadine islands and cays, has the distinction of being the world's largest producer of arrowroot, which is St. Vincent's second biggest export, next to bananas. Produced from a root, this is the white, powdery substance that's packed in small jars and sold in the herb and spice section of your supermarket. Used in place of flour or cornstarch, arrowroot is a flavorless thickener that produces translucent sauces and glazes.

While working at the Culinary Institute of America, I found arrowroot to be the thickener of choice for most chefs. Especially in low-fat cuisine, which doesn't have the fat and flour necessary to make a roux, arrowroot works beautifully to provide clear, yet thickened sauces, without the gumminess that flour and cornstarch can sometimes leave behind. If you're new to cooking with arrowroot, bear in mind that it reaches its maximum thickening power just before boiling, so don't overcook it. When substituting arrowroot for cornstarch, use an equal amount; when replacing flour with arrowroot, use half the amount.

Shrimp and
Mango-Stuffed Yellowtail

As part of a Thanksgiving buffet, my friend Chiqui, who now happily resides in Costa Rica, served a whole fish whose belly cavity was stuffed with a slightly spicy shrimp and mango mélange. Working from taste bud memory, I've attempted to create a similar dish that doesn't require using a whole fish. Yellowtail, a type of snapper, usually comes in thick enough fillets so that you may slice it horizontally, creating a hinged top and bottom. The stuffing is piled onto the bottom fillet, baked open face, with the top fillet flipped over for final baking. If you're cooking for a crowd, and want to go the whole-fish route, increase the amount of stuffing, based on the size of your impeccably fresh whole yellowtail or grouper, gutted and scaled by a reputable fish market. Pickapeppa Pepper Sauce, a Jamaican-produced condiment, has fairly wide distribution, and is sold next to other hot sauces. If you simply cannot find it, substitute Worcestershire sauce that's been thickened with a little tomato paste.

1 cup finely crumbled, dry French or
*   Italian bread*
4 ounces (^{2}/$_3$ cup) finely chopped shrimp
^{1}/$_2$ cup finely diced mango
2 tablespoons thinly sliced scallion
1^1/$_2$ tablespoons Worcestershire sauce
^{1}/$_2$ teaspoon turmeric
^{1}/$_2$ teaspoon ground allspice

^{1}/$_2$ teaspoon ground ginger
^{1}/$_2$ teaspoon salt
^{1}/$_8$ teaspoon cayenne pepper
2 (8-ounce) yellowtail fillets, each about
* ^{1}/$_2$–^{3}/$_4$ inch thick*
2 teaspoons Pickapeppa Pepper Sauce
*   (see Headnote)*

1. Preheat the oven to 375°. Coat a baking pan with nonstick cooking spray. In a medium bowl, combine all the ingredients except the fish and Pickapeppa Pepper Sauce until well moistened.

2. Slice the fillets almost in half, horizontally, leaving the top and bottom barely attached. Lay the fillets, open face, on the baking pan, and spread the stuffing on the two bottom fillets. Bake for 10 minutes, or until the bottom fillet appears almost thoroughly cooked and the stuffing is piping hot. Flip the top fillet onto the stuffing, and spread the Pickapeppa Pepper Sauce over the top. Bake another 5 minutes, until the fish flakes easily when tested with a fork. Cut each stuffed fillet into two pieces.

Makes 4 servings

Per Serving: Calories: 240; Fat: 7 g; Cholesterol: 45 mg; Sodium: 500 mg; % Daily Value: Niacin 44%, Vitamin C 39%, Vitamin B$_{12}$ 30%, Vitamin A 15%, Thiamine 15%

Almond Crunch Sea Bass

When crushed nuts are used as an outer coating on fish or chicken, they're usually held on with a flour dusting, then an egg wash dip. But as I watched my banana trees churn out more fruit than I could ever hope to use, I began to think about what else I could do with those ripe, yellow fingers. A mashed, ripe banana has the ideal consistency for letting other things, such as nuts, adhere to it. The fillets are first quickly seared, for a browned bottom, then finished in the oven. A small quantity of paper-thin, presliced almonds gives the crunchy topping effect, without wasting a lot of calories. The result is a combination of textures and flavors that will make your taste buds happy. Instead of sea bass, grouper would work well in this recipe, since it, too, provides thick fillets.

1 cup ripe, mashed bananas
¹/₄ cup thinly sliced scallions, green part
   only
1 tablespoon curry powder
2¹/₂ teaspoons grated fresh ginger

¹/₄ teaspoon salt
2 garlic cloves, minced
4 (5-ounce) sea bass fillets
1¹/₂ ounces sliced almonds, toasted

1. Preheat the oven to 425°. Coat a shallow ovenproof sauté pan or skillet large enough to comfortably hold the 4 fillets with nonstick cooking spray.

2. In a small bowl, combine the first six ingredients, and spread the mixture over the fillets. Heat the pan over high heat, then add the fillets. Cook for 1 minute, to brown the fillet bottoms, then transfer the pan to the oven.

3. Bake for 10 minutes, until the fish flakes easily when tested with a fork. Remove from the oven, and lay the almonds on top of the fillets.

Makes 4 servings

Per Serving: Calories: 260; Fat: 9 g; Cholesterol: 60 mg; Sodium: 235 mg; % Daily Value: Vitamin B_6 49%, Magnesium 28%, Riboflavin 20%, Niacin 16%, Thiamine 15%, Dietary Fiber 10%

Nuts about Nuts

While it's true that nuts are high in fat, most of it is unsaturated fat. These no-cholesterol goodies are also packed with protein and a host of other micronutrients. A 1-ounce serving of almonds, for example, provides 8 percent of your Daily Value for calcium, and is a really good source of Vitamin E (the Almond Crunch Sea Bass, page 166, has 9 percent Daily Value, per serving, for Vitamin E). Yet, the same 1-ounce serving has 167 calories and 15 grams of fat. Cashews, a tropically grown nut, have about the same calorie and fat profile as almonds. So, while you do have to be judicious about their use, nuts can make a significant nutritional contribution to your diet.

Chile Rum Glazed Grouper

Glazes, or "paints" as they're often called in the chef world, have a thick, syrupy consistency and a very concentrated flavor. In this recipe, dark brown sugar, hot peppers, and rum, all used over and over again in Caribbean cooking, contrast and complement each other very nicely. The glaze also gives the grouper a deep mahogany color. Grouper, a thick, meaty fish, holds up well to this strong-flavored paint job. While you could substitute swordfish or tuna, I wouldn't suggest using a mild-tasting, thin fish fillet like snapper or dolphinfish.

½ cup dark brown sugar
1 tablespoon undiluted orange juice
*   concentrate*
3 tablespoons dark rum
¼ teaspoon cayenne pepper

1 small dried bird pepper, minced, with
*   seeds*
2 garlic cloves, minced
4 (6-ounce) grouper fillets

1. In a small saucepan over low heat, combine the sugar, orange juice concentrate, rum, peppers, and garlic. Stir and heat about 15 minutes, until the sugar is totally melted to a syrupy consistency. Remove from the heat, and set aside. The glaze may be prepared in advance and kept refrigerated. If so, bring it to room temperature before using.

2. Coat the grill rack with nonstick cooking spray. Using a pastry brush, paint both sides of the fillets with the rum glaze. Grill on both sides over medium heat for a total of 10–15 minutes, until the fish flakes easily when tested with a fork. Just prior to removing the fillets from the grill, glaze again on both sides, using any remaining glaze. If using the oven broiler, coat baking pan with nonstick

cooking spray. Broil grouper 6 inches from heat on both sides for a total of 10–12 minutes, until fish flakes easily.

Makes 4 servings

Per Serving: Calories: 295; Fat: 2 g; Cholesterol: 60 mg; Sodium: 90 mg; % Daily Value: Potassium 21%, Vitamin B$_{12}$ 15%, Magnesium 15%, Thiamine 12%

When Groupers Have Cheeks

Groupers can grow quite large, up to 100 pounds. These are not agile, spirited fish, but lazy bottom feeders that hang at the ocean floor, often buried under a coral rock or in a hole. Even though they're not spunky, pulling one up on a fishing line is like retrieving a wet army blanket. While most of us are accustomed to buying their thick fillet meat, large groupers also have medallion-like cheek meat. These are little pockets of succulent meat in what would be the cheek area of the fish's head. It's a delicacy you probably won't experience unless you've caught your own big fish and someone knows how to expertly retrieve the nuggets.

Baked Avocado Tilefish

High-fat avocado is not off limits if paired with other low-fat foods such as fish fillets. In this way, fat calories can be "stretched," and still result in a finished dish that is moderate in calorie, fat, and cholesterol content. Although avocado contains fat, it has no cholesterol, as is the case with all plant foods. The fish contributes such an insignificant amount of cholesterol that you get a 0 value for the whole recipe. Normally, you sprinkle lemon or lime juice over avocado to prevent browning, but in this recipe the yogurt's active acidophilus culture seemed to do the same job. Tilefish is a warm-water, lean, and mild-flavored fish; if you can't find it, choose some other mild fish, such as snapper or flounder.

$^{1}/_{3}$ *cup ripe avocado pulp*

2 tablespoons plain nonfat yogurt

2 tablespoons unpeeled, grated cucumber, squeezed dry

1 tablespoon minced scallion, green part only

2 garlic cloves, minced

1 teaspoon Worcestershire sauce

$^{3}/_{4}$ *teaspoon ground ginger*

$^{1}/_{4}$ *teaspoon salt*

4 (6-ounce) tilefish fillets

$^{1}/_{3}$ *cup finely diced tomato*

Coarsely ground black pepper

1. In a small bowl, whisk together all the ingredients except the fish, tomato, and black pepper until thoroughly blended. The recipe may be prepared in advance up to this point. If so, cover, and refrigerate.

2. Preheat the oven to 350°. Coat a baking pan with nonstick cooking spray. Place the fillets on the baking pan, and lightly coat the top side of each fillet with 2 tablespoons of the avocado mixture. Bake for 10 minutes, until the fish flakes easily when tested with a fork.

3. Meanwhile, in a small saucepan set over low heat, warm the remaining avocado mixture. When the fish is done, spoon the warmed mixture over the top of each fillet. Garnish with the tomato and pepper. This also works nicely with chicken breasts: Make a slit on the breast and fill it with a small bit of the mixture. Use the rest on top, after baking.

Makes 4 servings

Per Serving: Calories: 225; Fat: 9 g; Cholesterol: 0; % Daily Value: Phosphorous 33%, Potassium 23%,
Magnesium 13%

Mack the Knife

If you remember this Bobby Darin song, you'll know immediately this is a shark dish. While some may cringe at the thought of dining on Jaws, shark is a firm, steaklike fish, becoming more readily available on restaurant menus and at seafood counters. If you can't find it, or don't want to use shark, either swordfish or wahoo, a meaty fish from the mackerel family but with a lower fat content, makes an excellent alternative. Papaya and hearts of palm are the tropical components for a bed of uncooked salsa. To keep those ingredients firm, I choose to warm just the seasoned oil/stock mixture. This vegetable/fruit salsa would also work beautifully with grilled chicken or any other type of grilled fish.

1 cup peeled, diced papaya

1 cup 1/4-inch-thick slices hearts of palm

1 cup seeded, diced tomatoes

1/2 teaspoon salt

1 teaspoon coriander seeds, crushed

1 teaspoon coarsely ground black pepper

14 ounces shark steak, swordfish, or wahoo

2 tablespoons olive oil

2 tablespoons minced shallots

3 garlic cloves, minced

1/2 cup reduced-sodium chicken stock

1. In a bowl, combine the papaya, hearts of palm, and tomatoes. Set the salsa aside at room temperature.

2. In a small cup, combine 1/4 teaspoon of the salt, the coriander seeds, and the black pepper; sprinkle this mixture on both sides of the fish. Coat the grill rack with nonstick cooking spray. Grill the fish on both sides over high heat for a total of 10–12 minutes, until it flakes easily when tested with a fork. If using the

oven broiler, coat baking pan with nonstick spray. Broil fish, 6 inches from heat, on both sides, a total of 12–15 minutes, until fish flakes easily.

3. Meanwhile, in a small saucepan, warm the oil, add the shallots and garlic, and cook for 2 minutes. Add the stock and heat an additional 3 minutes.

4. When the shark is done, slice off the surrounding, outer skin, and cut the fish into four portions. Pour the heated oil/stock (reserving 2 tablespoons) into the salsa, and toss. To serve, place a portion of the salsa on a plate, sit a piece of fish on top, then drizzle a bit of the remaining oil/stock over the fish.

Makes 4 servings

Per Serving: Calories: 270; Fat: 12 g; Cholesterol: 50 mg; Sodium: 365 mg; % Daily Value: Vitamin C 56%, Vitamin B$_{12}$ 24%, Vitamin B$_6$ 24%, Vitamin A 23%, Niacin 18%, Vitamin E 18%

Dolphinfish Rangoon

Snapper Rangoon has been a signature dish for years at the Bagatelle Restaurant, a longtime establishment here in Key West. While the restaurant's version is dredged in flour and pan-sautéed in butter, I lighten up the recipe by grilling the fish, and use dolphinfish, commonly called mahimahi in other parts of the country. Dolphinfish, by the way, is a beautiful blue, green, and yellow fish, not the lovable, friendly descendant of Flipper. Instead of the original cream of coconut and butter sauce–base, I use a small bit of butter, "lite" coconut milk, and I thicken the sauce with arrowroot. The combination of fruits can vary, depending on what is available to you. I find that a slice of juicy, sweet pineapple nicely covers the fillet and adds moisture to the dish. I choose also to use sliced starfruit and kiwi, which hold their shape better if left unheated. For a different fruit medley, try lightly heated cantaloupe or honeydew melon slices, and finish with banana and strawberries.

4 (5-ounce) dolphinfish fillets
¾ teaspoon salt
¼ teaspoon black pepper
1½ tablespoons butter
4 half-moon pineapple slices, core
  removed
¼ cup dark rum
⅓ cup "lite" coconut milk
1 tablespoon fresh lime juice

2 teaspoons corn syrup
¼ teaspoon white pepper
½ teaspoon arrowroot
3 tablespoons water
1 medium starfruit, sliced
1 medium kiwi, peeled and sliced
2 tablespoons thinly sliced fresh mint
  leaves

1. Season the fish on both sides with $\frac{1}{2}$ teaspoon of the salt and the black pepper. Coat the grill rack or a grill tray with nonstick cooking spray. Grill the fish on both sides over medium heat for a total of 7–8 minutes, until it flakes easily when tested with a fork. If using the oven broiler, coat broiler with nonstick cooking spray. Broil fish, 6 inches from heat, on both sides for a total of 8–10 minutes, until fish flakes easily.

2. Meanwhile, in a large skillet, melt the butter. Warm the pineapple on both sides over low heat for 2–3 minutes. Stir in the rum, and heat for 2 minutes. Add the coconut milk, lime juice, corn syrup, white pepper, and the remaining $\frac{1}{4}$ teaspoon of the salt. Heat an additional 3 minutes.

3. In a cup, stir the arrowroot into the water until dissolved. Stirring constantly, add it to the pan and heat for 1 minute, until the sauce is slightly thickened.

4. To serve, plate the fillets and spoon a small bit of sauce over each one. Lay a pineapple slice on top, then add the starfruit and kiwi slices. Spoon the remaining sauce over the top, and garnish with fresh mint.

Makes 4 servings

Per Serving: Calories: 260; Fat: 7 g; Cholesterol: 115 mg; Sodium: 570 mg; % Daily Values: Vitamin C 55%, Potassium 21%, Iron 12%

Seafood Enchiloua

Enchiloua, or the quick slang "chiloua," is a Cuban-style tomato-based seafood sauce. There are a few subtle tricks to this dish, and most of them I have learned not from Cuban cooks but from my Irish friend Chip, who is as good a fisherman as he is a lawyer. Chip says the secret to making any good, red seafood sauce is to use anchovies. I believe him, and you will too, once you've made this dish. You will never see or taste them, but they're an integral ingredient, trust me. When faced with the dilemma of whether to use beer or sherry (and I've seen it done both ways), Chip's sage advice is, "Use sherry in the kitchen, use beer if you're 70 miles offshore and cooking on a boat." Makes perfect sense to me. Based on this logic, here you have the kitchen, sherry version. When it's lobster season, and we've caught our own, I would make this dish entirely from lobster. But if price is a consideration, then this lobster, shrimp, and calamari combo is equally terrific. This is a slow-simmered dish, so make it when you're hanging around the house for the afternoon. It's the ultimate sauce for pasta and rice, or can be eaten with a spoon, directly from the pot, for those who can't wait. It makes an excellent meal for a crowd, or freeze it, in portioned containers, for future use.

1 tablespoon olive oil

1 cup finely diced onion

1/2 cup finely diced green pepper

5 garlic cloves, minced

2 teaspoons dried oregano

2 teaspoons dried basil

2 bay leaves

1 teaspoon salt

1/2 teaspoon red pepper flakes

1/4 teaspoon black pepper

1½ pounds medium shrimp, with
    heads on
2 tablespoons tomato paste
1 (2-ounce) tin rolled anchovies stuffed
    with capers, packed in oil, drained
1 cup medium-dry sherry

1 cup water
1 (28-ounce) can tomato puree
1 (28-ounce) can crushed tomatoes with
    added puree
3 (8-ounce) lobster tails
6 ounces calamari, cut into ¼-inch rings

1. In an 8-quart saucepan, warm the oil over low heat. Add the onion, green pepper, garlic, 1 teaspoon each of the oregano and basil, the bay leaves, ½ teaspoon of the salt, ¼ teaspoon of the red pepper, and the black pepper, and cook for 15 minutes. Stir occasionally until soft.

2. Meanwhile, remove and discard the antenna from the shrimp heads. Remove the heads and set them aside. Peel the shrimp, leaving the tails intact. Refrigerate the shrimp, and freeze the shells for another use.

3. Stir the tomato paste and half the anchovies into the pan. Using the back of a wooden spoon, mash the anchovies, so they will easily disintegrate into the sauce. Stirring occasionally over low heat, and cook for 10 minutes.

4. Stir in ½ cup of the sherry and the 1 cup water, scraping up any browned bits from the bottom of the pan. Add the shrimp heads, cover, and cook over low heat for 15 minutes. Don't stir or move the heads around too much. Remove the heads with a slotted spoon or a fork, taking care not to scoop up a lot of sauce with them. This step has infused the sauce with lots of shrimp flavor.

5. Stir in the tomato puree, crushed tomatoes with their puree, and another ¼ cup of the sherry. Cover, and cook over low heat, for 20 minutes, until the sauce comes to a full simmer. Add the lobster, calamari, and the remaining teaspoon each of oregano and basil, the ½ teaspoon of salt, and the ¼ teaspoon of red pepper flakes. Mash the remaining anchovies with a fork, and stir them into the sauce. Cover and cook, over very low heat, for 2 hours.

(Seafood Enchiloua continued from page 177)

6. Add the remaining ¹/₄ cup of sherry, and the shrimp. Heat another 5 minutes, remove the bay leaves, then spoon the sauce and seafood over cooked linguine or white rice.

Makes 14 servings

Per Serving (seafood and sauce only): Calories: 170; Fat: 2 g; Cholesterol: 130 mg; Sodium: 870 mg; % Daily Value: Vitamin C 66%, Vitamin B$_{12}$ 31%, Niacin 20%, Vitamin A 17%, Iron 16%, Zinc 15%, Magnesium 14%

Creole Shrimp and Dolphinfish

Originally, Creole referred to a mixture of French and Spanish heritage, commonly found in both Louisiana and the Caribbean. Today, the term is used more loosely, and with respect to cuisine it often refers to dishes of mixed heritage (whatever they may be), but usually tomato-based, and with hot peppers. A Creole sauce is inherently a low-fat sauce because it calls on tomato, peppers, and onion as the base, with very little added fat. Although any type of fish or chicken could be poached in a Creole sauce, this recipe uses a combination of mild-tasting dolphinfish and shrimp. White rice is the best accompaniment to soak up those savory Creole flavors.

2 teaspoons olive oil

1¹/₃ cups finely diced onions

1¹/₃ cups finely diced green bell peppers

1¹/₂ teaspoons arrowroot

2 cups peeled, finely chopped plum
   tomatoes

4 garlic cloves, minced

³/₄ teaspoon salt

¹/₂ teaspoon minced Scotch bonnet pepper

³/₄ cup Island Shrimp Stock (page 36)

³/₄ cup white wine

¹/₂ teaspoon ground thyme

¹/₂ teaspoon ground oregano

4 (4-ounce) dolphinfish fillets

¹/₂ pound small, peeled shrimp

¹/₃ cup minced cilantro leaves

1. In a large skillet with a tight-fitting lid, warm the oil over medium heat. Add the onions and green peppers; cook for 10 minutes, until soft. Stir the arrowroot directly into the vegetables and cook for 1 minute.

2. Add the tomatoes, garlic, salt, and Scotch bonnet pepper. Bring to a boil, reduce the heat to low, and

(Creole Shrimp and Dolphinfish continued from page 179)

simmer for 20 minutes, until the sauce starts to thicken slightly and the tomatoes have lost most of their moisture.

3. Add the stock, wine, thyme, and oregano. Bring to a boil, and add the fish. Reduce the heat to low, cover, and simmer for 5 minutes, until the fish almost flakes easily when tested with a fork. Add the shrimp, cover, and heat an additional 1–2 minutes, until the shrimp are pink and no longer translucent. Remove from the heat and stir in the cilantro.

Makes 4 servings

Per Serving: Calories: 275; Fat: 4 g; Cholesterol: 170 mg; Sodium: 620 mg; % Daily Value: Vitamin C 156%, Iron 24%, Vitamin B$_6$ 22%, Copper 16%, Vitamin A 14%

Fête des Cuisinières

Guadeloupe's (*Festival of the Cooks*) is probably one of the Caribbean's most vibrant and colorful food events. And mind you, this is a party celebrating only female cooks.

Taking place during the first week of August, this day-long event brings together restaurant owners, professional chefs, and culinary amateurs to pay homage to the art of cooking. Dating back to 1916, the fête honors St. Laurent, the patron saint of cooks. Some 200 cooks from all over the island gather in Pointe-à-Pitre, Guadeloupe's largest town, where they prepare a five-hour banquet. Starting at about 3 or 4 A.M., each woman cooks her specialty. By 6 in the morning, it's time to start dressing for the church processional. This is not just any dress-up event, but one where traditional Creole costumes have all been made from the same fabric, which changes annually. Dressed in the identical fabric, the women don their madras headdresses, silk shawls, starched white linen aprons, and full petticoats. Add the gold earrings, bracelets, and beads, and you have a sight to behold.

Carrying flower baskets trimmed with miniature cooking utensils, the women proceed, en masse, to the cathedral, for the only solemn part of the day. After the service, the group marches to a nearby school yard, where banquet tables wait to receive the culinary specialties of the day; huge crawfish, salt cod fritters, land crab tarts, stuffed lobster, turtle, and octopus, often ending with a butterfly-shaped cake (Guadeloupe's shape from the air). The bells are rung, the music begins, the rum starts to flow, and everyone settles in to enjoy a fabulous banquet and give thanks to the cooks of the island.

Papaya Cream Grilled Shrimp

Pureed papaya makes a perfect sauce base because of its texture and gorgeous color. In this recipe, papaya's deep orange-pink color turns to pastel with the addition of light cream. Cream in a light cookbook? This recipe, once again, speaks to the mantra of big flavors, which says, "Use small amounts of high-quality, big-flavor ingredients to get the most bang for your fat buck." Just $1/4$ cup of light cream gives this sauce a velvety texture, and the creamy taste you'd expect when eating a higher-fat sauce. You will see that the natural sweetness of the papaya tempers the heat of the Scotch bonnet pepper, creating an unexpected flavor. Try this sauce on grilled boneless chicken breasts as well. A calorie count of only 180 means there's plenty of room for rice, and at least two vegetable side dishes, to round out a delightful meal.

2 cups (1 medium fruit) peeled, seeded,
cubed papaya
$1/3$ cup beer
$1/4$ cup light cream
1 tablespoon minced shallot
$1/2$ teaspoon minced Scotch bonnet pepper
$1/2$ teaspoon table salt

1 teaspoon ground coriander
$1/8$ teaspoon kosher salt
1 pound large, peeled shrimp
$1/2$ cup blanched, sliced asparagus cut
$1/8$ inch thick
1 tablespoon Mint and White Wine
Dressing & Marinade (page 28)

1. In a blender, combine the papaya, beer, cream, shallot, pepper, and table salt. Puree until smooth. The dish may be prepared in advance up to this point. If so, cover and refrigerate. Stir before proceeding.

2. Pour the pureed mixture into a small saucepan and, over low heat, warm it for 5–8 minutes. Don't overheat it, as it will thicken up too much.

3. Meanwhile, combine the coriander and kosher salt, and toss the shrimp with it. Coat a grill tray with nonstick cooking spray. If you don't have a tray, skewer the shrimp. Grill on both sides over high heat, for a total of 3–4 minutes, until the shrimp are pink and no longer translucent.

4. In a small bowl, toss the asparagus with the vinaigrette. To serve, pour a little papaya sauce on the bottom of each plate. Arrange the shrimp in a semicircle, then scatter the sliced asparagus over all. The pale orange sauce, slightly charred shrimp, and green asparagus make a picture-perfect plate.

Makes 4 servings

Per Serving: Calories: 180; Fat: 5 g; Cholesterol: 185 mg; Sodium: 560 mg; % Daily Value: Vitamin C 79%, Vitamin A 22%, Iron 18%, Folic Acid 16%

Red Curry Shrimp

Nowhere in the Caribbean is curry more prevalent than in Trinidad, where a large percentage of the population is of Indian ancestry. Using curry powder is an acceptable shortcut, but in this recipe, I've taken the more time-consuming route and made a curry mixture from a variety of herbs and spices. Curries vary dramatically in their flavor profile; some pack an immediate fire, while others are more subtle in their heat. They all, however, should have multiple flavor nuances, not just the heat from the pepper. This curry has a slow flavor build, which creeps up on your taste buds. Heating the spices, especially the seeds, releases their flavor so the oil can better soak it up. The resulting pureed, low-fat sauce is thick and aromatic, perfect for serving with plain white rice.

2 teaspoons minced garlic

1 teaspoon minced fresh ginger

1 teaspoon coriander seeds

1 teaspoon black peppercorns

3/4 teaspoon turmeric

1/2 teaspoon ground mustard

1/2 teaspoon fennel seeds

1/2 teaspoon ground cumin

1/4 teaspoon cinnamon

1/4 teaspoon salt

1/8 teaspoon ground cloves

1 tablespoon vegetable oil

1/4 cup minced onion

1 (14 1/2-ounce) can whole tomatoes, with their liquid

2 tablespoons red wine

1 pound large, peeled shrimp, tails on

2 cups cooked white rice

6 slivered scallions, green part only, cut into 2-inch pieces

1. In a mortar and pestle, combine the garlic and all the spices, crushing the whole spices and peppercorns as fine as possible. The slight moisture from the garlic and ginger will help the mixture stick together.

2. In a large skillet, warm the oil over medium heat. Add the onion and cook for 5 minutes, stirring occasionally, until soft but not browned. Stir in the curry blend, and cook an additional 3 minutes.

3. Using clean hands, add the tomatoes and their juice to the pan while squishing them into a pulp. To further soften the tomatoes, making them more pulpy and less whole, flatten them with a fork and remove the hard, green cores. Add the wine, and bring the mixture to a boil. Reduce the heat, cover, and simmer for 20 minutes.

4. Transfer the tomato mixture to a blender and puree it on high speed for 30 seconds, until smooth. Pour the mixture back into the pan; heat over a low heat for 5 minutes. Add the shrimp, cover, and cook for 5 minutes, until the shrimp are pink and no longer translucent.

5. To serve, spoon some of the sauce onto the bottom of each plate. Pack a $\frac{1}{2}$ cup measuring cup with rice, and invert it onto the center of the sauce. Place the shrimp around the rice, adding a little more sauce over the top of the rice. Garnish with the scallions.

Makes 4 servings

Per Serving: Calories: 265; Fat: 5 g; Cholesterol: 175 mg; Sodium: 500 mg; % Daily Value: Vitamin C 32%, Iron 29%, Niacin 22%, Vitamin B$_{12}$ 21%, Thiamine 15%

All Shrimp
Are Not Created Equal

Only recently have different types of shrimp become available to American consumers. Before that, size was the only distinguishing characteristic. While most people still think bigger is better, there's more to shrimp selection than meets the eye.

Shrimp come from salt water or fresh water, warm or cold, and they're either harvested wild or farm-raised. Warm-water shrimp make up the majority of our supply, and are categorized by their shell color: white, brown, pink, and black tiger. There's also rock shrimp, encased in a hard shell.

Most of what we eat here in the United States is white shrimp, which has a grayish-white shell that turns pink when cooked. Brown shrimp, harvested from the Gulf of Mexico, have a more distinctive, briny flavor, while pink shrimp are primarily found in the Caribbean and Central America. Here in Key West, we have a fairly significant shrimping industry, although not nearly the size it was years ago. As a result, our local markets carry pink shrimp, which are characterized not only by a pink shell but also a pink dot on their heads. The cooked meat is also pink, with a dense, sweet texture. Tiger shrimp are primarily farm-raised in Asia, and have a noticeable black-and-gray-striped shell. Because of their higher moisture content, the meat is less dense than other varieties.

Colossal shrimp and jumbo shrimp always seemed like culinary oxymorons, and, in fact, they are. While "shrimp" connotes small, everyone's always looking for the biggest. Serious cooks know, however, that use should dictate size. By using this handy, shrimp guide you'll never again wonder how many to expect per pound.

SHRIMP SIZE	APPROXIMATE NUMBER OF SHRIMP PER POUND
Tiny	70
Extra Small	61–70
Small	51–60
Medium	41–50
Medium Large	36–40
Large	31–40
Extra Large	26–30
Jumbo	21–25
Extra Jumbo	16–20
Colossal	12–15
Extra Colossal	10

Conch Asopao

Asopao, meaning "soupy," is a thick, rice-based brothy stew flavored with chicken, meat, or seafood. My conch version is a cross between conch chowder, a Bahamian tomato-based soup, and a Puerto Rican asopao. As you dig into the thick yet soupy consistency, you'll wonder, "Is it soup, a wet rice dish, or what?" Everyone sees it differently, and that's part of the fun. Asopao is eaten as a main dish, and you will find it quite filling. The Spanish-style flavors and tomato puree give the broth a richness, and a slight spiciness that is just terrific. If ground conch is unavailable in the market, substitute finely chopped shrimp or scallops.

3 tablespoons fresh lime juice

1 pound ground conch

2 teaspoons olive oil

¹/₂ cup finely chopped red bell pepper

¹/₂ cup finely chopped green bell pepper

¹/₂ cup finely chopped onion

¹/₃ cup finely chopped celery

5 garlic cloves, minced

¹/₂ teaspoon minced Scotch bonnet pepper

1 teaspoon ground thyme

1 teaspoon ground allspice

1 teaspoon ground oregano

1 teaspoon salt

2 bay leaves

¹/₂ cup tomato puree

¹/₂ cup peeled, seeded, finely chopped tomato

4 cups water

1 cup beer

¹/₂ cup uncooked long-grain rice

¹/₂ teaspoon arrowroot

2 tablespoons each minced fresh flat-leaf parsley, chives, and scallion

1. Stir the lime juice into the conch, and let it sit while preparing the vegetables.

2. In an 8-quart saucepan over medium heat, warm the oil, then add the bell peppers, onion, celery, garlic, Scotch bonnet, thyme, allspice, oregano, salt, and bay leaves and cook for 15 minutes, until soft but not browned.

3. Add the conch, and cook for 5 minutes. Reserve 1 tablespoon of the tomato puree and stir in the rest along with the chopped tomato, water, and beer. Bring to a boil, reduce the heat, cover, and cook for 1 hour, until the conch is tender.

4. Increase the heat to high and stir in the rice. Bring to a boil, reduce the heat, cover, and cook for 20 minutes, stirring occasionally, until the rice is tender.

5. Mix the arrowroot into the reserved tomato puree, stir it into the pan, and heat for 2 minutes. Stir in the parsley, chives, and scallion. Serve in soup bowls.

Makes 6 servings

Per Serving: Calories: 180; Fat: 3 g; Cholesterol: 30 mg; Sodium: 495 mg; % Daily Value: Vitamin C 128%, Magnesium 43%, Iron 22%, Vitamin A 21%

Grilled Lobster Tail
with Roasted Corn Stuffing

One of Key West's favorite, dinosaur bartenders, Chris Robinson, relayed this recipe to me. It uses local Caribbean, spiny lobster, also known as langouste. Unlike its Northern cousins, these lobsters have no claws, but make up for the lack with succulent tail meat. Buying a 5-ounce tail will yield approximately 4 ounces of lobster meat. For a nice presentation, the lobster tail is first grilled in a foil pouch, the meat is pulled from the shell, partially slit down the middle (for stuffing), then nestled back into the shell. You now have a fanned-out tail for holding the delicious roasted corn stuffing. Cooking the lobster in foil preserves moisture and eliminates the need for lots of oil or butter. While this recipe is for 2 tails, proportions can be doubled or tripled for 4 or 6 tails. But don't wait until company comes to make this dish.

2 (5-ounce) lobster tails (4 ounces meat
*   in each)*
1¹/₂ teaspoons olive oil
2 garlic cloves, minced
Coarsely ground black pepper
1 small ear fresh corn, shucked
3 (¹/₄-inch) slices (¹/₂ ounce) dry French
*   or Italian bread*

1 tablespoon (¹/₂ ounce) finely chopped
*   chorizo sausage*
2 tablespoons finely chopped scallion,
*   green part only*
1 tablespoon finely chopped red bell
*   pepper*
¹/₈ teaspoon salt

1. With a pair of scissors, cut the hard, back side of each lobster tail shell down the middle and cut the meat part of the way through so that the two sides open up and the tail sits flat, still in its shell. Place each tail in a piece of aluminum foil, rub the meat with $1/2$ teaspoon of the olive oil, sprinkle with 1 clove of the minced garlic, and season it with the black pepper. Crimp the foil around each tail, leaving some space at the top, and creating an encased pouch.

2. Cook the corn in boiling water for 5 minutes, then transfer it to the grill and, over high heat, grill it for 5–10 minutes, until the kernels are lightly browned. When cool enough to handle, remove the kernels with a knife. (This should yield about $1/3$ cup.)

3. Reduce the grill heat to medium, or use a cooler side of the grill, and cook the lobster pouches for 10–12 minutes, until the meat is no longer translucent. Pull the lobster tail out of the shell, and slit it down the middle again as the meat may have curled in slightly. Transfer the tails to a baking sheet.

4. Meanwhile, place the bread on a baking sheet or a piece of aluminum foil, and broil, on both sides for a total of 1 minute, until crisp and lightly browned. Cut, blend, or process the bread into tiny, crumb-like pieces, yielding about $1/3$ cup.

5. In a small saucepan over medium-low heat, cook the chorizo for 2 minutes, until crisp. Add the scallion, red pepper, and the remaining minced garlic clove, and cook for 2 minutes. Add the corn, and cook for 1 minute. Stir in the bread crumbs, and heat for 1 minute. Remove from the heat and stir in the remaining teaspoon of olive oil.

6. Preheat the oven to broil. Spoon the stuffing mixture down the center of each tail. On a rack about 6 inches from the broiler, broil for 1–2 minutes, until the stuffing is golden brown.

Makes 2 servings

Per Serving: Calories: 290; Fat: 8 g; Cholesterol: 80 mg; Sodium: 760 mg;
% Daily Value: Copper 106%, Vitamin B$_{12}$ 54%, Vitamin C 34%, Zinc 24%, Potassium 16%, Niacin 15%,
Thiamine 15%, Vitamin B$_6$ 13%

Walkin', Talkin' Protein

❈ ❈ ❈ ❈ ❈ ❈ ❈ ❈ ❈ ❈ ❈

When it comes to animal foods, Caribbean menus have traditionally included beef, pork, goat, and chicken. There's a historical reason why some islands have more meat, especially beef, in their culinary heritage. In the early 1500s, Spain owned Hispaniola (the island that includes the Dominican Republic and Haiti), Jamaica, Cuba, and Puerto Rico, all of which have significant land mass. Livestock was successfully produced on these islands, in part to feed the sailors and soldiers from the mother country. Because of this, land on the Spanish islands was not as readily converted into sugar plantations as was the case on French- and English-owned islands. To this day, Spanish menus still emphasize beef, although not necessarily the choicest cuts. Pigs, goats, and chickens, on the other hand, don't require as much grazing space, can be modestly housed in backyards or left to roam the roads. Goats, especially, with their surefootedness, can handle island terrain, and seem quite at home straddling the road, holding up traffic.

Because in years past much of the meat had been less than first quality, slow, low-heat cooking methods were used to turn tough hens, old goats, and skinny pigs into fall-off-the-bone tender meals. Of course, today, resort kitchens and high-end restaurants offer just about anything you can think of: the best steaks, prime cuts of veal and lamb, as well as exotic game. The recipes in this chapter stick to the basics—beef, pork, and chicken—with only a token nod to veal and lamb. These are homey comfort dishes prepared with a lighter hand, and some newly created dishes, as well.

Many people concerned with health still want the diversity that meat lends to a diet. These recipes indicate how beef and pork, as well as dark meat chicken, can be worked into a calorie-wise diet.

Coconut Kerry Chicken

When emancipation was granted to African slaves, servants from India and China began arriving in the Caribbean, bringing their curry and their cooking methods. In the French islands, curry is known as colombo, while Dutch islanders refer to it as kerry. Regardless of the name, most people agree that it helps you perspire and cool off in a hot climate. Curries typically have hot and sweet components, the latter often being coconut milk. To reduce calories and fat, I use canned "lite" coconut milk, a handy ingredient for Thai cooking as well.

2 tablespoons fresh lime juice

4 (6-ounce) skinless chicken breasts,
*   bone-in*

$^1/_2$ teaspoon salt

$^1/_4$ teaspoon black pepper

1 teaspoon Annatto Oil (page 31)

2 tablespoons water

$^1/_3$ cup finely chopped onion

$^1/_4$ cup thinly sliced scallions, green part
*   only*

3 garlic cloves, minced

1 tablespoon curry powder

1 cup seeded, finely chopped plum
*   tomatoes*

$^1/_2$ cup "lite" coconut milk

$^1/_2$ cup reduced-sodium chicken broth

2 cups cooked white rice

1. Rub the lime juice over the chicken. Coat the chicken with $^1/_4$ teaspoon of the salt and the pepper. In a large skillet, warm the oil over medium-high heat and brown the chicken, meaty side down first. Cook on both sides for a total of 5 minutes, until nicely browned. Remove from the pan and set aside.

(Coconut Kerry Chicken continued from page 195)

2. Reduce the heat to medium and add the water, scraping up any browned bits from the bottom of the pan. Cook the onion, scallions, garlic, curry, and the remaining ¼ teaspoon of salt for 5 minutes, or until the onion is tender. Add the tomatoes, coconut milk, and broth.

3. Bring the mixture to a full simmer and add the chicken to the pan, meaty side down. Cover and simmer, turning once, for 15 minutes, until the chicken is no longer pink inside. Resist the urge to turn up the heat as this will toughen the breast meat. Serve the chicken and sauce over the rice.

Makes 4 servings

Per Serving: Calories: 295; Fat: 7 g; Cholesterol: 70 mg; Sodium: 340 mg; % Daily Value: Niacin 63%, Vitamin B$_6$ 32%, Vitamin C 26%, Iron 14%

In a Nutshell

Coconut milk, coconut cream, and cream of coconut are three distinctly different products, but sometimes the terms are used interchangeably, and incorrectly.

Coconut milk is produced and canned (or can be made at home) by heating equal amounts of water and shredded fresh coconut. The mixture is then strained, and the resulting liquid is coconut milk, which is used in a "lite" version in many of these recipes. Coconut cream is similarly made, except the proportions are 1 part water or milk to 4 parts coconut, yielding a richer, creamier product. Neither of these products is sweet. Cream of coconut is the sweetened, very thick, canned product used almost exclusively for making tropical cocktails and desserts.

Tamarind Scallion Chicken Bundles

Tamarind is used in many different global kitchens, from Indian to Hispanic to Dutch. It's a tree-growing fruit whose pod contains seeds and an edible sour pulp. The dark brown, gooey pulp is used as a flavoring for beverages and curries and is a standard ingredient in Worcestershire sauce. When combined with other ingredients, it lends a unique flavor. It's usually sold in supermarket produce sections, or in Latin, Asian, and Indian markets. See The Tale of Tamarind (page 45) for more info.

1¹/₄ cups "lite" coconut milk
2 ounces sweetened tamarind paste
2 teaspoons ground thyme
2 teaspoons ground cumin
¹/₂ teaspoon black pepper
4 (5-ounce) skinless and boneless chicken
  thighs

8 scallions, green part only, cut into
  5-inch-long pieces
¹/₄ cup reduced-sodium soy sauce
4 garlic cloves, minced

1. In a small bowl, combine ¹/₄ cup of the coconut milk, the tamarind paste, 1 teaspoon each of the thyme and cumin, and the black pepper. Lay the chicken thighs out flat, and spread this mixture on the inside. Place 2 scallions in the center of each thigh, roll into a bundle, and secure it with a toothpick.

2. In a wide, shallow dish, combine the remaining coconut milk, thyme, and cumin, the soy sauce, and the garlic. Add the chicken, turning to coat it. Cover and refrigerate for several hours, turning once.

(Tamarind Scallion Chicken Bundles continued from page 197)

3. Coat the grill rack with nonstick cooking spray and grill the chicken on both sides over medium heat for a total of 10–15 minutes, until the meat is nicely browned on the outside and no longer pink on the inside. If using the oven broiler, coat broiling pan with nonstick cooking spray. Bake chicken at 450°, for 12–15 minutes, until no longer pink on the inside.

4. Meanwhile, in a small saucepan, heat the marinade to a boil, reduce the heat, and simmer for 10 minutes. Use a whisk, if necessary, to smooth out the coconut milk.

5. To serve, put the chicken thighs on a plate, and pour the sauce over them. You might want to serve some plain white rice for soaking up this delicious soy-flavored, coconut sauce.

Makes 4 servings

Per Serving: Calories: 280; Fat: 13 g; Cholesterol: 80 mg; Sodium: 600 mg; % Daily Value: Niacin 31%, Iron 21%, Vitamin B$_6$ 18%, Zinc 16%, Riboflavin 15%

Chicken with Raisin-Orange Sauce and Fried Ginger

I found that using raisins in a sauce not only delivers great flavor, but that, when pureed, they act as a thickener. So, without any flour or fat, you can produce a slightly thickened, creamy sauce. And because very little fat is used in the overall recipe, we can afford to fry the ginger. This little crispy addition adds a texture contrast, as well as an unmistakable flavor. This one recipe incorporates several island flavors: raisin, orange, ginger, and allspice. When adding the whole allspice, try to remember how many berries you put in. It'll make it easier to pick them out from among the raisins.

2 teaspoons Annatto Oil (page 31)

4 tablespoons peeled, paper-thin, julienned ginger strips

1/2 cup minced onion

3 oranges, peeled, sectioned, pith and membrane removed and juice reserved

4 tablespoons raisins

2 garlic cloves, smashed

5–6 allspice berries

4 (4-ounce) skinless and boneless chicken breasts

1. In a small saucepan, bring the oil to a light simmer over medium heat. Quickly fry the ginger, turning and tossing it for about 1 minute, until crispy and browned. Remove from the pan with a slotted spoon and set aside.

2. In the same pan, cook the onion in the remaining oil for 3 minutes. Add two thirds of the orange

(Chicken with Raisin-Orange Sauce and Fried Ginger continued from page 199)

sections, all of the reserved juice, the raisins, garlic, and allspice. Reduce the heat to low, cover, and cook for 30 minutes, until the orange has cooked down and is very soft.

3. Coat the grill rack with nonstick cooking spray. Grill the chicken over medium heat, on both sides, for a total of 10 minutes, until the meat is no longer pink inside. Alternatively, coat a large skillet with cooking spray, and pan-sauté the chicken on both sides for a total of 10 minutes until done.

4. Remove the allspice berries from the sauce, transfer the sauce to a blender, and puree it for 1 minute, until smooth.

5. To serve, plate the chicken, pour the sauce over the top, garnish the chicken with the ginger, and arrange the remaining orange sections around the plate.

Makes 4 servings

Per Serving: Calories: 240; Fat: 5 g; Cholesterol: 70 mg; Sodium: 60 mg; % Daily Value: Vitamin C 91%, Niacin 57%, Vitamin B$_6$ 30%

Barbacoa

The Arawak Indians left a cooking legacy for which we can all be thankful; it's called barbecuing. Barbecuing began on a barbacoa, a grating of thin green sticks upon which thinly sliced meat was grilled over an open fire. Apparently, the Arawaks used the same word for a frame bed fashioned in a similar manner. The early Caribbean settlers called this method of cooking boucaning, and it was much tastier than leaving meat out to dry in the sun. Oddly enough, it seems the pirates, or "buccaneers," of the seventeenth century also derived their name from this cooking technique. They lived in the wild and boucaned native game and birds to sustain themselves when they weren't pillaging trading ships.

Arroz con Pollo
y Chorizo y Cerdo

(Rice with Chicken, Chorizo Sausage, and Pork)

If you're familiar with paella, you know what this dish is all about. And like Spanish paella, there are many different ways to make chicken and rice. Every household throughout the Caribbean has its own family-style way of stretching a small amount of chicken into a filling and tasty meal. My version calls on chorizo, lean pork, and olives to heighten the flavor. I like to use thigh meat because it stays moist throughout the cooking process and, besides, the dish can afford the dark meat's fat content since there's no added oil. This is one-pot cooking that tastes even better the next day.

GARLIC PASTE

4 garlic cloves

1 teaspoon red wine or balsamic vinegar

1¹/₂ teaspoons dried oregano leaves

¹/₂ teaspoon salt

¹/₄ teaspoon black pepper

*6 (3-ounce) skinless and boneless chicken
    thighs*

*1 ounce chorizo sausage (about half
    a 3-inch link), finely chopped*

2 tablespoons water

*3 ounces boneless pork loin or lean ham,
    diced*

³/₄ cup chopped onion

¹/₂ cup chopped green bell pepper

3 garlic cloves, minced

¹/₄ cup seeded, chopped plum tomato

¹/₄ *cup chopped Spanish olives or salad*
   olives
1¹/₂ *cups uncooked Valencia short-grain*
   rice
3¹/₂ *cups reduced-sodium chicken broth*

¹/₃ *cup white wine*
¹/₂ *10-oz. package frozen peas, thawed*
3 *canned (not marinated) drained*
   artichoke hearts, cut into quarters

1. Combine the garlic paste ingredients in a mortar and pestle. Rub the paste over the chicken, and refrigerate it while you chop, dice, and prepare the other ingredients, which should take about 20 minutes.

2. In a shallow pan about 10–12 inches in diameter, cook the chorizo over medium heat 3–5 minutes, until crispy, spreading it around so the bottom of the pan gets greased. Remove the chorizo, and set it aside. Add the chicken, and brown it on both sides for a total of 10–15 minutes. Remove from the pan, and set it aside.

3. Add the water to the pan, scraping up any browned bits from the bottom. Over medium heat, cook the pork, onion, green pepper, and garlic for 5 minutes. Add the tomato, olives, and chorizo, and cook an additional minute.

4. Add the rice, and stir to coat it thoroughly. Add the broth, wine, and chicken. Bring the mixture to a boil, stirring occasionally, and cook 15–20 minutes, adding water if rice is not yet fully cooked, until all the liquid is absorbed and the rice is tender. About 5 minutes before you think the rice will be done, gently stir in the peas and artichoke hearts. You will need nothing more than a simple salad to go with this hearty meal.

Makes 6 servings

Per Serving: Calories: 370; Fat: 10 g; Cholesterol: 55 mg; Sodium: 420 mg; % Daily Value: Vitamin C 38%,
Niacin 31%, Thiamine 30%

Chicken and Shrimp Asopao

The literal translation of asopao is "soupy." This particular version of asopao uses chicken as the protein source, although it could easily be seafood, beef, or pork. Most traditional chicken asopao recipes use a whole cut-up chicken, which, after browning, gets deboned. I found it much easier to simply start with skinless and boneless chicken thighs. But do not substitute chicken breasts in this recipe, as the white meat will dry out during the prolonged cooking. You can see how these one-pot peasant dishes have sustained generations of people; they're extremely well rounded in their nutritional value.

1 teaspoon dried oregano leaves

1/2 teaspoon salt

4 garlic cloves

3/4 pound skinless and boneless chicken thighs

1 teaspoon olive oil

1/3 cup finely diced onion

1/3 cup finely diced green bell pepper

1/2 pound small, peeled shrimp

1 ounce lean ham, diced

1 cup peeled, seeded, diced plum tomatoes

2 tablespoons plus 1/2 cup water

1 1/2 cups uncooked long-grain rice

2 (14 1/2-ounce) cans reduced-sodium chicken broth

1/4 cup dry sherry

1 cup frozen peas, thawed

1/4 cup green Spanish olives

2 tablespoons sliced pimento

1 tablespoon drained capers

1. In a mortar and pestle, combine the oregano, salt, and garlic, and rub it over the chicken.

2. In a 4-quart saucepan, warm the oil over medium-high heat, and brown the chicken on both sides

for a total of 10 minutes, until a nice crust forms. Remove the chicken and set it aside. When cool enough to handle, cut it into 1-inch-long strips.

3. Reduce the heat to medium and add the onion and green pepper. Cook for 5 minutes, scraping up any browned bits from the bottom of the pan. Add the shrimp, and cook for 2 minutes, until pink. Remove the shrimp from the pan and set it aside.

4. Reduce the heat to low, add the ham, tomatoes, and 2 tablespoons water, and cook for 2 minutes. You'll now have a little more moisture in the pot to fully scrape up those flavorful browned bits from the bottom of the pan. Return the cut-up chicken to the pan, and toss to coat it with the tomato mixture. Cover, and cook over a very low heat for 15 minutes.

5. Stir in the rice, broth, remaining 1/2 cup water, and the sherry. Cook for 20–25 minutes, over low heat, until most of the liquid has been absorbed and the rice is tender. If rice is not yet fully cooked, add more water until the rice is cooked to a thick, wet consistency; moist enough to plop off a spoon.

6. Stir in the peas, olives, pimento, capers, and the shrimp. Heat thoroughly for 2 minutes, and serve immediately.

Makes 6 servings

Per Serving: Calories: 380; Fat: 8 g; Cholesterol: 100 mg; Sodium: 600 mg; % Daily Value: Vitamin C 44%, Niacin 40%, Thiamine 32%, Iron 27%, Zinc 17%, Dietary Fiber 10%

Stuffed Banana Lime Voodoo Chicken

This recipe is based on a Haitian dish that actually calls for two different stuffings. To make things simpler, I concocted a version that blends the flavors of those two stuffings into one. And it's a stuffing unlike any you've ever made. With bananas, lime, rum, and a little chorizo, it will cast a spell on your appetite. In the islands, people would most likely use an old hen, but we have the luxury of selecting a nice, plump roasting chicken. Removing the skin dramatically cuts back on fat, cholesterol, and calories, so that the brown sugar mixture is applied directly to the bird, resulting in a rich, mahogany color.

1 (3½-pound) roasting chicken

1 ounce chorizo sausage, minced

2 garlic cloves, minced

2 slices white bread, crust removed, cut
    into ¼-inch cubes

1 cup (1 large fruit) diced banana cut
    into ¼-inch cubes

3 tablespoons fresh lime juice

3 tablespoons dark rum

1⅓ tablespoons dark brown sugar

1 tablespoon chopped flat-leaf parsley

2 teaspoons freshly grated lime zest

½ teaspoon freshly grated nutmeg

½ teaspoon salt

⅓ teaspoon cayenne pepper

Coarsely ground black pepper, to taste

1. Preheat the oven to 375°. Remove the gizzards, neck bone, and chicken skin.

2. To make the stuffing, in a large skillet, cook the chorizo and garlic over medium low heat for 3 minutes, until lightly browned. Add the bread cubes and cook for 2 minutes, stirring occasionally, so that the bread becomes coated with the chorizo oil. Remove the pan from the heat.

3. Stir in the banana, 2 tablespoons each of the lime juice and rum, $1/3$ tablespoon of the brown sugar, the parsley, lime zest, $1/4$ teaspoon of the nutmeg, the salt, and the cayenne pepper, until well combined. Stuff the chicken cavity with this mixture, and place the bird breast side up in a 13×9-inch roasting pan.

4. In a small bowl, combine the remaining lime juice and rum, the remaining brown sugar and nutmeg, and the black pepper. Using your fingers, rub this mixture over the outside of the chicken.

5. Loosely cover the bird with aluminum foil and roast it for 30 minutes. Remove the foil, and cook an additional 1 hour, until the juices run clear when the thigh is pierced. Remove the chicken from the oven and let it sit for 5 minutes before slicing and scooping out the stuffing.

Makes 4 servings

Per Serving: Calories: 435; Fat: 14 g; Cholesterol: 125 mg; Sodium: 545 mg; % Daily Value: Niacin 68%, Vitamin B$_6$ 51%, Zinc 21%, Riboflavin 20%, Magnesium 14%, Iron 13%

Blue Bird with Clay Cooked Vegetables

This is a spin on something I often cook; a whole chicken and veggies done in a clay cooker. A clay cooker is a great way to prepare low-fat meals because the clay holds moisture, and retains juices without a speck of oil. If you don't own a clay cooker, use a deep-sided, ovenproof pan with a tight-fitting lid. To give this recipe an island twist, and thus its name, Blue Bird, the chicken is marinated in orange juice and curaçao. Curaçao, the blue liqueur from its namesake island, also has an orange flavor, and combined with the o.j., makes a sweet-tart basting medium. A blue-colored marinade might seem a little odd at first, but I found it kind of fun. It will impart some of its color to the chicken, although both the chicken and the marinade become light brown once cooked. The vegetable medley includes boniato instead of sweet potato, carrots (calabaza makes a good alternative), onion, and tomatillos.

1 (3–3¹/₂-pound) roasting chicken

MARINADE

1 cup orange juice
2 tablespoons curaçao
1 teaspoon seeded, minced Scotch bonnet
  pepper
¹/₂ teaspoon garlic powder

¹/₂ teaspoon onion powder
¹/₂ teaspoon salt

1 cup unpeeled, coarsely chopped boniato
  (see page 143)
4 tomatillos, peeled and quartered
2 carrots, cut into 1-inch pieces
1 medium onion, coarsely chopped

¹/₄ teaspoon salt

2 tablespoons herbes de Provence, or any
    assorted dry herbs

Coarsely ground black pepper, to taste

¹/₂ cup frozen peas

1. In a shallow dish big enough to comfortably hold the chicken, combine all the marinade ingredients. Add the chicken and turn it to coat, leaving it breast side down to marinate. Cover, and refrigerate overnight, turning twice, so most of the marinating is done on the breast side.

2. When ready to cook, preheat the oven to 375°. Fill the top and bottom of the clay cooker with water, and let it sit for 10 minutes. This helps the clay to absorb moisture, which is released during cooking. Discard the water and add the boniato, tomatillos, carrots, onion, and salt to the clay cooker. Add 1 tablespoon of the herbs and the black pepper, and toss.

3. Remove the chicken from the marinade, and pour the marinade over the vegetables. Sit the chicken on top of the vegetables and rub the breast and legs with the remaining 1 tablespoon of herbs. Cover and cook for 45 minutes. Stir the peas into the other vegetables. Cover and cook an additional 15 minutes, until the chicken juices run clear when the thigh is pierced. This dish is best served in shallow bowls, with plenty of juice spooned over the vegetables and chicken. Some good-quality, sourdough bread would be nice for dunking.

Makes 4 servings

Per Serving: Calories: 395; Fat: 10 g; Cholesterol: 110 mg; Sodium: 545 mg;
% Daily Value: Vitamin A 106%, Vitamin C 85%, Niacin 67%, Vitamin B₆ 45%,
Folic Acid 18%, Riboflavin 18%, Iron 15%, Dietary Fiber 15%

Taste of the Caribbean

Foodie types who like to plan vacations with a culinary theme in mind might want to consider the Taste of the Caribbean. In an effort to enhance consumer interest in Caribbean cuisine, the Caribbean Hotel Association and the Caribbean Culinary Federation, the two host groups, have opened up this formerly trade-only event to the public. The cornerstone of the 4–5 day affair is the culinary competition that takes place among some 15 or so teams of chefs, each representing a different island. Each team works from a different mystery basket (they have no advance knowledge of what the ingredients will be), and within 5 hours must create a terrific three-course meal for 60 people. These are the meals the media, trade attendees, and you, the public, feast on. Winners are announced in several categories, including best team, best signature dish for an individual chef, best pastry dish, and a cocktail beverage award. In addition, there's an assortment of seminars on food and kitchen trends, plus wine and liquor tastings. The event has been held in Puerto Rico for the past two years, although future locations may vary.

Pineapple, Pork, and Boniato Stew

I like to put just one odd new ingredient in a recipe so it's not too intimidating. Boniato is probably a new one for most people. It's a variety of sweet potato that has white flesh, bumpy red skin, a slightly sweet flavor, and a less dense, but drier texture than a regular potato. It's grown in the tropics and subtropics, and is what you are served in the islands when you order sweet potato. Many major supermarkets, especially city stores, stock boniatos in their produce department. They don't store well, so buy just what you need, which is 1 medium potato for this recipe. This one-dish meal is definitely nutritionally balanced, providing meat, fruit, vegetable, and complex carbohydrates all in one pot.

5 garlic cloves

³/₄ teaspoon salt

¹/₂ teaspoon freshly ground black pepper

³/₄ pound boneless pork loin, cut into
    ¹/₂-inch cubes

6 tablespoons Sour Orange Mix (page 18)

1 cup scallions cut into 1-inch pieces,
    green part only

¹/₂ cup finely chopped onion

1 tablespoon crushed coriander seeds

1 bay leaf

¹/₂ tablespoon cider vinegar

2 cups water

1 cup boniato cut into ¹/₂-inch cubes

¹/₂ cup diced carrots

²/₃ cup diced fresh pineapple

¹/₄ cup seeded, diced plum tomato

(Pineapple, Pork, and Boniato Stew continued from page 211)

1. In a mortar and pestle, combine two of the garlic cloves, ¼ teaspoon of the salt, and the pepper. Rub the mixture over the pork cubes. Heat a 4-quart saucepan over medium-high heat (we're not using any oil here, the pork will brown in its own fat). Working in two batches so as not to crowd the pan, brown the pork on all sides for about 5 minutes. Do not turn the pork too quickly; let it caramelize and brown so it's easier to turn over. Remove from the pan.

2. Add 2 tablespoons of the Sour Orange Mix to the pan, scraping up any browned bits from the bottom. Add the scallions, onion, coriander seeds, bay leaf, cider vinegar, the remaining ½ teaspoon salt, and the remaining 4 tablespoons of Sour Orange Mix. Mince the remaining 3 garlic cloves and add to the mixture. Cook for 5 minutes, until the onion is tender.

3. Add the water, boniato, carrots, and the pork. Bring to a boil, reduce the heat to medium-low, and cover. Simmer for 20 minutes, until the carrots and boniato are tender. Add a little more water, if necessary, during cooking to make sure the boniato is always covered with liquid, otherwise it tends to turn gray. Turn off the heat and add the pineapple and tomato. Let the stew sit for 10 minutes before serving, to lightly heat the pineapple and tomato. Remove the bay leaf.

Makes 5 servings

Per Serving: Calories: 200; Fat: 6 g; Cholesterol: 30 mg; Sodium: 380 mg; % Daily Value: Vitamin C 47%,
Vitamin A 40%, Thiamine 40%, Vitamin B$_6$ 24%

The Hospitable Pineapple

Contrary to what most people think, pineapples are not native to Hawaii, but were one of the first plants brought there by westward-bound American settlers. Pineapples originated in South America and moved with the Carib Indians when they ventured into the Caribbean islands. Within the Indian culture, there was a mystique about the fruit, and it played an important role in their culture. Young boys would run through pineapple fields, proving their manhood by avoiding the prickly spears of the plant. The fruit was also placed on doors, and considered a sign of hospitality to strangers. Europeans adapted this idea by using the pineapple as a decorating motif on gateposts and homes. Even in the Caribbean today, the pineapple is used as a decorative element. I can personally vouch for this fact, since the back fence at my home was recently constructed with a pineapple-and-heart cutout design. Conveying hospitality and love can only bring good karma, I hope.

Calypso Candied Pork Chops

This is based on an old Jamaican recipe to which I've made some lighter changes. Instead of a whole roast, I've used lean loin pork chops, while dark corn syrup replaces white sugar for the "candied" coating. Traditionally served with a thickened sauce, this version uses clear pan juices, which have fewer calories, and don't compete with the rum-flavored coating.

3/4 teaspoon ground ginger

1/4 teaspoon ground cloves

1/4 teaspoon salt

1/4 teaspoon black pepper

4 garlic cloves

2 bay leaves

3 tablespoons dark rum

2 tablespoons dark corn syrup

4 (6-ounce) trimmed, bone-in, loin pork chops

1/2 cup reduced-sodium chicken broth

1. Preheat the oven to 400°. In a mortar and pestle, combine the ginger, cloves, salt, pepper, garlic, and bay leaves into a rub. Stir in the rum and corn syrup, then cover the top side of the chops with this mixture.

2. Put the chops in an ovenproof skillet, and bake them for 15–17 minutes, until medium rare (page 215). Remove the chops from the pan and set them aside on a serving platter.

3. Return the skillet to the stove top, and, over medium-low heat, add the broth, and scrape up any browned bits from the bottom. Bring the mixture to a boil, remove bay leaves, then pour it over the chops.

Makes 4 servings

Per Serving: Calories: 230; Fat: 10 g; Cholesterol: 60 mg; Sodium: 205 mg; % Daily Value: Thiamine 35%, Zinc 19%, Niacin 18%, Vitamin B₆ 17%

Lean, Happy Pork

The pork producers have done an excellent job of redeeming their product in the eyes of a nutritionally conscious American public. Over the last few decades, revamped breeding practices have produced leaner pigs, thus, new, leaner retail cuts of pork. For example, a trimmed, cooked boneless loin roast has 45 percent less fat and 23 percent fewer calories than it's chubby counterpart from the early 1980s. Maybe the animals are even happier not carrying around all that extra weight. Who knows?

In general, leaner meats take less time to cook than fattier cuts. So don't rob your pork of its natural juices by overcooking it because you're concerned about trichinosis. Today's pork supply is quite safe, and by cooking it to an internal temperature of 160°, you can still maintain a juicy texture and a slightly pink center. Following is a listing of the leanest cuts on the market today, and the percentage of fat reduction in those cuts, compared to 1983, according to the National Pork Producers' Council.

CUT	FAT (g)*		% REDUCTION
	1983	CURRENT	
Blade Steak	15.6	10.6	32 %
Center Rib Chop	12.7	8.5	33 %
Center Loin Chop	8.9	6.9	22 %
Top Loin Chop	12.7	6.6	48 %
Sirloin Roast	11.2	8.8	22 %
Tenderloin	4.1	4.1	0

* Figures given per 3 oz. cooked meat.

Cuban Roast Pork

In my opinion, no one cooks roast pork like the Cubans. Part of their secret is the long (48-hour) marinating process. Using an acid-based marinade, such as Garlic Mojo (page 32), helps break down muscle fibers, making the meat you-won't-need-a-knife-tender. Instead of preparing a cooked mojo marinade, you could also season Sour Orange Mix (page 18) with oregano, salt, and pepper, and use that for a marinade instead. Many people still cook pork until it's shoe-leather-done and wonder why it doesn't taste good. Lean pork will be much too dry if you cook it much past medium-rare (page 215), so please keep an eye on it. Since a serving comes in at only 210 calories, the dinner plate can be rounded out with a filling portion of black beans, yellow rice, and some grilled plantains.

2 pounds trimmed, whole boneless   *¹/₂ cup Garlic Mojo (page 32)*
    pork loin

1. Place the pork loin in a shallow, nonreactive, ovenproof roasting pan. Add the mojo, turning the meat to coat it on all sides, and cover with plastic wrap. Refrigerate for 48 hours, turning it every 6–8 hours. You will see the outside of the meat start to lose its bright red color and turn slightly brown. That's okay, it's an indication that the acid is breaking down the muscle fibers.

2. Preheat the oven to 350°. Drain and reserve the marinade. Place the meat back in the pan and roast it for 35–40 minutes, until the center is still slightly pink, to an internal temperature of 160°F. Remove the pan from the oven and set the meat on a plate to rest for 5 minutes before slicing. Add the reserved mari-

nade to the roasting pan, and on the stove top, heat whatever is left in the roasting pan to a boil for 1 minute. Pour over the sliced meat.

Makes 6 servings

Per Serving: Calories: 210; Fat: 11 g; Cholesterol: 65 mg; Sodium: 130 mg; % Daily Value: Thiamine 41%, Niacin 22%, Riboflavin 15%, Zinc 13%

Down Island
Smoked Pulled Pork

Pork butt is a good cut to use for smoking because it's inexpensive and becomes amazingly tender during the long, slow, cooking process. In this recipe, the butt gets a double flavor hit because it's first coated in Smokin' Rub (page 19), then bathed in Jolly Mon Bubba Barbecue Sauce (page 38). Trim as much fat as you can from the meat before putting on the rub. Then, after it's smoked, you will be able to pull, shred, or slice it into very small pieces. It's at this point that you will trim away any remaining fat. While a pork butt is not the leanest cut of meat, the end result is quite moderate in fat and calories. There's no fat added during the cooking, only lots of flavor from the rub, the sauce, and the smoking itself. In order to limit the portion size (it's very tempting to just eat this stuff right out of the bowl), $^1/_2$ cup per sandwich makes a generous smoked pork sandwich. Use plain, soft white buns that will soak up the sauce. Forget the fancy bread because the pork is the star. Please read Smoking Basics (page 220), before proceeding with this recipe.

1 (5–6 pound) pork butt or shoulder
blade roast, well trimmed of fat
$^1/_2$ cup Smokin' Rub (page 19)

$1^1/_2$ cups Jolly Mon Bubba Barbecue
Sauce (page 38)

1. Coat the entire piece of pork with the Smokin' Rub, and let the meat come to room temperature, about 20 minutes; just long enough to take the chill off the meat, which helps minimize the temperature drop in the smoker when the meat is added.

2. Prepare a charcoal, wood, or electric smoker according to manufacturer's directions. Make sure you've reached the ideal temperature before adding the pork to the smoker.

3. Place the pork butt on the smoker grate and put on the lid. A 5–6 pound pork butt will take about 7–8 hours. Have a thermometer handy so you can check for a finished internal temperature of at least 160°. You will, over the course of 7–8 hours, add more fuel, chips, and water, but resist the temptation to remove the lid and check your smoking butt until it has cooked 4 hours. Removing the lid lets a lot of heat escape and brings down the temperature.

4. Once the meat is done, working with your hands or a knife, pull the meat off the bone or cut it into small chunks, discarding any remaining fat. This does not have to be done with any kind of precision, just get it all into a bowl. Add about 1–1¼ cups of Jolly Man Bubba Barbecue Sauce, tossing well to coat the pork. Add the barbecue sauce, tossing well to coat the pork. If you're not serving all the pork immediately, reserve ¼ cup of the sauce to moisten the pork for future use.

Makes 16 sandwiches

Per sandwich, with sauce (roll not included): Calories: 170; Fat: 5 g; Cholesterol: 40 mg; Sodium: 670 mg; % Daily Value: Thiamine 22%, Zinc 18%, Riboflavin 11%, Iron 10%

Smoking Basics

Before getting started on this discussion, there are a few terms that need clarifying: grilling, barbecuing, and smoking.

Grilling is what most of us do in the backyard, with our burgers, chicken, pork chops, and fish. It means cooking over high heat for a short period of time. As you've thumbed through this book, you've noticed a variety of grilled recipes that include chicken, fish, vegetables, and even fruit.

Barbecuing and smoking, or smoke cooking as it's sometimes called, are really interchangeable terms for the same cooking method. And that is, to cook over low, indirect heat for a long time. While smoking can be done directly over a low fire, it's more common to have the food farther away from the heat, thus the term indirect heat. The beauty of smoking is that the meat doesn't have to be constantly watched, as when grilling, and it imparts a fabulous flavor without adding one single calorie.

Smokers range from a 55-gallon drum that's been cut in half, to a small, black-hooded, backyard smoker with a temperature gauge. You can make a smoker out of almost any heat-resistant vessel that allows space for indirect heating. Many smokers include a water pan, which provides moisture during the cooking process.

Once you have a smoker, you must decide on a fuel: charcoal or hardwood. Charcoal is easy to buy, although you will need to add hickory, mesquite, or another similar wood for added fuel and flavor. Hardwood logs certainly lend flavor all by themselves, and are considered by smoking purists the only way to go. Once you make a fire, let it turn into hot embers before adding the meat. You cannot smoke with flames a-blazing.

Next comes the part that requires patience. You put the meat on in the morning, check the fuel situation throughout the day, replenish the water, and that's it. It's not hard to do, but you can't leave and go shopping for the day. Someone has to baby-sit the smoker.

As you would expect, bigger pieces of food, such as a whole turkey or a pork butt, will take longer to smoke than fish fillets or ribs. I have found that the 5–6-pound pork butt used in the Down Island Smoked Pulled Pork recipe (page 218), and my 12-pound Thanksgiving turkey take the same 7–8 hours to smoke. Although the turkey is bigger, its cavity is hollow, while the center of a solid pork or beef cut must reach at least 160°. Most backyard smokers come with a booklet that gives approximate cooking times for different foods.

In the islands, smoking is a time-honored cooking method, either in a hole dug in the sand or in a closed pit. Historically, it was a good way to preserve food and to turn poor-quality meats and old hens into tender forkfuls. Which is exactly why you would not want to smoke a filet mignon. The slow, low heat, which breaks down tough muscle fibers, is ideal for tenderizing cheaper cuts of less tender beef and pork. Don't spend a lot of money to smoke an expensive cut of meat that's already tender.

Seasoning rubs, pastes, and finishing sauces are usually pretty close to fat-free. I like to put a dry rub or spicy paste on the meat before smoking, with a finishing sauce slathered on at the end. You could also choose to use a basting sauce during cooking instead of a dry rub. When going this route, baste at the beginning, once during cooking, and again when the food is finished. Taking the cover off once during smoking will add about 20 minutes

(Smoking Basics continued from page 221)

to your cooking time. There's an infinite combination of spices you can concoct yourself, or buy prepared spice blends. Either way, pack a lot of it onto the surface of whatever you're smoking. To turn a rub into a paste, add a small amount of fruit juice, Worcestershire sauce, soy sauce, or any other liquid that seems to make sense.

Smoking is a social kind of cooking. It's fun to do when there's a house full of people, who will want to take turns checking the fire and making bets on exactly when the food will be done. This also gets you off the hook with some of the work. After you've tried the Down Island Smoked Pulled Pork, and you're a convert to the lip smackin' flavor of smoked foods, try your hand at a whole turkey, chicken, or Cornish hen, pot roast cuts, a whole fish, oysters and clams, potatoes, corn on the cob, and whole onions.

Three-Pepper Pork

Peppers are one of the cornerstones of Caribbean cooking, and this dish makes use of three different types. Fresh and dried peppers, like lots of other produce, go by different names, depending on what part of the country you live in. Cubanelle peppers are light green fresh peppers with an oblong shape and a mild, non-fiery flavor. In my mother's kitchen, they're referred to as Italian frying peppers, and very often that's how they're labeled in the market. The second pepper must lend some heat to the dish, and for this, I suggest any variety of fresh, dark green, skinny chile peppers. The third pepper should be red or yellow bell pepper for added color. Peppers, vinegar, wine, collard greens, and lemon zest come together to create a strong-flavored dish that requires only a small amount of olive oil to get things started. While it seems like a long list of ingredients and instructions, everything gets done in the same pan, is prepared in small components, then assembled at the last minute.

7 garlic cloves, minced

*1/2 teaspoon plus 1/8 teaspoon dried
    oregano*

1/2 teaspoon onion powder

1 1/8 teaspoons salt

4 (4-ounce) boneless pork loins

1 tablespoon olive oil

4 medium cubanelle peppers

4 fresh, dark green, skinny chile peppers

*1 large red or yellow bell pepper, seeded
    and quartered*

1 medium red onion, sliced

2 tablespoons cider vinegar

Coarsely ground black pepper, to taste

1/2 cup red wine

2 cups torn collard greens or kale

1/2 teaspoon finely grated lemon zest

1/4 cup water

(Three-Pepper Pork continued from page 223)

1. In a mortar and pestle, combine 5 cloves of the minced garlic, $1/2$ teaspoon of the dried oregano, the onion powder, and $1/4$ teaspoon of the salt. Coat both sides of the pork with this mixture, and refrigerate.

2. Using a 10- or 12-inch skillet with a tight-fitting lid, warm 2 teaspoons of the olive oil over medium heat. Add all three types of peppers, and the onion. Cook, turning occasionally, for about 10 minutes, until the peppers start browning on the outside. Cover, and cook an additional 15 minutes, until the onion is soft and the peppers are softened but still slightly firm to the touch. Transfer the mixture to a large bowl and toss with the vinegar, 1 teaspoon of the olive oil, $1/2$ teaspoon of the salt, and black pepper to taste. Cover and set aside. The dish can be made a few hours in advance up to this point.

3. Add $1/4$ cup of the wine to the skillet and, over low heat, scrape up any browned bits from the bottom. Add the greens, cover, and cook 8–10 minutes, until wilted. Add the lemon zest, the remaining minced garlic, $1/4$ teaspoon of salt, and black pepper to taste. Transfer the greens to the same bowl as the peppers and onion, but do not mix.

4. Add the pork to the skillet and over medium-high heat, cook it on both sides for a total of 8–10 minutes, until medium-rare (page 215). Remove the pork from the pan and set it aside.

5. Add the remaining $1/4$ cup of wine to the skillet, scraping up any browned bits from the bottom. Stir in the water, the remaining $1/8$ teaspoon of dried oregano, and the remaining $1/8$ teaspoon of salt. Heat for 1 minute.

6. To serve, portion the greens onto four plates, lay the pork on top, spoon on some sauce, and top with peppers and onions.

Makes 4 servings

Per Serving: Calories: 265; Fat: 10 g; Cholesterol: 50 mg; Sodium: 665 mg; % Daily Value: Vitamin C 380%, Vitamin A 58%, Thiamine 37%, Vitamin B$_6$ 30%, Niacin 20%, Dietary Fiber 17%, Vitamin E 12%

Ropa Vieja

Pronounced "rope-a vee-a-ya," this Spanish dish literally means "old clothes." Because the meat is first stewed in a broth, the broth is often used as a soup by itself, the meat considered a hand-me-down, or old clothes. This is a shredded beef dish, and I find it's easiest to shred by pulling it with your hands (as you do with string cheese), not slicing it, as many recipes suggest. Cachucha peppers, sometimes called rocotillo, look like Scotch bonnets but are always green, a little rounder in shape, and most important, not hot. If you can't find them, substitute green bell peppers. The sauce is not really a sauce, but a flavorful, moist mixture that simply holds the meat together. It's a rustic, peasant-style dish that doesn't win any prizes for beautiful plate presentation, but is home-style cooking at its best.

BEEF AND BROTH
2 pounds trimmed beef brisket
1 onion, coarsely chopped
1 carrot, coarsely chopped
1 teaspoon black peppercorns
1 bay leaf
8–10 cups water

SAUCE
1/2 teaspoon Annatto Oil (page 31)
1/2 cup finely chopped onion

2 tablespoons minced cachucha peppers
*   (or green bell peppers)*
3 garlic cloves, minced
1 (14 1/2-ounce) can peeled, diced
*   tomatoes, drained*
1/2 teaspoon salt
1/8 teaspoon ground cinnamon
1/8 teaspoon ground cloves
1/2 cup water
2 tablespoons capers
Coarsely ground black pepper, to taste

(Ropa Vieja continued from page 225)

1. In an 8-quart saucepan, combine all the beef and broth ingredients, making sure you use enough water to adequately cover the beef. Bring it to a boil, reduce the heat, cover, and cook for $1^1/_2$–2 hours, until the beef is shredding consistency. Remove the beef from the broth and set it aside until cool enough to handle. Discard the broth, or save it for a beef soup base, but reserve the carrot for later use in the recipe. The beef should be shredded into thin strips by pulling the meat along the grain. If the strips are long, cut them to about 6 inches in length. The dish can be made a day in advance and refrigerated up to this point.

2. In a 4-quart saucepan over medium heat, warm the oil and cook the onion, peppers, and garlic for 10 minutes, until soft but not browned. Add the tomatoes, salt, cinnamon, and cloves. Mash the reserved carrot and add it to the pan. Cook for 20 minutes, until the mixture starts to reduce and most of the liquid has evaporated.

3. Add the water, capers, and shredded beef to the pan. Heat for 5 minutes, stirring to make sure the beef is coated. Small flecks of carrot and tomato should cling to the beef, with just enough liquid for moistness. Season with black pepper to taste. Ropa Vieja is typically served with a side of black beans and white rice.

Makes 6 servings

Per Serving: Calories: 225; Fat: 9 g; Cholesterol: 80 mg; Sodium: 460 mg; % Daily Value: Zinc 41%, Vitamin A 38%, Vitamin B$_{12}$ 38%, Vitamin C 34%

Two Potato
and Malanga Beef Stew

This recipe uses malanga, an unfamiliar tropical root tuber, in a very familiar way: in beef stew. As with many other Caribbean vegetables, there's a name confusion with malanga. If you're in a Puerto Rican market, it's called yautia; in a Cuban neighborhood store, it's malanga. See Malanga Is Not a Dance (page 98) for more malanga details. Malanga will seem right at home in a beef stew, side by side with white and sweet potatoes. You'll be hard-pressed to find many other entrees that deliver such an assortment of nutrients.

1/2 teaspoon salt

1/2 teaspoon black pepper

1 tablespoon fresh lime juice

5 garlic cloves, chopped

1 1/4 pounds round beef tips, cut into
    1-inch chunks

1/4 cup plus 2 tablespoons red wine

1 cup sliced onion

1/2 cup diced celery

2 cups plus 2 tablespoons water

1 (15-ounce) can beef broth

1 1/2 teaspoons ground coriander

1 teaspoon ground cumin

1/2 teaspoon dried oregano

1/4 teaspoon cayenne pepper

2 bay leaves

1 cup peeled malanga cut into 1-inch
    cubes

1 cup unpeeled sweet potato cut into
    1-inch cubes

1 cup unpeeled white potato cut into
    1-inch cubes

2 teaspoons arrowroot

1 cup seeded, diced plum tomatoes

(Two Potato and Malanga Beef Stew continued from page 227)

1. In a mortar and pestle, combine the salt, pepper, lime juice, and garlic to form a paste. In a medium bowl, combine the beef and paste, tossing to coat the meat.

2. Heat an 8-quart saucepan over high heat for about 1 minute. Working in three batches (so as not to crowd the pan—otherwise the meat will steam, not brown), brown the meat on all sides, letting it caramelize before attempting to turn it. We don't need oil because the natural fat in the meat will help with the browning. Set the beef aside.

3. Reduce the heat to medium and add ¼ cup of wine to the pan, scraping up any browned bits from the bottom. Stir in the onion and celery, and cook for 10 minutes, until the vegetables are slightly tender.

4. Add 2 cups of the water, the broth, coriander, cumin, oregano, cayenne pepper, bay leaves, and the beef to the pan. Bring to a boil, reduce the heat, cover, and simmer for 1 hour, until the beef is fork-tender.

5. Bring the mixture to a boil and add the malanga and sweet and white potatoes. Cover and cook for 10 minutes, until the malanga and potatoes are done. Meanwhile, in a cup, combine the remaining wine, water, and arrowroot. Stir the mixture into the pan and heat for 1–2 minutes, until slightly thickened. Add the tomatoes, turn off the heat, and let the stew sit for 5 minutes to lightly cook the tomatoes.

Makes 6 servings

Per Serving: Calories: 245; Fat: 5 g; Cholesterol: 45 mg; Sodium: 500 mg; % Daily Value: Vitamin A 64%, Vitamin B$_6$ 31%, Vitamin C 41%, Vitamin B$_{12}$ 32%, Zinc 21%, Iron 15%, Dietary Fiber 12%

The Skinny 6

I'm a firm believer that beef can be part of a well-balanced, healthful diet. When lean cuts are chosen, beef dishes can be comparable in calories, fat, and cholesterol to chicken, lean pork, and seafood recipes. The real story behind beef is not what it lacks but what it can provide. To that end, beef is an excellent source of protein, Vitamins B_6 and B_{12}, iron, and zinc. The Skinny 6, a term coined by the National Livestock and Meat Board, are the leanest cuts of beef available on the market today, typically from the loin or round. Because these have less internal marbling (fat) than, for example, a rib eye steak, cooking methods make a difference. You will find quick, high-heat, or moist-cooking techniques such as braising and stewing will yield the most tender results.

	CALORIES*	FAT(g)*	PROTEIN(g)*	CHOL(mg)*	IRON(mg)*	ZINC(mg)*
Eye Round	143	4	24	60	1.6	4
Top Round	153	4	27	71	2.4	4.7
Round Tip	157	6	24	70	2.5	6
Top Sirloin	165	6	26	76	2.8	5.5
Top Loin	176	8	24	65	2.1	4.4
Tenderloin	179	8.5	24	76	3	4.7

* Values are based on 3 oz. cooked meat.

Palomilla Steak Chimichurri

Palomilla is a name, used on Cuban menus, to describe a very thin, boneless sirloin steak served with fried onions on top. Often the steaks are so big, they're draped over the sides of the plate. This recipe carries through the same idea, but scales down the portion size and replaces the onions with Parsley Dill Chimichurri (page 46). You'll need a paper-thin, boneless sirloin, about $^1/_8$ inch thick. If you can't find anything that thin, buy a slightly thicker cut, and pound it.

1$^1/_2$ pounds boneless, trimmed sirloin
palomilla steak, $^1/_8$ inch thick, cut
into 4 portions

$^1/_2$ cup Sour Orange Mix (page 18)
$^1/_2$ cup Parsley Dill Chimichurri
(page 46)

1. In a shallow dish, combine the steaks and the Sour Orange Mix. Cover and refrigerate at least 1 hour.

2. Discard the marinade and grill the steaks over high heat, on both sides, for a total of 4–5 minutes, until medium-rare/medium. These are super-thin and will cook quickly, so don't walk away from the grill. Alternatively, heat a cast-iron skillet over high heat and cook to the same doneness. Remove the steaks from the grill and immediately spoon some chimichurri on top of each portion.

Makes 4 servings

Per Serving: Calories: 280; Fat: 13 g; Cholesterol: 100 mg; Sodium: 220 mg; % Daily Value: Vitamin C 66%,
Vitamin B$_{12}$ 51%, Zinc 49%, Vitamin B$_6$ 28%, Iron 26%, Niacin 25%

Caribbean Rim Meat Loaf

Trying to create a Caribbean version of meat loaf, I came up with this one that combines meat, starch, and vegetables all in one dish. The tasty beef and pork mixture is seasoned with Jerk Rub (page 24) and then used as the stuffing base. With a nod to the tropics, West Indian pumpkin, called calabaza, is one of several vegetables used in the open-face stuffing. And in place of melted butter or margarine, typically used to moisten stuffing, chicken broth makes a fine low-cal substitute. This whole dish can be assembled ahead, refrigerated, and baked whenever you're ready.

1/2 pound ground sirloin

1/2 pound ground pork

1/2 cup fine bread crumbs

1 egg

2 tablespoons Jerk Rub (page 24)

1 tablespoon Worcestershire sauce

1 tablespoon ketchup

2 teaspoons commercial yellow mustard, not Dijon

STUFFING

1 teaspoon olive oil

1/2 cup finely chopped onion

1/2 cup diced calabaza

1/4 cup finely chopped green bell pepper

2 cups (2 ounces) 1/4-inch cubes dry Italian or French bread

1 tablespoon drained capers

1/3 cup drained canned corn

2 teaspoons dried thyme leaves

1/4 teaspoon salt

2 garlic cloves, minced

1/2 cup reduced-sodium chicken broth

(Caribbean Rim Meat Loaf continued from page 231)

1. Preheat the oven to 375°. In a large bowl, thoroughly combine the first eight ingredients. On a baking sheet with an edge, form the meat loaf into approximately an 8 × 6-inch rectangle. Create a shape that comes up slightly on all four sides, making a well in the middle to hold the stuffing.

2. To make the stuffing, in a large skillet, warm the oil over medium heat and cook the onion, calabaza, and pepper for 10 minutes, until tender. In a large bowl, combine this mixture with the bread, capers, thyme, salt, and garlic. Stir in the broth to thoroughly moisten the stuffing. Spread the corn in the well, then spoon the stuffing on top.

3. Tent the meat loaf with foil and bake it for 40 minutes. Remove the foil, then increase heat to broil, and cook for an additional 5 minutes. Cut into quarters, and serve.

Makes 4 servings

Per Serving: Calories: 325; Fat: 10 g; Cholesterol: 115 mg; Sodium: 770 mg; % Daily Value: Vitamin C 41%, Thiamine 35%, Zinc 32%, Niacin 29%, Vitamin B_{12} 25%

Picadillo

Picadillo is a homespun dish, with each family's version made just a little bit differently. One common thread, however, is that most recipes call for some combination of capers, green olives, and raisins. Using ground sirloin really helps to reduce the overall fat content of the finished dish, and Pepper Sherry (page 17) adds some liquid to the drier, leaner beef. By serving a 2:1 ratio of rice to meat you have a meal rich in complex carbohydrates that's full of important vitamins, yet moderate in calories and fat.

1 teaspoon olive oil

1 cup finely chopped onion

1 cup finely chopped green bell pepper

3 garlic cloves, minced

1 pound ground sirloin

$1/2$ cup water

6 tablespoons Pepper Sherry (page 17)

$1/3$ cup raisins

$1/3$ cup pitted, chopped pimento-stuffed
   green olives

2 tablespoons tomato paste

2 tablespoons capers, drained

$1/4$ teaspoon salt

6 cups cooked hot white rice

Finely minced onion, for garnish
   (optional)

1. In a large skillet with a tight-fitting lid, warm the oil over medium heat and cook the onion, green pepper, and garlic about 10–15 minutes, until soft but not browned. Push everything to one corner of the skillet.

2. Increase the heat to high and add the ground sirloin. Brown the meat for 5 minutes, breaking it up with a fork. Stir in all the remaining ingredients except the rice and optional garnish. Reduce the heat to

(Picadillo continued from page 233)

low, cover, and simmer for 30–40 minutes, stirring occasionally. The resulting dish should have a moist but not soupy consistency; something like a taco filling.

3. To serve, measure 1 cup of rice, top with ½ cup of picadillo and garnish with minced onion, if desired.

Makes 6 servings

Per Serving: Calories: 390; Fat: 6 g; Cholesterol: 45 mg; Sodium: 470 mg; % Daily Value: Vitamin C 76%, Zinc 27%, Vitamin B$_{12}$ 23%

Grilled Beef with Spicy Tamarind Sauce

Thinly cut, lean sirloin steak is stuffed, folded, skewered, and grilled into delicious little packages. The recipe would be great if it ended right there, but the tamarind sauce adds a spicy, sweet flavor to the already well-seasoned meat. Tamarind, a sour-tasting, tropical fruit, is available in juices and nectars widely sold in Hispanic and Indonesian markets. Using tamarind nectar as the sauce base contributes a few calories, yet big flavor results. This is a great summer dinner because everything can be made ahead, skewered, and be ready to go on the grill whenever you're ready to eat.

1 tablespoon olive oil

1 cup finely diced mushrooms

$^1/_3$ cup fresh chives cut into $^1/_2$-inch pieces

2 tablespoons reduced-sodium soy sauce

$^1/_4$ teaspoon black pepper

2 tablespoons minced fresh flat-leaf parsley

1$^1/_2$ pounds boneless sirloin steak, $^1/_4$ inch thick

$^1/_2$ teaspoon ground coriander

$^1/_2$ teaspoon ground cumin

$^1/_8$ teaspoon red pepper flakes

$^1/_3$ cup minced onion

2 garlic cloves, minced

$^3/_4$ teaspoon arrowroot

7 ounces tamarind nectar

1. In a small skillet, over medium-low heat, warm 2 teaspoons of the oil and cook the mushrooms and chives for 3 minutes. Add 1 tablespoon of the soy sauce and the black pepper and cook an additional 5 minutes, until the mushrooms are soft. Stir in the parsley and set aside.

(Grilled Beef with Spicy Tamarind Sauce continued from page 235)

2. Cut the steak into four pieces. With a mallet, rolling pin, or another heavy object, pound the meat and flatten each piece to an 8 × 4-inch rectangle.

3. In a small dish, combine the coriander, cumin, and red pepper flakes. Sprinkle half this mixture over one side of the meat. Spoon some of the mushroom mixture into the middle of each piece of meat. Fold in the two long sides, then fold up one of the short sides (so the filling won't fall out). Thread a small skewer through the three sides, ending with the last side flapped over, creating a rectangular meat pocket. Sprinkle the remaining spice blend over the outside of the meat.

4. Grill the meat over medium heat, turning it once, for a total of 10 minutes, until medium-rare/medium. This is a thin cut, so it won't take long to cook.

5. Meanwhile, prepare the gravy. In a small saucepan, heat the remaining 1 teaspoon of oil and cook the onion and garlic for 5 minutes, until soft. Over very low heat, add the remaining 1 tablespoon of soy sauce. Stir the arrowroot into the tamarind nectar, add it to the pan, and bring to a boil for 2 minutes.

6. To serve, remove the steaks to a serving platter, carefully remove the skewers, and pour the sauce over the steaks.

Makes 4 servings

Per Serving: Calories: 285; Fat: 11 g; Cholesterol: 100 mg; Sodium: 345 mg; % Daily Value: Zinc 49%, Niacin 28%, Iron 25%, Riboflavin 24%, Vitamin C 21%, Potassium 18%

Buche Boliche

Boliche, also known as Cuban pot roast, is a classic dish, made with an eye round roast and a ham stuffing. I made some changes, for nutrition's sake, still maintained the basic essence of the dish, and actually came up with something that, I think, is more interesting than the original. Eye round is a lean cut of meat to start with, so it was the filling that needed some revamping. The ham stuffing has been replaced with a sweet and savory mixture of dates, banana, and capers. Looking for a gravy alternative, I thought about another Cuban classic: high-test espresso coffee, also known as *buche* (boo-chee). Dark brown, brewed coffee works beautifully as a gravy base, providing deep color, rich flavor and no fat.

1 teaspoon salt

1 teaspoon dried oregano leaves

³/₄ teaspoon black pepper

3 garlic cloves, minced

1¹/₂ pounds trimmed eye round roast

¹/₃ cup finely chopped ripe banana

6 pitted dates, finely chopped

1 tablespoon drained capers

²/₃ cup diced onion

¹/₂ cup diced carrot

1 cup brewed espresso coffee, at room temperature

¹/₄ cup dry red wine

1. In a mortar and pestle, combine ¹/₂ teaspoon of the salt, the oregano, ¹/₂ teaspoon of the pepper, and the garlic; set this aside.

2. With a long, narrow, nonserrated knife, make a 1-inch hole through the center of the roast. Insert the knife in one end and twist it around as you pierce all the way through the roast, coming out the other end. You may need to stick the knife back in and turn it a few times to get a nice circular hole for the stuffing.

(Buche Boliche continued from page 237)

3. In a small bowl, mash the banana, dates, capers, and half the seasoning blend, until the mixture holds together. Using your fingers and working from both ends, push the stuffing into the hole until filled.

4. Rub the remaining seasoning blend over the outside of the roast. Place the onion and carrot in a shallow pan and sit the roast on top of the vegetables. Combine the coffee and wine and pour it over the meat. Cover and refrigerate for 3–4 hours, turning occasionally.

5. Drain and reserve the marinade. In a 4-quart saucepan with a tight-fitting lid; brown the roast on all sides over medium heat for a total of 10 minutes. Reduce the heat, push the roast to one side of the pan, and add the onion and carrots from the marinade, the remaining ½ teaspoon of salt, and the remaining ¼ teaspoon of pepper to the pan, scraping up any browned bits from the bottom. Cook the vegetables for 10 minutes, until soft. Add the coffee-wine marinade, turn the roast once, cover, and simmer over medium-low heat for 3 hours, until the meat is fork-tender.

6. When done, remove the roast from the gravy and let it sit for 5 minutes before slicing. Cut into ½-inch slices, transfer to a serving platter, and spoon the gravy over the meat. Eating this is like biting into a Tootsie Roll pop. The soft center makes attractive slices that taste as good as they look.

Makes 4 servings

Per Serving: Calories: 260; Fat: 4 g; Cholesterol: 80 mg; Sodium: 700 mg; % Daily Value: Vitamin B$_{12}$ 40%, Vitamin A 39%, Zinc 37%, Vitamin B$_6$ 32%, Niacin 24%, Iron 16%

Lamb and Eggplant Colombo

Colombo is the French-Caribbean term for curry. While many curried dishes use coconut milk, this one uses white wine, a common French variation. When it comes to curried meats, goat is often on the menu. Since most of us can't get goat at the local supermarket, lamb is an ideal substitute. As in many of the other island one-pot meals, long braising and stewing turns a chewy, inexpensive cut of meat into a tender morsel. Use a vegetable peeler to make the paper-thin calabaza strips. All the flavors stay right in the pot, making for a tasty gravy, and a nutritious low-fat meal.

1 pound boneless, trimmed stewing lamb,
    cut into 1-inch cubes
1 teaspoon olive oil
1½ cups peeled, diced eggplant
1 cup diced onion
1 tablespoon curry powder
3 garlic cloves, minced

½ teaspoon salt
1 cup white wine
1 cup water
½ cup peeled, paper-thin calabaza,
    pumpkin, or winter squash strips
    (see Headnote)
1 tablespoon fresh lime juice

1. Place a 4-quart saucepan over high heat. Once the pan is hot, add the lamb and working in batches, brown the meat on all sides for a total of 1–2 minutes per batch. Set the meat aside.

2. Reduce the heat to medium, add the oil to the pan, and cook the eggplant and onion for 5 minutes, scraping up any browned bits from the bottom. Stir in the curry, garlic, and salt. Add the wine and water, continuing to scrape up any browned bits.

(Lamb and Eggplant Colombo continued from page 239)

3. Bring the mixture to a boil, then add the lamb. Reduce the heat to a simmer, cover, and cook for 45 minutes, until the lamb is fork-tender. Add the calabaza, cover, and cook an additional 5 minutes. Stir in the lime juice, remove from the heat, and serve.

Makes 4 servings

Per Serving: Calories: 190; Fat: 6 g; Cholesterol: 50 mg; Sodium: 310 mg; % Daily Value: Vitamin B_{12} 23%, Zinc 19%, Niacin 19%, Iron 11%, Riboflavin 11%

Celebrating French Food in the Caribbean

St. Barthélemy, more commonly called St. Bart's, is a piece of France floating in the Caribbean Sea. Probably more than any other island, its food heritage is closely tied to France. To celebrate the food and wine of France, St. Bart's now hosts a Festival Gastronomique during the last week of April. Each day, a different region of France is promoted by featuring its local products. Winemakers from the highlighted regions are on hand for presentations and wine tastings. In the evenings, local restaurants adapt French regional menus to a Caribbean setting. The week winds up with a pastry competition, a contest for chefs to create a local fish specialty, and a sailing regatta.

Veal with Sweet Potatoes, Mangoes, and Plantain Chips

This is a recipe I adapted from the National Culinary Team of Aruba, which took first place at the 1996 Caribbean Culinary Federation's annual competition. I revised their technique to save calories, and simplified the number of ingredients. A veal shoulder has replaced a veal breast; and regular pears step in for Asian pears. The original version was served in a fried plantain basket, which looked great but is too high in fat for our purposes, not to mention a little time-consuming to make. To achieve a similar taste and texture, this recipe uses plantain chips, which are readily sold in snack food sections, next to the potato chips and pretzels.

1 teaspoon olive oil

12 ounces trimmed veal shoulder, cut
    into $1/4$-inch cubes

$1/2$ cup minced onion

2 garlic cloves, minced

$1/2$ teaspoon curry powder

$1/8$ teaspoon cayenne pepper

$1/4$ cup white wine

$1^1/3$ cups reduced-sodium chicken stock

1 cup peeled, diced sweet potatoes

1 teaspoon Worcestershire sauce

$1/2$ teaspoon ground cumin

$1/2$ teaspoon salt

1 cup semiripe, diced mango

$1/2$ cup peeled, diced pear

1 tablespoon chopped cilantro

1 tablespoon chopped fresh flat-leaf
    parsley

1 teaspoon arrowroot

1 ounce plantain chips

(Veal with Sweet Potatoes, Mangoes, and Plantain Chips continued from page 241)

1. In a medium saucepan, over medium heat, warm the oil, then cook the veal, onion, and garlic for 5 minutes, until the meat is lightly browned. Stir in the curry and cayenne pepper, and cook for 2 minutes. Add the wine, scraping up any browned bits from the bottom of the pan. Add all but 2 tablespoons of the stock. Cover, and simmer for 30 minutes.

2. Meanwhile, in a small saucepan, boil the potatoes in water to cover for 7–10 minutes, until done. Drain, and set aside.

3. Stir the Worcestershire sauce, cumin, and salt into the pan with the veal. Carefully add the mango, pear, potatoes, cilantro, and parsley. Do not stir, as the fruits and potatoes will start to fall apart. Over medium heat, warm for 2–3 minutes.

4. Meanwhile, stir the arrowroot into the remaining 2 tablespoons of stock. Stir the mixture into the pan and bring to a light boil for 1 minute, until the mixture thickens.

5. To serve, ladle into individual soup bowls and garnish with the plantain chips.

Makes 4 servings

Per Serving: Calories: 310; Fat: 8 g; Cholesterol: 55 mg; Sodium: 365 mg; % Daily Value: Vitamin A 161%, Vitamin C 58%, Niacin 29%, Vitamin B$_6$ 23%, Riboflavin 21%, Dietary Fiber 20%, Zinc 17%

The Many Faces of Plantain

This is produce that, when unripe, acts like a vegetable and gets more like a fruit as it ripens. Throughout its life span, a plantain takes on multiple personalities in the kitchen.

When they're hard, green, and bland, plantains are suitable for boiling and adding to stews and soups, just as you might a potato. This is also the perfect stage for paper-thin slicing, and frying to make plantain chips. Not a low-fat food, but okay to use in small quantities. At their full yellow stage, plantains can be slit lengthwise and grilled with their skins still on. These are not as easy to peel as bananas, requiring a crosswise, not length-wise peeling motion. As they ripen and the skins turn black, looking as if they should be tossed in the garbage, the flavor becomes quite sweet. This stage is ideal for adding to vegetable purees or a mashed potato medley (Sweet Potato, Boniato, and Plantain Mash, page 144).

My suggestion is to buy plantains at the stage you require them, because they don't ripen anywhere nearly as quickly as bananas. I've had green plantains hanging on a tree out back for a month, and once picked, it may take at least a week before they start to blacken.

Sweet
Sunsets

❋ ❋ ❋ ❋ ❋ ❋ ❋ ❋ ❋ ❋ ❋

⫘   ⫘   ⫘

Dessert in the islands, as eaten by the locals, has historically consisted of plain tropical fruits, sugary coconut concoctions, and dense, starchy sweet breads. With few exceptions, these sweets would have made for a rather unhealthy dessert chapter. But times have changed, and many restaurants across the Caribbean are using a wide assortment of their native, tropical fruits to create inspiring, drop-dead desserts. This chapter, too, relies on the gorgeous colors and fabulous flavors of tropical fruits as the basis for many of the desserts and other bread-basket goodies.

Creating lower-fat baked goods is perhaps the biggest challenge to cooks. Desserts and baked goods rely so heavily on butter, cream, and oil for a creamy mouth feel, moisture, and to tenderize the gluten in flour. Generally speaking, reduced-fat bakery items have a short shelf life. Make only what you need, and plan to use it as soon as it's made.

While many of the recipes are original creations, I have used classical desserts, such as flan and coconut bread, as springboards for their lighter counterparts. Browse through this section carefully, because many items are what I consider crossover recipes. Bread pudding, sweet bread, corn bread, and muffins can work at breakfast and brunch, as dinner accompaniments, or as dessert.

Key Lime Tart

Key Lime pie is an incredibly simple dessert to make, but when made in the traditional style, it's packed with calories and fat. A so-called typical piece of Key Lime pie has approximately 465 calories and 18 grams of fat. Its basic ingredients, sweetened condensed milk, egg yolks, and a graham cracker crust, are real heavyweights. I've found that fat-free condensed milk, and just a little gelatin provide the creamy texture of the original. To help control the portion size, it's made in a shallow tart or quiche pan, not the traditional pie plate, so the slices aren't quite so thick. Using just a bottom crust, with no sides, saves on more calories. Low-fat meringue topping instead of whipped cream further reduces the fat content. Most key lime pies don't require heating, but when eggs are involved, I prefer to cook them for food-safety sake. Here in Key West, where there are more recipes for Key Lime pie than you can imagine, this one can take its rightful place alongside the other belly-busting versions.

1¹/₂ tablespoons margarine, melted
1¹/₂ tablespoons water
1 cup (about 5 [5-inch] squares) finely crushed low-fat graham crackers
¹/₂ teaspoon ground nutmeg
2 eggs, separated

¹/₂ tablespoon plus ¹/₄ cup sugar
1 (14-ounce) can fat-free sweetened condensed skim milk
1 teaspoon unflavored gelatin
¹/₂ cup fresh lime juice
¹/₄ teaspoon cream of tartar

1. Preheat the oven to 325°. Coat a 9-inch, 1¹/₄-inch-deep tart or quiche pan with nonstick cooking spray.

2. In a small bowl, combine the melted margarine and water. In a medium bowl, combine the graham cracker crumbs and nutmeg. Slowly drizzle the margarine into the crumbs, tossing with a fork until the

(Key Lime Tart continued from page 247)

crumbs are thoroughly moistened. Press this into the bottom of the tart pan. Bake for 15 minutes, until crisp and firm. Remove from the oven and cool completely before filling.

3. Increase the oven temperature to 350°. In a medium bowl, using an electric mixer, beat the egg yolks and $1/2$ tablespoon sugar on medium speed for 30 seconds. Add the condensed milk, and beat an additional 15 seconds. In a cup, stir the gelatin into the lime juice until dissolved, and pour this into the egg mixture. Beat for 15 seconds to thoroughly combine. Pour the filling into the pie crust, and bake for 8 minutes.

4. Meanwhile, prepare the meringue topping. In a clean, small bowl, using clean, grease-free beaters, whip the egg whites on high speed for 20 seconds, until foamy. Add the cream of tartar, beat an additional 3–5 minutes, gradually adding the remaining $1/4$ cup sugar, until stiff, glossy peaks form.

5. When the pie appears firm, remove it from the oven and increase the heat to 400°. Using a spatula or butter knife, spread the meringue over the entire pie top, making small peaks and swirls. Return the pie to the oven for 4–5 minutes, until the peaks lightly brown. Don't walk away from the stove because the meringue can burn in a matter of seconds. Remove the pie and cool it at room temperature for $1/2$ hour, then refrigerate for at least 3 hours before slicing.

Makes 8 servings

Per Serving: Calories: 300; Fat: 3 g; Cholesterol: 60 mg; Sodium: 120 mg;
No other significant nutritional values.

Key Limes

Key limes are a product of south Florida and Latin America. There are no commercially grown Key limes in the Florida Keys; there's little land mass, and what there is has been gobbled up by residential and commercial building. Some large growers, like Brooks Tropicals, in Homestead, Florida, have extended distribution beyond Florida borders, so look for these small, yellow limes in your produce section. Luckily, the key lime tree in my yard keeps me nicely supplied for the year. Once the summer crop starts waning, I squeeze and freeze as much juice as possible.

For any of the recipes in this book, fresh lime juice from Persian limes, the everyday variety, will do just fine. To get the maximum juice out of a lime, roll it back and forth a few times, pressing down (as though massaging it), before cutting. Although Key limes are much smaller than regular limes, they yield a lot of juice for their small size; about 2 tablespoons per fruit. The flavor is a little more limey, rather than just tart, which is what makes it a nice cooking ingredient. The cardinal sin in any of these recipes would be to use bottled lime juice instead of fresh. Please go to the trouble of squeezing; it's well worth it.

Mamey Cheesecake

I've eaten a lot of reduced-fat cheesecakes over the years. Most of them have overdosed on the gelatin, tasting more like a creamy Jell-O than cheesecake. My idea of cheesecake heaven is the dense, New York–style stuff I ate while growing up in New Jersey. This recipe comes closest to the cheesecakes I love, but with a dramatic reduction in calories and fat. Make no mistake, any cheesecake worth its weight will never be 100 calories a slice. But by using a combination of skim ricotta cheese, Neufchâtel cheese, and "lite" cream cheese, the texture in this cake is right on the money. The flour helps to eliminate moisture from weeping out of the cake, a common occurrence when fat is reduced in a batter. The randomized swirl design is a decorating tip I saw used in Susan Purdy's, *Have Your Cake and Eat it, Too.*

CRUST

2 tablespoons margarine, melted

2 tablespoons water

1 teaspoon rum extract

1¼ cups (about 7 [5-inch] crackers) finely crushed low-fat graham crackers

FILLING

1 (15-ounce) container skim ricotta cheese

1½ pounds Neufchâtel cheese, softened

1 cup sugar

¼ cup all-purpose flour

1 teaspoon almond extract

¼ teaspoon salt

3 egg whites

2 cups pureed mamey (page 252) or papaya

1. Preheat the oven to 400°. Coat the bottom and sides of a 10-inch springform pan with nonstick cooking spray. To prepare the crust, in a cup, combine the melted margarine, water, and rum extract. In a medium bowl, slowly drizzle the margarine mixture into the crumbs, tossing with a fork until thoroughly moistened. Press this into the bottom of the pan. Bake for 8 minutes, until slightly crisp. Cool completely before filling. Reduce the oven temperature to 350°.

2. If you have a food processor with at least an 8-cup capacity, you can prepare the filling, from start to finish, in the processor. If not, first process the ricotta, Neufchâtel, and cream cheese until smooth, then transfer the mixture to a large mixing bowl and complete the recipe with an electric mixer. If you don't have a food processor, puree the ricotta cheese in a blender, transfer it to a bowl, and continue by creaming the Neufchâtel and cream cheese with a mixer until smooth.

3. In a food processor, puree the ricotta, on medium speed, until smooth and pourable. Add the Neufchâtel cheese a little at a time through the feeder tube while the processor is running. Repeat with the cream cheese. At this point, you should have a thick white mixture. This is where you transfer to a bowl, if necessary.

4. Add the sugar, flour, almond extract, and salt; process until combined. Add the egg whites, and process on low speed just until combined. Don't overprocess the egg whites. Reserve ¹/₃ cup of this batter and set it aside. On low speed, add the pureed mamey to the remaining batter, until just combined.

5. Pour the fruit batter into the springform pan. Place four dollops of the reserved batter on top, and drag the point of a knife over the surface of the cake, creating a random swirl pattern, resulting in white streaks through the pink-colored batter. Don't overwork it; a few twists and turns will do.

6. Carefully place the cake in the oven, and bake for 1 hour. Turn off the heat and let the cake sit in the oven for another hour. This gradual cooling down in the oven sometimes helps to prevent surface cracks, although cracking is sometimes difficult to prevent. Cool the cake completely at room temperature, then refrigerate it overnight, or at least 4 hours. If cracks are really bothersome, cover them up with diced

(Mamey Cheesecake continued from page 251)

mamey or other fresh fruit. Cheesecake should be sliced with a sharp, nonserrated knife dipped in hot water, between slices.

Makes 16 slices

Per Slice: Calories: 245; Fat: 12 g; Cholesterol: 35 mg; Sodium: 290 mg; % Daily Value: Vitamin C 33%, Vitamin A 27%, Riboflavin 10%, Phosphorus 10%

Marvelous Mamey

If you see mamey (pronounced ma-may) on a menu, please order it. And if you're able to buy it fresh at the produce market, jump at the chance. You would never imagine that inside this tropical fruit, which looks like a football, is the most beautiful color you've ever seen. It's a vibrant, salmon-pink, similar to the afterglow of a hot sunset.

Mamey is ripe when it yields to a gentle squeeze, and it should be spoonably soft. It can be used in blenderized drinks, fruit salads, and frozen desserts. Forget about heating it, as it will fall apart fairly easily. Since there are two growing seasons, June to September and again January to April, keep a lookout at both times of the year. If you turn up empty-handed, look for frozen mamey pulp. Fresh, ripe papaya is also a good substitute in any recipe where you would use mamey. The color will not be as intense, but you'll still have a glorious-tasting dessert.

Deep Dish Sweet Potato Plantain Pie

Sweet potato pie is no stranger in the American South, where the African influence helped make this an old-time favorite dessert. The same influence has prevailed in the Caribbean, where a variety of desserts use American-style sweet potatoes. This recipe takes a shortcut by using canned sweet potatoes packed in a light syrup, and gets the island touch from the plantain chips used to form the crust. It's best eaten soon after it's made, when the crust is plenty crunchy, before the chips get soggy. Rich in Vitamin A because of the potatoes, the pie can be jazzed up with a drizzle of Orange Caramel Sauce (page 276).

1 (12-ounce) can drained sweet potatoes,
    packed in light syrup (reserve ¹/₄ cup
    syrup)
³/₄ cup evaporated skim milk
²/₃ cup sugar

2 eggs
1 egg white
1 teaspoon vanilla extract
¹/₄ teaspoon lemon extract
1 ounce plantain chips

1. Preheat the oven to 350°. In a food processor, puree the sweet potatoes to a creamy consistency. Add all the remaining ingredients, including ¹/₄ cup syrup from the potatoes, except the plantain chips, and process for 2–3 minutes, until well combined. If using an electric mixer, whip the potatoes before adding the other ingredients.

2. Spray a 9-inch, deep dish pie pan with nonstick cooking spray. Using a rolling pin, crush the plantain chips. Don't pulverize them to fine crumbs, but leave a little crunch. Coat the bottom of the pie pan

(Deep Dish Sweet Potato Plantain Pie continued from page 253)

with the crumbs. Slowly pour the filling over the plantain chips. Since the chips are not stuck firmly to the bottom of the pan, they will move about a little as you pour in the filling; that's okay.

3. Bake for 60–70 minutes, until a toothpick inserted in the center comes out clean. Cool, then refrigerate for at least 2 hours before slicing.

Makes 10 servings

Per Serving: Calories: 140; Fat: 2 g; Cholesterol: 45 mg; Sodium: 55 mg; % Daily Value: Vitamin A 28%

Scotch Bonnet Chocolate Baby Cakes

I f you think the idea of using Scotch bonnet peppers in a chocolate dessert is crazy, just one bite will make you a believer. Credit for the original recipe goes to Terrence Shaw, Pastry Chef for the 1996 Cayman Islands National Culinary Team. After tasting Terry's version, I made my own revisions to reduce calories and fat. One of the ways I did this was by substituting cocoa powder, which is virtually fat-free, for the original semisweet chocolate. The result is an individual soft-centered chocolate cake that reveals a hint of heat once it's in your mouth for a few seconds. The chocolate, spicy flavor contrast is just one of the things that makes this such an intriguing dessert. The outer texture is cakelike while the interior gets gooey, adding even more interest. And since this is served warm from the oven, a tiny bit of light whipped cream literally puts the icing on the cake.

2 Scotch bonnet peppers, seeded and cut into a few pieces	*$^1/_3$ cup sugar*
2 ounces unsalted butter, melted	*$^1/_2$ teaspoon vanilla extract*
1 tablespoon hot water	*$^1/_2$ cup unsweetened cocoa*
2 eggs, beaten	*3 tablespoons all-purpose flour*
6 tablespoons skim milk	*$^1/_8$ teaspoon salt*
	2 tablespoons whipped cream

1. Preheat the oven to 375°. Coat six (4-ounce) ramekins or disposable foil cups with nonstick cooking spray. In a cup, add the peppers to the melted butter, and steep for 10 minutes. Remove the peppers and stir in the hot water.

(Scotch Bonnet Chocolate Baby Cakes continued from page 255)

2. In a medium bowl, using a whisk, combine the eggs, 2 tablespoons of milk, the sugar, and the vanilla.

3. In a separate medium bowl, slowly drizzle the pepper butter into the cocoa, stirring it with a fork. You should have a rather thick and stiff chocolate mixture. Slowly add the remaining 4 tablespoons of milk, stirring constantly with a fork to a smooth, somewhat pourable consistency.

4. Stir the egg mixture, a third at a time, into the chocolate, until well blended. Stir in the flour and salt.

5. Pour the batter into the prepared cups, and place the cups on a baking sheet. Bake for 12 minutes, or until the outer edges feel firm, but the center is still wobbly. Remove from the oven and run a knife around the outer edge of each cake. Invert onto dessert plates, squirt a smidgin of whipped cream on top, and serve immediately.

Makes 6 servings

Per Serving: Calories: 175; Fat: 10 g; Cholesterol: 90 mg; Sodium: 80 mg; % Daily Value: Vitamin C 37%, Iron 16%, Vitamin A 12%

Brandy and Allspice Streusel Cake

You've seen numerous recipes throughout the book that use allspice in many savory ways, as is typical of Caribbean cooking. It's also used in the way you would expect, in baking. This light, crumbly-textured cake uses a combination of flour and cornmeal, and gets its flavor from both brandy and allspice. Brandy, a throwback to the French and Spanish, can be found next to the rum in most island liquor cabinets. Wrap this cake tightly to prevent it from drying out, a common problem for many lower-fat baked goods. The gingerbread-like texture is terrific for brunch, with an afternoon cup of tea, or served as dessert with a scoop of low-fat vanilla frozen yogurt.

$1/4$ cup raisins	1 tablespoon ground allspice
1 tablespoon plus $1/4$ cup brandy	1 teaspoon baking powder
2 tablespoons chopped walnuts	$1/2$ teaspoon baking soda
$1/2$ tablespoon plus 1 cup cake flour	$1/2$ cup granulated sugar
1 tablespoon dark brown sugar	2 tablespoons margarine
$1/2$ teaspoon ground cinnamon	1 egg
$1/4$ cup cornmeal	$1/4$ cup skim milk

1. Preheat the oven to 350°. Coat a 9-inch round baking pan with nonstick cooking spray. In a small bowl, combine the raisins and 1 tablespoon of the brandy. In another small bowl, combine the nuts, $1/2$ tablespoon of the flour, the brown sugar, and the cinnamon. Set both bowls aside.

(Brandy and Allspice Streusel Cake continued from page 257)

2. In a medium bowl, combine the remaining 1 cup of flour, the cornmeal, allspice, baking powder, and baking soda.

3. In a large bowl, using an electric mixer, cream the granulated sugar and margarine. Gradually add the egg, milk, and the remaining ¼ cup of brandy. Add half the dry ingredients to the wet, beat for 30 seconds until well combined, then gradually mix in the remaining dry ingredients. Do not overbeat; just mix to a smooth batter.

4. Pour the batter into the pan and sprinkle the brandy-soaked raisins over the top, including any brandy remaining in the bowl. Sprinkle the nut mixture over the raisins. Bake for 20 minutes, until a toothpick inserted in the center comes out clean. Cool 30 minutes before cutting.

Makes 8 servings

Per Serving: Calories: 210; Fat: 5 g; Cholesterol: 25 mg; Sodium: 170 mg; % Daily Value: Thiamine 11%

Allspice, the Workhorse

In the United States, we trot out our allspice at the holidays, for baking cookies and sweet breads, and then it goes back on the spice rack until the following year. It's a spice opportunity missed, because allspice is an incredibly versatile seasoning. Nontraditional allspice uses can be found in Jerk Rub (page 24), Conch Asopao (page 188), and Shrimp and Mango–Stuffed Yellowtail (page 164).

The Europeans found allspice growing in the Caribbean and named it such because it tasted like a combination of cinnamon, nutmeg, and cloves. It grows on the pimento tree, and is sometimes called Jamaican pepper, or pimento. Supposedly, this name came about because the dried spice berries look like black peppercorns. Similar to nutmeg, there is a world of difference between using freshly grated allspice and the packaged ground variety.

In Jamaica, a major exporter of allspice, the local varieties have a more pungent, dramatic flavor than allspice grown elsewhere. Jamaicans have been very thrifty with the pimento tree. Not only do they utilize the berry, but pimento is the wood of choice lending a special flavor to jerk barbecues. And last but not least, the ripe allspice berries are used to make a locally produced liqueur called Pimento Dram.

Banana, Mango, Nutmeg Ice Cream

Sound like an exotic new flavor from Ben & Jerry's? It tastes exotic, doesn't have nearly the amount of fat as premium ice creams, and you can create this one at home. This is not start from scratch ice cream, but simply uses high-quality, store-bought low-fat vanilla ice cream. When mangoes are nearing the end of their season, which is late summer, I freeze lots of mango pulp so I can whip up this recipe any time. Make your own mango pulp with a few quick hits in the food processor, or buy it frozen. For those who live in the North, this ice cream will be like a little ray of sunshine in your January dessert bowl.

2 cups semisoft, low-fat vanilla ice cream   *¹/₂ cup quartered banana slices*

²/₃ cup mango pulp   *1¹/₂ teaspoons freshly grated nutmeg*

1. In a food processor, pulse the ice cream and mango at low speed 2–3 times, so that the mango is streaked through the ice cream. Alternatively, if you don't have a food processor, stir the mango into the softened ice cream until you get the same effect.

2. Stir in the banana and nutmeg, and refreeze to the desired hardness.

Makes 4 servings

Per Serving: Calories: 165; Fat: 3 g; Cholesterol: 10 mg; Sodium: 60 mg; % Daily Value: Vitamin C 28%, Vitamin A 22%, Calcium 20%, Dietary Fiber 10%

Shortcut Skinny Flan

Baked custards are known around the world as French crème caramel, Italian crema caramella, and Spanish flan. The flan eaten in the Spanish islands, like all these desserts, varies not just regionally but from one family to the next. Like its French cousin, crème caramel, flan is typically served inverted, so the caramel sits right on top. To make life easier, this version is not inverted, but eaten right from the cup. When you dip your spoon in for a bite, the gooey syrup on the bottom is a sweet and pleasant surprise. Instead of caramelizing the sugar to make the caramel coating, I short-cut the process and use dark corn syrup. By adjusting and altering the normally high-fat ingredients like egg yolks, eggs, whole milk, sweetened condensed milk, and sugar, this flan comes in with an incredibly low 1 gram of fat, a dramatic cholesterol reduction, and a healthy dose of calcium and Vitamin A.

2 egg yolks
¹/₂ cup frozen egg substitute, thawed
1 (14-ounce) can nonfat sweetened
  condensed milk

1 (12-ounce) can evaporated skim milk
1 tablespoon vanilla extract
¹/₂ cup dark corn syrup
Cinnamon, to taste

1. Preheat the oven to 300°. In a medium bowl, whisk together all the ingredients except the corn syrup and cinnamon.

2. Pour 1 tablespoon of the corn syrup into each of eight ¹/₂-cup ramekins or disposable aluminum foil cups (not baking muffin cups). Tilt the cups to cover the entire bottom with the syrup. Set the ramekins in a 13 × 9-inch baking pan and pour ¹/₂ cup of custard into each one. Set the pan on the oven rack, then

(Shortcut Skinny Flan continued from page 261)

fill it with enough hot water to come halfway up the sides of the ramekins. The water bath cooks the custard evenly, for a smooth, creamy texture, and helps prevent cracking.

3. Bake for 1 hour, until golden-colored on top and firm to the touch. Remove the ramekins from the water bath, and cool the custards at room temperature for 30 minutes, then refrigerate for at least 1 hour before serving. Serve with a cinnamon sprinkle on top.

Makes 8 servings

Per Serving: Calories: 235; Fat: 1 g; Cholesterol: 60 mg; Sodium: 135 mg;
% Daily Value: Calcium 14%, Vitamin A 14%

Calabaza Rum Custard Flan

The texture of this flan is slightly grainy because of the calabaza. The added vegetable tones down the overall sweetness of the dessert and loads it up with Vitamin A. To reduce cholesterol (most flans use lots of egg yolks), there is just 1 egg, with arrowroot providing additional body and structure. Fresh, cooked, or canned pumpkin would also work just fine. Because the whole dish can be made in advance, it's ideal company dessert.

1 pound peeled calabaza or pumpkin, cut into 2-inch cubes

1 (12-ounce) can evaporated skim milk

²/₃ cup sugar

¹/₄ cup dark rum

2 tablespoons arrowroot

1 teaspoon vanilla extract

1 egg

Freshly grated nutmeg, to taste

1. Preheat the oven to 350°. In a large saucepan, heat 2 inches of water to boiling. Add the calabaza, cover, and cook for 15–20 minutes, until the calabaza is very soft and can easily be pierced with a knife. Drain, and transfer to a food processor.

2. On low speed, process the calabaza for 1–2 minutes, until very smooth. With the processor still running, add the evaporated milk, ¹/₃ cup of sugar, the rum, arrowroot, and vanilla. Turn off the processor, and test the temperature. If it's pleasant to touch, and doesn't scald your finger, turn the machine back on and add the egg. If it's too hot, wait a few minutes until it cools, or stick it in the fridge for a few minutes. If the mixture is too hot when the egg is added, you'll have instant cooked egg—not a good thing for this recipe.

(Calabaza Rum Custard Flan continued from page 263)

3. Do this step immediately before pouring in the custard. To caramelize the sugar, pour the remaining ¹/₃ cup of sugar into a 4-cup heatproof mold. Melting the sugar right in the mold means less chance for error, and one less dirty pot. Place the mold over medium-low heat until the sugar has melted. Using pot holders, carefully tilt the mold so the bottom and sides get covered with the syrup. Work quickly, and at a low temperature, so the syrup doesn't turn hard.

4. Pour in the custard and set the mold in a baking pan just large enough to hold it. Set the pan on the oven rack, and fill it with enough hot water to come halfway up the sides of the mold.

5. Bake for 1¹/₂–1³/₄ hours, until a skewer or knife inserted in the middle comes out clean. Cool on a wire rack for 30 minutes, then refrigerate for at least 6 hours, or overnight, before serving. Slide a small knife around the outside of the flan to loosen it up. Place a serving plate over the mold, and invert it. This is always a nervous moment, but it usually comes out quite easily. If it doesn't come out on the first try, wet the knife with hot water and slide it around the flan again. Gently tap the mold on the counter a few times to help loosen it. Slice, and top each portion with grated nutmeg.

Makes 8 servings

Per Serving: Calories: 155; Fat: 1 g; Cholesterol: 30 mg; Sodium: 65 mg; % Daily Value: Vitamin A 23%, Calcium 14%, Riboflavin 11%, Potassium 10%

Piña Colada Custard Pie

Pineapple and coconut are two tropical flavors that just seem to be made for each other. Smooth custard, juicy pineapple tidbits, and shredded coconut provide a combination of textures that lets you forget this is a reduced-fat dessert. The pie keeps well in the refrigerator for several days, is simple enough for an everyday family dessert, and refined enough for a dinner party.

1 cup skim milk

1/2 cup frozen egg substitute, thawed

1/2 cup light brown sugar

1/3 cup "lite" coconut milk

2 eggs

1 teaspoon rum extract or flavoring

1/2 cup finely diced fresh pineapple

2 tablespoons shredded, sweetened coconut

1. Preheat the oven to 300°. In a medium bowl, whisk together the milk, egg substitute, sugar, coconut milk, eggs, and rum extract, until smooth. Stir in the pineapple.

2. Coat a 9-inch, 1¼-inch-deep tart or quiche pan with nonstick cooking spray, then set it in a baking pan just large enough to hold it. Place the pan on the oven rack and pour the custard into the tart pan. Fill the baking pan with enough hot water to come halfway up the sides of the tart pan. This will help eliminate cracking.

3. Bake for 1 hour, until a toothpick inserted in the center comes out clean and the top is lightly browned. Meanwhile, toast the coconut in the oven on a piece of aluminum foil for 5–7 minutes, until lightly browned. When the custard is removed from the oven, sprinkle the coconut over the top. Refrigerate for 2 hours before cutting.

Makes 8 servings

Per Serving: Calories: 105; Fat: 2 g; Cholesterol: 55 mg; Sodium: 65 mg; No other significant nutritional value

A Coconut Conversation

Coconut, in the form of grated meat or milk, is widely used in Caribbean cooking. Besides being used in sweet dishes, it's a flavor that mingles nicely with curry, hot peppers, and savory herbs, a perfect example of contrasting flavors.

Coconut palms, grown in tropical climates, crank out their nuts for some 70-odd years, making coconut an abundant agricultural export for many islands. When the nut is immature and green, the inside meat is soft and jellylike. As it ripens, the meat becomes dry and hard, a perfect texture for shredding and grating. When buying fresh coconuts, choose one that makes a sloshing sound when you shake it. That's the clear coconut water inside.

The hard part, for most people, is figuring out how to get the meat out, without taking off their fingers in the process. An easy trick is to bake the coconut at 350° for 15 minutes, then freeze it until the shell cracks or refrigerate for several hours. Grate as much as you need; wrap and refrigerate the rest. One medium coconut will yield about 3–4 cups grated coconut. If you're buying prepackaged coconut, there is sweetened and unsweetened, and you will find both types used in this book.

Unfortunately, coconut is high in fat, especially saturated fat. But true to the idea of big-flavored ingredients, it can be used in small amounts and still accomplish the job. Because coconut palms are so prolific, it's no wonder that coconut oil has been a commonly used cooking fat for islanders and commercial food manufacturers. But some years back, in response to consumers' nutritional concerns, food companies stopped using highly saturated coconut oil, and it has all but disappeared from product ingredient labels.

Lemon Natilla

Natilla is a pudding relative of flan. My Cuban neighbors usually make this in individual little cups, and I've chosen to do the same. You could, however, make it in a serving bowl and spoon out portions as needed. The basic ingredients—eggs, milk, and in this case, evaporated skim milk—are slightly thickened by the addition of arrowroot. In general, I find Cuban desserts to be very sweet, and I really cut back on the sugar, to satisfy both my taste buds and the calorie count. I think the lemon extract in this recipe cuts the sweetness a bit, and gives the custard an ever-so-slight, refreshingly tart flavor.

1 (12-ounce) can evaporated skim milk	$^1/_3$ cup sugar
$^3/_4$ cup skim milk	1 tablespoon honey
1 (2-inch-long) piece of lemon zest	$^1/_2$ teaspoon lemon extract
$1^1/_2$ tablespoons arrowroot	$^1/_4$ teaspoon vanilla extract
2 eggs, beaten	

1. In a small saucepan, over low heat, heat the evaporated milk, skim milk, and lemon zest, just to boiling. Cool to the touch, at room temperature or in the fridge. Remove the surface skin that has formed, and the lemon zest.

2. In a small bowl, stir the arrowroot into a few tablespoons of the cooled milk, until dissolved. Whisk this back into the remaining milk, then whisk in the eggs.

3. Transfer the mixture to a medium saucepan. Stir in the sugar, honey, and extracts and, over low heat, cook for 10–15 minutes, stirring frequently, until the pudding starts to thicken. Resist the temptation

(Lemon Natilla continued from page 267)

to turn up the heat because you will only curdle the eggs and scorch the bottom of the pan. Thickening custard is a slow, careful process that can't be hurried. Pour the mixture into six 4-ounce ramekins or aluminum foil cups and refrigerate several hours before serving.

Makes 6 servings

Per Serving: Calories: 150; Fat: 2 g; Cholesterol: 75 mg; Sodium: 110 mg; % Daily Value: Calcium 23%, Riboflavin 19%, Vitamin A 12%

Baked Grapefruit and Coconut Brunch Bread

This is a fruit version of the casserole brunch dish that usually contains lots of cheese and sausage. This version is not a main course, but can take the place of both fruit and a breakfast bread on your brunch menu. The tart grapefruit and sweet coconut work well as a complementary combination. Vitamin C–rich grapefruit has a lot of moisture, so be sure to drain the fruit as well as possible to keep the finished dish from becoming soggy. The whole recipe can be prepared in advance, then baked just before serving. After baking, it firms up the longer it sits.

2½ cups Italian or French bread, cut into ½-inch cubes

1½ cups well-drained pink grapefruit sections, membranes and pith removed

1½ cups "lite" coconut milk

¼ cup plus 1 tablespoon dark brown sugar

2 eggs

1 teaspoon coconut extract

¼ teaspoon freshly grated nutmeg

⅛ teaspoon salt

2 tablespoons shredded, sweetened coconut

1 teaspoon flour

2 teaspoons butter

1. Coat an 8 × 8-inch square baking pan with nonstick cooking spray. Place the bread cubes in the bottom of the pan and top with the grapefruit sections.

2. In a small bowl, with a whisk, combine the coconut milk, ¼ cup of the brown sugar, the eggs,

(Baked Grapefruit and Coconut Brunch Bread continued from page 269)

coconut extract, nutmeg, and salt. Pour this mixture over the bread and fruit. Cover, and refrigerate overnight, or at least 8 hours, until well soaked.

3. When ready to bake, preheat the oven to 350°. Bake for 30 minutes. Meanwhile, in a small bowl, combine the shredded coconut, flour, and the remaining 1 tablespoon of brown sugar. Cut in the butter with a knife, so it resembles small, pebble-like pieces. Sprinkle this mixture over the bread pudding, bake for an additional 20–30 minutes, until the pudding is firm and the liquid has been absorbed. Cool at room temperature for 30 minutes before serving. Cut into six squares. The final moisture of the dish will vary somewhat, depending on the juiciness of the grapefruit.

Makes 6 servings

Per Serving: Calories: 175; Fat: 7 g; Cholesterol: 75 mg; Sodium: 160 mg; % Daily Value: Vitamin C 36%

Guava Raisin Bread Pudding

Guava is a small, round fruit, with a yellow-green skin, and a flesh that ranges from white to yellow to red, depending on the variety. Because fresh guava is often hard to find, readily available guava nectar can be used in many recipes. If you've never seen the nectar, you will be impressed by its striking pink color, fragrant aroma, and illusive taste, sometimes described as pineapple, banana, and strawberry combined. To intensify the flavor of the dish, guava paste, an incredibly sweet product made from guava pulp, sugar, and pectin is also used. To help control calories, the guava paste is spread on the bread, where your tastebuds will notice it, rather than blended into the custard. Guava paste comes packaged in small boxes or tins, and is sold in the Hispanic section of your supermarket. Buy the smallest package possible, because a little goes a long way. Serve this alone, or accompanied by Starstruck Guava Dessert Sauce (page 273).

1 (12-ounce) can evaporated skim milk

1 (7-ounce) can guava nectar

$1/2$ cup frozen egg substitute, thawed

$1/2$ cup sugar

2 tablespoons all-purpose flour

1 teaspoon almond extract

$1/2$ teaspoon freshly grated nutmeg

12 slices (6 ounces) Italian or French bread, cut $1/2$ inch thick

$1^1/2$ ounces guava paste

$1/3$ cup raisins

$3/4$ cup Starstruck Guava Dessert Sauce (page 273) (optional)

1. Preheat the broiler. In a medium bowl, combine the evaporated milk, guava nectar, egg substitute, sugar, flour, almond extract, and nutmeg, and set it aside.

(Guava Raisin Bread Pudding continued from page 271)

2. Place the bread on a baking sheet and broil it on both sides, for a total of 1–2 minutes, until golden. Remove from the oven and turn the temperature down to 325°. Spread the guava paste on one side of the bread. The paste is sticky and difficult to spread, but the heat from the broiled bread should make it more spreadable. Cut six slices of bread into three lengthwise strips each, leaving six slices intact.

3. Coat an 8 × 8-inch baking pan with nonstick cooking spray. Place the bread strips, guava side up, in the pan. Sprinkle half the raisins over the bread, then pour on half the custard filling. Place the remaining six bread slices on top, and repeat with the remaining raisins and custard. Press down with a spoon, if necessary, to submerge the bread, soaking it thoroughly.

4. Cover with aluminum foil and bake for 45 minutes. Remove the foil and bake an additional 5 minutes. Cool for at least 10 minutes before cutting into six portions according to where the top bread slices are placed. Serve warm or at room temperature. If using the dessert sauce, use 2 tablespoons per serving.

Makes 6 servings

Per Serving (without sauce): Calories: 270; Fat: 1 g; Cholesterol: 0; Sodium: 275 mg;
% Daily Value: Calcium 22%, Vitamin C 20%, Thiamine 15%, Vitamin A 13%

Starstruck Guava
Dessert Sauce

One of the most striking things about cooking with tropical fruits is their wild colors. Cooking with a palette of pinks and purples is not what most of us are accustomed to, but that's exactly what you get with this recipe. This sauce starts out as a shade of fuchsia, then, after adding the cream and rum, deepens to a rich purple. There's just enough cream in this to make it seem indulgent, yet it has only 1 gram of fat per 2-tablespoon serving. The flavor of star anise permeates the sauce, for a wonderful accompaniment to Guava Raisin Bread Pudding (page 271), or your own favorite bread pudding recipe.

1 (7-ounce) can guava nectar
4 tablespoons light cream

1 tablespoon dark rum
1 star anise

In a small saucepan over very low heat, warm all the ingredients for 15 minutes. Remove the star anise and serve the sauce warm.

Makes 8 servings

Per 2 Tablespoons: Calories: 30; Fat: 1 g; Cholesterol: 5 mg; Sodium: 0; % Daily Value: Vitamin C 13 %

Cooking with a Star

If you like the flavor of anise seeds and anisette liqueur, you're going to love cooking with star anise. As its name implies, the seed is in a star shape, and is common to Chinese cooking. In fact, it is one of the spices contained in oriental five-spice powder. Since the Chinese passed through the Caribbean during early settlement, it's no wonder their food influences are still felt.

Whole star anise does its job by infusing its flavor into whatever you're cooking. Let it steep during the cooking process, then remove it at the end. For presentation purposes, it's a nice touch, and a conversation piece, to scatter some of the little stars around the rim of the serving dish.

Mint Pineapple Sauce

This pale green dessert sauce will shock your taste buds, simply because you're not expecting something green to taste like pineapple. As always, fresh fruit is preferable, and in this case, fresh mint is essential. For a further twist, you might use other mint varieties, such orange mint, apple mint, and, yes there is, pineapple mint. The sauce has a clean, refreshing taste, that is great poured over fresh pineapple slices, or spooned over bread or rice pudding. Adding to its versatility, the sauce tastes equally good either chilled or slightly warmed. And how often does a dessert sauce come with a respectable amount of Vitamin C?

1 cup cubed fresh pineapple   *1 tablespoon chopped fresh mint*

¹⁄₄ cup pineapple juice   *1 tablespoon sugar*

2 tablespoons light cream

In a blender, combine all the ingredients and puree to a pale mint green color with a creamy, mint-flecked consistency. Use immediately, or reblend before serving, as the sauce will separate after standing.

Makes 4 servings

Per Serving: Calories: 55; Fat: 2 g; Cholesterol: 5 mg; Sodium: 0; % Daily Value: Vitamin C 13%

Orange Caramel Sauce

Caramel sauces are sweet, gooey, and, in my book, the ultimate dessert topping. Yet they can be real calorie busters. Evaporated skim milk helps trim down some of the calories and fat, while the double citrus whammy of orange juice and orange extract lends new flavor to an old favorite. Although we tend to think of citrus fruits as being indigenous to the New World, it was Columbus himself who first brought citrus plants to the Caribbean rim, where they've been grown extensively since the sixteenth century.

3/4 cup sugar	*3/4 cup evaporated skim milk*
1/3 cup orange juice	*1 teaspoon dark corn syrup*
3/4 tablespoon unsalted butter	*1/2 teaspoon orange extract*

1. In a small saucepan over medium heat, heat the sugar and orange juice to a boil. Stirring occasionally, cook at a light boil for 10–15 minutes.

2. Remove the pan from the heat and stir in the butter. Stirring constantly, add the evaporated milk, a little at a time. Over low heat and stir for 1 minute, to ensure a perfectly smooth consistency. Turn off the heat and stir in the corn syrup and orange extract. Cool at least 30 minutes before serving, to thicken.

Makes 16 servings

Per Serving: Calories: 55; Fat: 1 g; Cholesterol: 0; Sodium: 15 mg;
No other significant nutritional contribution

Electric Carambola Compote

Carambola, also known as starfruit, is often used for its unusual shape, while only a second thought is given to its juicy, slightly tart flavor. This recipe makes good use of both attributes. The carambola-based fruit compote is flavored and colored by candied ginger and dried papaya, the later providing the shocking, "electric" orange color. This dish is so versatile, it could also have been at home in the Big-Flavor Accompaniments chapter, cuddling up to grilled fish, shrimp, or chicken. But it found its way into the dessert chapter because it's outrageously good served as a warm topping for frozen vanilla yogurt or angel food cake.

1 (7-ounce) can pineapple/passion fruit nectar (if unavailable, use pineapple juice)

1 teaspoon vanilla sugar*

1 star anise

2 medium carambola, sliced

$^{3}/_{4}$ cup thinly sliced dried papaya

2 tablespoons raisins

1 tablespoon candied ginger strips

1. In a medium saucepan, heat the pineapple nectar, vanilla sugar, and star anise to a boil. Reduce the heat, and keep at a full simmer for 10–15 minutes, until the liquid has slightly reduced. Add the remaining ingredients and cook for an additional 10–15 minutes, until the carambola softens slightly but still holds its shape, and the liquid becomes "electric" orange.

* Vanilla sugar is made by storing vanilla beans with sugar in a tightly covered container. One bean to $^{1}/_{2}$ pound of sugar, stored for a week, lends a wonderful flavor, which is carried through to the finished dish. Remove the bean before using the sugar. Vanilla beans can be purchased at specialty food stores.

(Electric Carambola Compote continued from page 277)

2. Remove the star anise and allow the compote to cool slightly before serving, so the juices will thicken and become syrupy.

Makes 6 servings

Per Serving: Calories: 95; Fat and Cholesterol: 0; Sodium: 10 mg; % Daily Value: Vitamin C 103%, Vitamin A 17%, Potassium 14%

Carambola Goes Mainstream

Carambola is coming onto the food scene with the same popularity that the once un-known kiwi did. It is now readily available in produce sections across the country, and is as delicious to eat as it is fun to cook with.

Carambola also goes by the name starfruit, and it is easy to identify. Usually yellow in color, it has five lengthwise ribs running down its oblong, 4–5-inch egg shape. When sliced, it's these ribs that create the characteristic star shape. The fruit needs no peeling or seeding and can be eaten right out of your hand, like an apple. To assure a ripe fruit, look for a deep yellow color and ribs that are slightly brown. Once ripe, use it in a day or two, or store it in the refrigerator for up to 2 weeks.

Carambolas are great in stir-fry dishes or other entrees where they're in and out of the heat fairly quickly. As with most high-moisture fruits, they'll lose their shape if over-cooked. Use them in a fresh salsa, a fruit salad, or a tossed green salad. For blenderized drinks, puree the fruit, reserving a few slices for garnish. A star-shaped slice of carambola will add a tropical touch to any plate, yet a whole fruit has only about 40 calories and is a good source of Vitamin C and potassium.

Cashew Waffles with Nutmeg Syrup

The native West Indies cashew tree does double duty by producing both a fruit and a nut. The nut grows from the bottom of the cashew apple, a tart fruit often made into jelly or wine but not generally found in the States. Like all nuts, cashews are fairly high in fat, so a little bit has to go a long way. Store any leftover cashews, tightly wrapped, in the refrigerator to prevent them from turning rancid.

1 cup reduced-fat all-purpose baking mix
5 ounces skim milk
1 egg white
1 teaspoon vegetable oil

¹/₂ teaspoon vanilla extract
1¹/₂ tablespoons finely chopped, unsalted, roasted cashews
4 tablespoons Nutmeg Syrup (page 58)

1. Spray the top and bottom of an 8 × 8-inch (4 [4-inch] waffles) waffle iron with nonstick cooking spray, then preheat the iron.

2. In a small bowl, combine all the ingredients, including half the cashews. Pour the batter onto the waffle iron, close, and cook for 5 minutes, until the steam stops and the waffles are lightly browned. Serve each waffle with 1 tablespoon of Nutmeg Syrup, and the reserved cashews sprinkled on top.

Makes 4 servings

Per Serving (with syrup): Calories: 210; Fat: 5 g; Cholesterol: 0; Sodium: 380 mg;
No other significant nutritional value

Banana Butter and Leek
Pocket Muffins

I'm constantly trying to find new and different things to do with bananas, since I have so many growing in my yard. I came up with what I called "banana butter," and then couldn't decide what to do with it. The answer was a pocket-filled muffin. The banana butter flavors the batter and also appears in the muffin's center. Not only is it fun to bite into, but the banana provides some tenderizing moisture, so that the recipe requires less oil overall. These muffins have a broad range of uses, from breakfast food to dinner bread.

BANANA BUTTER

1 teaspoon vegetable oil

*1/4 cup peeled, seeded, finely chopped
    tomato*

1/4 cup finely chopped scallions

*6 cachucha peppers, seeded and minced
    (if unavailable, use 1/4 cup minced
    green bell pepper)*

1/2 teaspoon turmeric

1/2 teaspoon ground cinnamon

1/4 teaspoon salt

2 cups very ripe, sliced bananas

3 tablespoons lemon juice

1/4 cup skim milk

BATTER

1/2 cup skim milk

1/4 cup vegetable oil

2 tablespoons sugar

1 egg

1/2 the banana butter mixture (see above)

2 cups cake flour

2 teaspoons baking powder

1/2 teaspoon salt

*1/3 cup sliced leeks (cut lengthwise, then
    sliced)*

1. To make the banana butter, heat the oil in a large skillet. Add the tomato, scallions, peppers, turmeric, cinnamon, and salt, and cook over low heat for 10 minutes, stirring occasionally, until soft. Add the bananas and cook an additional 10 minutes, until they're mushy but still have a little chunk left. Stir in the lemon juice.

2. Transfer to a blender, and slowly add the milk while pureeing to a smooth consistency. There should be red and yellow flecks throughout the banana butter when finished.

3. Preheat the oven to 400°. Coat a muffin tin (9 muffin cups) with nonstick cooking spray. To make the batter, in a small bowl, whisk together the milk, oil, sugar, egg, and half the banana butter, until thoroughly combined.

4. In a large bowl, combine the flour, baking powder, and salt. Gently add the wet mixture to the dry ingredients, stirring just until combined. Stir in the leeks. Do not overmix.

5. Fill the muffin cups one-third full with batter, then spoon a heaping teaspoon of the remaining banana butter into each. Top the muffins with batter to two-thirds full. Bake 20–25 minutes, until they are slightly golden on top, and the interior is dry when tested with a toothpick. Be sure to stick the toothpick slightly off-center when testing for doneness, so as not to go through the banana butter.

Makes 9 servings

Per Serving: Calories: 230; Fat: 8 g; Cholesterol: 25 mg; Sodium: 270 mg; % Daily Value: Vitamin C 41%, Vitamin E 28%, Thiamine 17%

Citrus, Coconut, Carrot
Sweet Bread

This sweet tea bread is a good example of how to use one ingredient in various forms to create a dominant theme; in this case, its orange flavor and color. Orange extract and orange juice concentrate, used in both the batter and the icing, come together for a powerful citrus taste. To take the orange idea one step further, orange-colored ingredients—grated carrots and dried papaya—add texture, flavor and color to the batter. The banana allows us to reduce the amount of oil, while the "lite" cream cheese and a small amount of coconut make for a seemingly rich icing. Orange, coconut, banana, and papaya represent Caribbean ingredients in an everyday sweet bread.

1 cup ripe mashed banana

1 cup grated carrots

1/2 cup dark brown sugar

1/4 cup vegetable oil

1/4 cup frozen orange juice concentrate,
thawed

2 teaspoons orange extract

1 teaspoon ground cinnamon

1 1/2 cups all-purpose flour

1 1/2 teaspoons baking powder

1/2 teaspoon baking soda

3 tablespoons (1-ounce) finely chopped
dried papaya

2 tablespoons shredded, sweetened
coconut

3 tablespoons "lite" cream cheese

2 teaspoons granulated sugar

1. Preheat the oven to 400°. Coat a 9 1/2 × 5-inch loaf pan with nonstick cooking spray.

2. In a medium bowl, thoroughly combine the first seven ingredients, using half the orange juice concentrate.

3. In a large bowl, combine the flour, baking powder, and baking soda. Stir the wet ingredients into the dry until thoroughly combined. Stir in the papaya. Pour the batter into the pan and bake 30–35 minutes, until a toothpick comes out clean when inserted in the center. Meanwhile, toast the coconut in the oven on aluminum foil for 3–5 minutes, until lightly browned. This can burn quickly, so watch it carefully.

4. While the bread is baking, prepare the icing. In a blender, puree the cream cheese, the remaining orange juice concentrate, and the granulated sugar until smooth.

5. Cool the bread for 5 minutes, invert, and turn right side up on a plate. Immediately spread the icing over the top, then sprinkle with the coconut. Cool for at least 1 hour before slicing.

Makes 16 servings

Per Serving: Calories: 135; Fat: 4 g; Cholesterol: 0; Sodium: 90 mg;
% Daily Value: Vitamin A 21%, Vitamin C 18%

A Party
for Coconut Groupies

Apparently, back in the 1800s all of Belize was one big coconut plantation. To celebrate its importance as a cash crop, then and even today, Belize hosts an annual Coconut Festival, usually during the second week of May. If you're planning a trip down that way, you might want to try your hand at the coconut hunt (for hidden money), or dress up for the costume contest, which allows that only coconut tree materials be used. Or how about climbing the tallest, greased coconut tree? Local food vendors and musicians round out a party you'll be nuts about.

Onion and Olive Skillet
Corn Bread

When Spanish explorers arrived in the Caribbean, corn was already being grown on some of the islands. Ground cornmeal, used by the native Caribbean Indians, was an extremely versatile and abundant ingredient. Over the years, corn breads and corn puddings have cropped up in infinite variations. This version has a Hispanic influence derived from oregano and Spanish olives. The olives not only add taste, they also contribute texture and a festive green and red splash of color. Baking in a cast-iron skillet gives the bread an earthy, peasant feel, but a 9-inch square or round baking pan works fine, too. Even though it's finely ground, cornmeal is an excellent source of dietary fiber, as well as Vitamin E and thiamine.

1 cup skim milk
2/3 cup drained canned corn
1/3 cup minced onion
1/3 cup vegetable oil
1 egg
1 cup all-purpose flour

1 cup yellow cornmeal
2 teaspoons baking powder
1 teaspoon dried oregano
1/8 teaspoon salt
1/4 cup chopped, Spanish, pimento-
       stuffed, salad olives

1. Preheat the oven to 400°. Coat a 10-inch cast-iron skillet with nonstick cooking spray. In a medium bowl, stir together all the wet ingredients (milk through egg) until thoroughly combined.

2. In a large bowl, combine all the remaining ingredients except the olives. Stir the wet ingredients into the dry until thoroughly mixed. Pour the batter into the skillet.

3. Sprinkle the olives over the top and bake 30 minutes, until the corn bread is lightly browned and a toothpick comes out clean when inserted in the center. Serve warm, or when reheating, cover with aluminum foil and warm in a 200° oven for 10 minutes.

Makes 10 servings

Per Serving: Calories: 185; Fat: 9 g; Cholesterol: 20 mg; Sodium: 240 mg;
% Daily Value: Vitamin E 21%, Thiamine 10%, Dietary Fiber 10%

Thirst-Quenching Libations

❈ ❈ ❈ ❈ ❈ ❈ ❈ ❈ ❈ ❈ ❈

In a hot, humid, Caribbean climate, thirst quenchers are an important part of the menu. Island beverages seem to fall into two categories: those made with rum and those made without rum. Practically considered the water of the Caribbean, rum has a long-running history in this part of the world (read more in The Legend of Rum, page 302). From the buccaneer pirate ships of the 1600s to today's all-inclusive luxury resorts, rum is used in an infinite number of drinks. Non-rum-containing drinks usually call on local fruits as their base, and are mixed with milk or sparkling water to make a refreshing libation.

Given the fact that rum is used in most of these drinks, low-calorie becomes a relative term. The Frozen Piña Colada recipe in this chapter (page 304) has had some calories shaved off, while the fresh fruits and juices used in other drinks contribute a small amount of nutrition. But let's face facts: cocktails are not considered part of a food group, and we don't drink them for their nutritional value. These beverage recipes are meant to be enjoyed as a moderate addition to an already healthy lifestyle.

So this chapter is really more about fun than anything else. Serving The Original Daiquiri (page 298) in pretty stemware might lend some Caribbean sophistication to your next cocktail party. A batch of Mojito Cocktails (page 296) at a backyard barbecue could really get the party rolling. Or how about offering fruit Batidos (page 291) as a change of pace for a brunch menu? And on a cold winter night, a Hot Apple Rum (page 295) will help put you in an idyllic, island state of mind.

Café con Leche

Long before specialty coffees, and coffee bars, became the rage, Cubans have been drinking their down-home version, called Café con Leche. There's nothing fancy about it; no foam on top, and no sprinkle of cinnamon or cocoa powder. True to its literal translation, it's simply "coffee with milk," although it should be more appropriately called, "milk with coffee." While the proportions do vary, most "con leche" is made with heated whole milk, or diluted evaporated milk, and a small amount of very strong espresso coffee. To lighten the calorie load, I've used a combination of skim milk and diluted evaporated skim milk, the latter lending a little sweetness. If you don't own a milk steamer, just heat the milk on the stove top or in the microwave. For people who aren't milk drinkers, it's an effortless way to get some daily calcium.

¹/₄ cup skim milk

¹/₄ cup evaporated skim milk

2 tablespoons water

¹/₂ cup hot, brewed espresso coffee

Sugar, to taste (optional)

In a small saucepan, heat the skim milk, evaporated milk, and water just to boiling. Alternatively, microwave on high for 30 seconds. Pour the milk into a mug, then stir in the coffee. Add sugar, if needed to suit your taste.

Makes 1 serving

Per Serving: Calories: 75; Fat and Cholesterol: 0; Sodium: 110 mg; % Daily Value: Calcium 26%, Riboflavin 16%, Potassium 10%

A Java Harvest Festival

The heart of Puerto Rico's coffee-growing region is on the western end of the island. And in the town of Maricao, in late February, you will find the annual Coffee Harvest Festival taking place. It's a big event, including handicraft exhibitions, live folk music, local food, and a parade complete with floats. To celebrate the island's coffee heritage, there are exhibitions of past and present tools and equipment used in harvesting the crop, as well as beverages and desserts that are made with—what else?—coffee.

Batidos

Batidos are tropical fruit milk shakes; the flavors depend on what's fallen off the tree that day. It could be papaya, mango, guanabana, or perhaps ripe pineapple. These drinks are more fruit than milk, and they should be so thick that you're tempted to use a spoon, but a straw will actually do. A batido can be a nourishing breakfast or an afternoon pick-me-up. There is a version that uses ice cream, but in the interest of nutrition, I stick with skim milk. Even if the fruit is ripe, I like to add a pinch of sugar. When tropical fresh fruit is not available, frozen pulp makes a fine substitute.

Pineapple Batido

1 cup diced fresh pineapple
½ cup skim milk

1 teaspoon sugar

In a blender, puree the pineapple, until smooth. Add the milk and sugar, then puree again. Pineapple has more moisture than papaya or mango, so less milk is used in this version than the following one.

Makes 1 serving

Per Serving: Calories: 135; Fat and Cholesterol: 0; Sodium: 65 mg; % Daily Value: Vitamin C 41%, Calcium 16%, Riboflavin 13%, Vitamin D 12%, Thiamine 12%

Papaya or Mango Batido

1 cup diced papaya or mango   *1 teaspoon sugar*
²/₃ cup skim milk

In a blender, puree the papaya or mango until smooth. Add the milk and sugar, then puree again.

Makes 1 serving

Per Serving: Calories: 130; Fat and Cholesterol: 0; Sodium: 90 mg; % Daily Value: Vitamin C 146%, Vitamin A 38%, Calcium 23%, Vitamin D 17%, Riboflavin 16%, Folic Acid 15%

Tamarind Soda

Tamarindade is a common drink in the islands, usually made with lots of sugar. It's true that tart tamarind (for more information, see The Tale of Tamarind, page 45) needs a sweetening boost, but I've found it doesn't take quite as much sugar as most recipes suggest. Adding carbonation with club soda or sparkling water makes this an extremely refreshing drink, one I enjoy at home all the time. I premix the tamarind pulp and sugar (just increase the ingredients proportionately), in a jar, so it's ready for the club soda any time I want a drink. If there are no maraschino cherries around the house, use a dash of grenadine or cranberry juice for color.

3 tablespoons frozen tamarind pulp,
thawed
2 teaspoons sugar
4–5 ice cubes

6 ounces club soda
1 teaspoon maraschino cherry juice
Freshly grated nutmeg, for garnish

In a tall glass, combine the ingredients except the nutmeg in the order listed, and stir until the sugar dissolves. Garnish with the nutmeg.

Makes 1 serving

Per Serving: Calories: 90; Fat and Cholesterol: 0; Sodium: 40 mg; No other significant nutritional value

Banana Lime Fizz

This is a variation on our fruit smoothies, which, delicious as they are, don't have any fizz or sparkle. The sweet banana flavor has been cut with the tart limeade, prepared from concentrate, and makes an excellent alternative to an alcoholic cocktail. The other fruit in this recipe can really be whatever is in season and available. I often use mango or papaya, but feel free to substitute any type of berry, peaches, or nectarines. Pineapple and melons contain more water and will give you a thinner consistency. Drinking one of these will definitely count toward your daily fruit group servings.

1 large, ripe banana
$^1/_2$ cup ripe, diced mango, papaya,
*   berries, peaches, or nectarines (see*
*   Headnote)*

$^1/_2$ cup limeade from concentrate
Ice cubes
$^1/_2$ cup club soda
2 slices lime

In a blender, puree the banana, mango, and limeade until thick and smooth. Pour into two tall, ice cube filled glasses. Stir in the club soda. Garnish each glass with a lime slice.

Makes 2 servings

Per Serving: Calories: 110; Fat and Cholesterol: 0; Sodium: 15 mg; % Daily Value: Vitamin C 34%,
Vitamin A 20%, Vitamin B$_6$ 19%

Hot Apple Rum

It sometimes gets nippy in the islands, when bone-chilling temperatures, at least here in Key West, can dip into the fifties. Big deal, you're saying, but with no heat in most homes, it sends us running for hot drinks. Hot apple cider, an old standby of life up North, teamed with island rum brings together the best of both worlds. Similar to a hot buttered rum drink, this one definitely has fewer calories and still warms the cockles of your heart.

2 cups apple cider	*½ cup light or dark rum*
5 cinnamon sticks	*4 teaspoons dark brown sugar*

In a small saucepan over low heat, warm the apple cider with 1 cinnamon stick, to a desired drinking temperature. To each of four heatproof glasses, add 2 tablespoons of rum and a teaspoon of sugar. Pour the cider over the sugar and rum and garnish each glass with a cinnamon stick.

Makes 4 servings

Per Serving: Calories: 145; Fat, Cholesterol, and Sodium: 0; No other significant nutritional value

Mojito Cocktail

I had my first mojito here in Key West, at a gallery reception showcasing recently arrived art work from Cuba. The bartender described the mojito as "the working man's cocktail," or the Cuban equivalent of drinking a Bud. As a daytime alternative to beer, or an evening cocktail, mojitos will certainly put you in an island state of mind. If you enjoy lime-based cocktails, such as vodka gimlets or margaritas, mojitos will be your drink. By keeping freshly squeezed, frozen lime juice on hand, you'll be ready to make these year-round. For entertaining purposes, simple syrup is quite handy and will keep in the refrigerator. Directions are provided for both multiple and single drinks.

SIMPLE SYRUP
1/2 cup hot water (from the tap is okay)
1/2 cup sugar

1/2 cup fresh lime juice
20–25 fresh mint leaves

1 1/2 cups light rum
4 cups club soda
Ice cubes

1. To make the simple syrup, in a heatproof container, stir the water and sugar until the sugar dissolves. Cool before using, so it can thicken slightly.

2. In a pitcher, combine the syrup, lime juice, and mint leaves. The recipe can be made in advance up to this point. Using a wooden spoon or another long utensil, muddle these ingredients, releasing the mint oils from the leaves. Stir in the rum and club soda; pour over ice.

Makes 8 Servings

Per Serving: Calories: 150; Fat and Cholesterol: 0; Sodium: 25 mg; No other significant nutritional value

For individual drinks, stir 2 tablespoons very hot tap water and 1 teaspoon sugar together until sugar dissolves. Add 1 tablespoon lime juice, 2–3 mint leaves, $1^1/_2$ ounces of rum, and $^1/_2$ cup of club soda.

The Original Daiquiri

Simple yet elegant, this is the way the daiquiri was meant to be enjoyed. There's nothing else to say, except get out your best "up" glass, and chill it.

3–4 ice cubes

3 ounces light rum

2 tablespoons fresh lime juice

2 teaspoons simple syrup (see Mojito Cocktail, page 296)

In a cocktail shaker or a jar with a tight-fitting lid, combine all the ingredients. Shake about 10–15 seconds, and strain into two chilled, straight-up glasses.

Makes 2 servings

Per Serving: Calories: 110; Fat, Cholesterol, and Sodium: 0; No other significant nutritional value

Thank You . . . Daiquirí, Cuba

We have a small town in eastern Cuba called Daiquirí, and an American miner named Jennings Cox to thank for the delectable daiquiri cocktail, which lost its accent and original pronunciation in the translation. Somewhere around the late 1800s, Cox, who was supervising copper mines in Daiquirí, had some unexpected American visitors, and he was fresh out of gin. While he himself would make do with the local rum in a pinch, he didn't think the Americanos would go for it in a big way. Trying to disguise the rum flavor, he added a bit of lime juice, some sugar, and chilled the potion. With an immediate hit on his hands, Cox introduced the drink to American soldiers during the Spanish-American War (which, as a point of interest, eventually forced Spain to relinquish control of the island). The military boys brought rum, and the daiquiri recipe, back to the States. The rest is cocktail history.

Starfruit Daiquiri

Just about any fruit can be used to make a frozen daiquiri, and starfruit (carambola) is no exception. Make sure the fruit is fully ripened, otherwise the drink will be way too tart (see page 278). Remember, you don't peel starfruit, so the whole thing, small seeds and all, goes into the blender. When making any frozen alcoholic beverage, the order in which ingredients go into the blender is very important. The key thing to keep in mind is pouring the alcohol over the ice, as described below.

1 medium starfruit
¹/₂ cup fresh lemon juice
¹/₂ cup simple syrup (see Mojito Cocktail, page 296)

2 cups ice cubes
4 ounces light or dark rum

1. Slice the starfruit, reserving four smaller slices for garnish.

2. In a blender, combine the starfruit, lemon juice, and simple syrup, then puree until smooth. Add the ice, then the rum. The alcohol is added last so that it helps break down the ice, creating a smooth, slushy drink with no ice chunks. Puree again, to a thick, slushy consistency.

3. Pour into four tall glasses, and garnish with the reserved starfruit slices. Serve immediately, as the ice will start to separate from the rest of the liquid. When making cocktails with thicker ingredients, such as cream of coconut in a piña colada, the drink doesn't separate quite as quickly, but don't give this too much thought, as you'll be heading back to the blender real soon to make another batch.

Makes 4 servings

Per Serving: Calories: 180; Fat, Cholesterol, and Sodium: 0; % Daily Value: Vitamin C 34%

Persimmon Daiquiri

Persimmons are not a tropically grown fruit, but their brilliant orange color and soft, ripe texture make a fiery, sunset-colored frozen cocktail. There's no need to peel the fruit; if it's ripe enough, the thin skin will blend right into the beverage. Persimmons, originally cultivated in Japan, China, and now in California, are usually available from late fall through winter, so these daiquiris can be a fun addition to any holiday drink menu. Don't forget, the order of ingredients is important, as noted in the Starfruit Daiquiri (page 300).

1 medium, unpeeled persimmon
¼ cup fresh lemon juice
2 tablespoons sugar

2 cups ice cubes
3 ounces light or dark rum

1. Cut the persimmon into small chunks, reserving four small slices for garnish.

2. In a blender, combine the persimmon, lemon juice, and sugar, then puree until smooth. Add the ice, then the rum. Puree again, to a thick, slushy consistency.

3. Pour into 8-ounce rock glasses and garnish with the persimmon slices.

Makes 4 servings

Per Serving: Calories: 85; Fat and Cholesterol: 0; Sodium: 20 mg; % Daily Value: Vitamin C 18%

The Legend of Rum

Most people are amazed to learn how many different types and brands of rum there are, most of them produced in the Caribbean. Rum, used ubiquitously for drinks and in cooking, now provides a neighborly thread throughout the islands. But this wasn't always the case.

Sugarcane, from which rum is produced, was first brought to the region by Columbus. Sugarcane was initially grown to help fill Europe's constant demand for sugar; rum production was a second thought. The French and British islands went full steam ahead on sugarcane production, which eventually created the need for slaves.

Back in the 1700s, rum did not enjoy a respectable reputation. It was given to slaves and servants as a means of keeping them content and quiet, while plantation owners sipped on European brandy. There was also the association between pirates and rum. Pirate skull and crossbones flags would often depict a skeleton holding a glass, which signified rum. Robert Louis Stevenson's *Treasure Island* didn't help any, either, with its "Fifteen men on the Dead Man's Chest, yo-ho-ho, and a bottle of rum." Today, however, rum has taken its place among the most respected of spirits.

Just like coffee connoisseurs, rum drinkers appreciate the nuances among different brands. To satisfy the most discriminating tastes, each island produces its own style of rum, with distinct flavor characteristics. Puerto Rico–based Bacardi is the world's most widely known and sold rum. From Jamaica, there's dark Myers's rum, and a variety of selections from Appleton Estates and Wray & Nephew's. Well-known Mount Gay and lesser-known, Cockspur come from Barbados.

Martinique exports Saint James and Bally brands, while Haiti's best-known exported rum is Barbancourt. Pusser's come from the British Virgin Islands, and Brugal hails from the Dominican Republic. While Venezuela has a long history of producing fine rums, some of them have just recently found their way into the mainstream American market. Although this list doesn't even touch the tip of the rum iceberg, it gives you some idea of how much choice there is. And, hopefully, the next time you travel to the islands, you'll remember to sample some of the local rums that never make it to our shores.

Rum production hasn't changed much since pirates roamed the seas. It's distilled directly from sugarcane juice or molasses, a by-product of sugarcane processing. There are three categories that make up the world of rum: light, dark, and black (also called *anejo,* pronounced ann-yeh-ho). The length of time a rum is aged in wooden casks determines its final color and flavor. Clear, or silver rum, is not aged very long, and spends little or no time in wood casks. Dark rums, sometimes labeled amber or gold, may mature in the casks anywhere from two months to two years. There is a lot of product variety in this category, ranging from slightly amber to deep, dark shoe polish brown. That far end of the spectrum is where I put Myers's rum. As with other distilled spirits, longer aging means bigger flavor, and a higher price tag. Black or *anejo* rums may spend two to four years aging to become robust, sipping rums, not ones you'd want to cook with.

When cooking with rum, either light or dark will do, although personally, I think dark rums stand up better to mixing with other ingredients. Of course, if you don't want the dish enhanced by rum's dark color, go with a light rum. Follow the same cardinal rule as you would when cooking with wine: don't use anything you wouldn't want to drink.

Frozen Piña Colada

No cocktail conjures up the image of a Caribbean vacation like a piña colada. But cream of coconut, the drink's staple ingredient, is way too high in fat for this book. To substitute, coconut extract delivers the flavor, while fresh pineapple gives the drink some body. The sweetness of this drink will ultimately depend on how ripe and flavorful a pineapple you use, so adjust the sugar or simple syrup as needed. Unless you have a real heavy-duty blender, make just two at a time, so the pineapple will be adequately pureed.

1 cup cubed fresh pineapple
1 teaspoon sugar or simple syrup
(see page 296)
1 teaspoon coconut extract

1 cup ice cubes
2 ounces light or dark rum
Pineapple wedges for garnish (optional)

In a blender, puree the pineapple until smooth. Add the remaining ingredients except the garnish, in the order listed. Puree again to a slushy consistency. Pour into two 8-oz. stem glasses, and garnish with pineapple wedges, if desired.

Makes 2 servings

Per Serving: Calories: 120; Fat, Cholesterol, and Sodium: 0; % Daily Value: Vitamin C 19%

Dark 'n Stormy

Some say this drink originated in Bermuda, because Gosling rum, a black Bermuda rum, is typically used to make it. Though Bermuda is not in the Caribbean, it's the mixer, ginger beer, that is produced and drunk in the Caribbean. Not a beer, but a carbonated soft drink, ginger beer has an incredibly spicy, ginger flavor. It's like ginger ale, but intensified about a thousand times. Ginger beer usually comes packaged in 10- or 12-ounce bottles, and is sold in specialty beverage sections, or in Caribbean and Latin American markets.

Ice cubes

3 ounces black rum

1 cup ginger beer

2 slices lime

Fill two tall glasses with ice. To each glass, add 1½ ounces of rum and ½ cup ginger beer. Stir, garnish each glass with a lime slice, and make believe you're on vacation.

Makes 2 servings

Per Serving: Calories: 160; Fat, Cholesterol, and Sodium: 0; No other significant nutritional value

Rum Barbados Punch

Legend has it that this drink originated in Barbados, where its special ingredient, falernum, is produced. A clear, nonalcoholic liquid, falernum is a sweet, spiced flavoring, reminiscent of cloves, mace, and allspice. It's not easy to find, but a good spirits shop should be able to order it for you if it's unavailable on the shelf. Once you have a bottle on hand, it will last for quite a long time. This punch is a great cocktail for those who don't want a drink that tastes strongly of liquor and like the idea of freshly grated nutmeg on top. Don't even think of making the drink without it.

Ice cubes
1/4 cup light rum
2 tablespoons fresh lime juice
2 teaspoons falernum

Dash red bitters
1 cup club soda
Freshly grated nutmeg

Fill two glasses with ice cubes. To each glass add 1/2 the rum, lime juice, falernum, bitters, and club soda. Stir, and top with nutmeg. These are nice to sip through a straw, so that you get the essence of nutmeg without the spice right on your tongue.

Makes 2 servings

Per Serving: Calories: 75; Fat and Cholesterol: 0; Sodium: 80 mg; No other significant nutritional value

Rum with a Punch

If you've been on vacation in the Caribbean, you know the scene I'm about to describe. You just left 30° weather, your winter coat is rolled up in a ball (banished for the week to the bottom of the hotel room closet), and you head to the nearest poolside bar. You can almost taste that fruity, refreshing rum punch you've been thinking about on the plane ride down. And when you finally take that first, thirst-quenching sip, all your worries slip away. You're not quite sure what's in this tropical mumbo jumbo in a glass, but who cares? You're in a mellow state of mind.

Well, that's usually how it goes, but not all the time. There's this French relative of the rum punch, called a petit punch, whose name, over time, has evolved into "ti-punch." I discovered this little punch while honeymooning on the tiny French island of Terre de Haut, off the coast of Guadeloupe. Being a vigilant food sleuth, and always searching for something new, I decided that ti-punch was the drink for me. What arrived was a very small glass filled with light rum, a tiny carafe of sugar syrup, and a piece of lime—no ice. The customer is left to his or her own devices to mix the proportions. I say, no matter how you mix it, it's still warm straight rum with a splash of sugar and lime: a mighty strong drink.

I'm glad I made the mistake, otherwise how would I have known about ti-punch. For the rest of you, when it comes to ordering rum drinks in the islands, I'd check with the bartender first.

Island Rum Sour

This is an extremely simple spin-off of the tried and true whiskey sour. The recipe calls for serving it straight up, but on the rocks is fine, too. Not a low-cal drink, but it's nice to know one can help meet one's daily Vitamin C requirement with a rum sour. If you can find kumquats, it's a nice change from the traditional orange slice garnish.

4–5 ice cubes

1 (6-ounce) can frozen lemonade,
  partially thawed

6 ounces light or dark rum

4 pineapple wedges

2 kumquats, cut in half

Put the ice cubes, lemonade, and rum in a glass shaker, or in a jar with a tight-fitting lid. Shake 10–15 seconds, and pour into four chilled, whiskey sour–style stemmed glasses. Garnish with the pineapple and kumquat.

Makes 4 servings

Per Serving: Calories: 200; Fat, Cholesterol, and Sodium: 0; % Daily Value: Vitamin C 26%

A No-Brainer Planter's Punch

You'll never go thirsty if you can remember "one of sour, two of sweet, three of strong, and four of weak." The translation for this no-nonsense recipe is: one part lime juice, two parts sugar, three parts rum, and four parts water. On British islands, where the word punch was derived from the Hindu word *panch*, meaning five, a planter's punch includes a fifth ingredient, a spice, most commonly grated nutmeg.

Rum Old-Fashioned

Retro cocktails, like martinis and old-fashioneds, are making a comeback. So it seemed fitting and fun to put a tropical twist on an old-fashioned, normally made with bourbon. The secret to making a good old-fashioned is in the muddling. Use your pestle for muddling, or the back of a wooden spoon.

2 fresh pineapple wedges, each 1 inch wide

2 maraschino cherries

2 teaspoons dark or light brown sugar

4 dashes Angostura bitters

Ice cubes

3 ounces light or dark rum

½ cup club soda

In each of two rocks glasses, place a pineapple wedge, a cherry, 1 teaspoon of sugar, and 2 dashes of bitters. Muddle these ingredients to a chunky pulp. Fill the glasses with ice cubes, add 1½ ounces of rum, and ¼ cup of club soda to each. Stir and sip.

Makes 2 servings

Per Serving: Calories: 135; Fat, Cholesterol, and Sodium: 0; No other significant nutritional value

Blue Dog

In cocktail lingo, a vodka and grapefruit juice is known as a Greyhound. By adding a touch of blue curaçao, the orange-flavored liqueur from its namesake island, the tart grapefruit flavor is softened and the drink becomes a pretty, sea blue-green. What a delicious way to get your Vitamin C.

Ice cubes

3 ounces vodka

1 cup grapefruit juice

1 tablespoon curaçao

Fill two 8-oz. tall glasses with ice cubes. Add half the vodka, grapefruit juice, and curaçao to each. Stir and swig.

Makes 2 servings

Per Serving: Calories: 150; Fat, Cholesterol, and Sodium: 0; % Daily Value: Vitamin C 65%

Caribbean Event Resource List

To obtain more information on the Caribbean events mentioned throughout this book, contact the following offices.

ANTIGUA

Antigua Tourist Board
610 Fifth Avenue, New York, NY 10020
(212) 541-4117

Trombone Associates (public relations agency)
420 Madison Avenue, New York, NY 10017
(212) 308-8880

BELIZE

Belize Tourist Board
415 Seventh Avenue, Eighteenth floor, New York, NY 10001
(212) 268-8798

Medhurst Associates (public relations agency)
1208 Washington Drive, Centerport, NY 11721
(516) 425-0900

GUADELOUPE

French Tourist Office
444 Madison Avenue, New York, NY 10022
(212) 838-7800, ext 228

Clement-Petrocik Company (public relations agency)
14 East Sixtieth Street, New York, NY 10022
(212) 593-1895

MARTINIQUE

French Tourist Office
444 Madison Avenue, New York, NY 10022
(212) 838-7800, ext 228

Clement-Petrocik Company (public relations agency)
14 East Sixtieth Street, New York, NY 10022
(212) 593-1895

PUERTO RICO

Puerto Rico Tourism Company
575 Fifth Avenue, New York, NY 10017
(800) 223-6530

ST. BART'S

French Tourist Office
444 Madison Avenue, New York, NY 10022
(212) 838-7800, ext 228

Clement-Petrocik Company (public relations agency)
14 East Sixtieth Street, New York, NY 10022
(212) 593-1895

ST. LUCIA

St. Lucia Tourist Board
820 Second Avenue, New York, NY 10017
(212) 867-2950

Middleton & Gendron Inc (public relations agency)
130 East Fifty-ninth Street, New York, NY 10022 (212) 980-9060

TRINIDAD

Trinidad Tourist Board
25 West Forty-third Street, New York, NY 10036 (212) 719-0540

TASTE OF THE CARIBBEAN
Sponsored by the Caribbean Hotel Association and
Caribbean Culinary Federation

Caribbean Hotel Association
18 Marseilles Street, Suite 2B, San Juan, Puerto Rico 00907
(787) 725-9139

Kahn Travel Communications
100 North Village Avenue
Rockville Centre, New York 11570
(516) 594-4100

Index